THE TRANSPARENT MARKET

The
Transparent
Market

MANAGEMENT CHALLENGES IN
THE ELECTRONIC AGE

Mats Larsson
David Lundberg

www.transparentmarket.com

MACMILLAN
Business

First published 1998 by
MACMILLAN PRESS LTD
Houndmills, Basingstoke, Hampshire RG21 6XS
and London
Companies and representatives
throughout the world

ISBN 0–333–73631–1 hardcover

A catalogue record for this book is available
from the British Library.

This book is printed on paper suitable for recycling and
made from fully managed and sustained forest sources.

10 9   8   7   6 5   4   3   2 1
07 06 05 04 03 02 01 00 99 98

Editing and origination by
Aardvark Editorial, Mendham, Suffolk

Printed in Great Britain by
Creative Print & Design (Wales), Ebbw Vale

Contents

Foreword

Over the past few decades the digitalisation of the business environment has revolutionised the way organisations think, plan and act. Through process after process, task after task, the digital revolution has invaded the workplace. In a little more than 30 years, computers have moved from being a scarce resource, through being a pervasive technology, to becoming an almost invisible but ubiquitous part of everyday life. Where once computers were thought of as giant calculators, they have increasingly become communicating appliances, providing information to anyone, anytime, anywhere.

The effects have been profound. The creative destruction unleashed by the digital revolution has enabled old industrial concepts to wither away and die, while new business models have allowed young enterprises to grow and prosper, based solely on the availability of cheap computing and communications power.

Simultaneously, the computer and communications industries have been busy reshaping themselves. From being classic examples of stability and vertical integration in the later 1970s, the combined computer and communications industries have turned into a vibrant, fluid and highly fragmented business. The emerging 'infocom' industry contains many markets, segments and niches. It employs millions of people and is today the main contributor to economic growth in most industrialised countries. Infocom has generated immense wealth, to individuals as well as to cities, regions and countries. All this, in a little over 30 years.

This dizzying pace of change is not letting up. Now, in the late 1990s, another phase has begun. Computers and communications once more are changing the way individuals and organisations behave, this time, through collaborative applications that enable everyday commercial transactions to go electronic. Ubiquitous computing and abundant communications are converging on an electronic marketplace where new ideas, new thinking and new business models are taking shape. Organisations and individuals alike can participate in on-line bids, speed up a supply chain, and reach new market segments in the blink of an eye, to name just a few examples of commercial life affected by the digital revolution. But reaping the rewards often requires a complete reassessment of how business is done in the modern economy.

Electronic commerce is fundamentally altering what we call a 'company', a 'firm' or an 'enterprise'. The modern corporation is increasingly becoming networked. The boundaries of organisations are no longer rigid and narrow. Often, a corporate organisation encompasses as true and intimate partners such 'outsiders' as suppliers, customers, developers and other third parties. We are talking about new businesses, defined by new concepts such as the extended enterprise and the networked corporation.

Electronic business, or e-business for short, potentially allows all members of a commercial value chain – manufacturers, suppliers, merchants and customers – to create wealth with drastically reduced transaction costs and significantly increased effectiveness. Any enterprise might soon engage in electronic commerce, no matter where, or when.

It is important to note, however, that electronic business is not simply about technology, although technology plays a fundamental part. Technology *per se* is often the least challenging part of any major change. More critical aspects include managing and establishing new relationships between key members of a physical or digital network. Such a network thus comprises customers, suppliers, competitors, as well as a wide range of third-party partners. Of course, an even bigger challenge is to integrate effectively all the major factors, technological and especially non-technological, to achieve outstanding and continuous competitive success in a rapidly changing marketplace.

This is indeed a different place, quite unlike any other, but with the potential to reshape radically organisations, enterprises and not least, individual behaviour. Where Nicholas Negroponte talked about the importance of being digital, where George Gilder hailed the bandwidth explosion and Frances Cairncross heralded the death of distance, Larsson and Lundberg now proclaim the emergence of the transparent market.

This book aims to produce a meaningful and pragmatic understanding of the transparent market. It describes and explains the underlying forces and business implications associated with the sweeping change before us. Reading the book will enable you to understand both the key technological and non-technological trends related to e-business. It will help you to uncover the impact of those trends on your own business, and in your own daily life. It will ultimately integrate salient variables and enable you to develop strategies for dealing with the great opportunities and perhaps even greater threats that e-business represents. In short, it will help you and your company to change. For as Charles Darwin once put it:

> It is not the strongest of the species that survive, nor the most intelligent. It is the one most adaptable to change.

Reading *The Transparent Market* goes a long way to helping you to become one who survives.

Mikael Edholm
DIRECTOR OF CORPORATE BUSINESS DEVELOPMENT
LM ERICSSON, LOS ALTOS HILLS, CA
April 1998

1 Introduction

Our approach

When we started to write this book, we both thought that the recent development of Internet technology and the effects that it could have on business and other aspects of society was an interesting area, well worth an in-depth study. However, as the book proceeded and we read more and more about this area in newspapers and magazines, and had new experiences as consultants in the field of management issues related to information technology (IT), we came to the conclusion that it could have even more serious effects than we had at first imagined. We have encountered a number of implications and possibilities that have the power to change much more than some limited parts of society. After reading this book, we hope that readers will agree with our conclusions and concerns, and will be ready to meet some of the challenges of this new marketplace and medium for the transfer of information.

The book is in three parts. First, we present some observations from the present market that foretell a new type of society arising from the new electronic marketplace. In the second part, we structure the ideas of the new market through the use of some key concepts, and in the third part, we discuss the challenges that face us as managers, citizens, governments and individuals.

Throughout the book, we use examples and quotes to support our reasoning. A number of these quotes come from two renowned books in the field of classical economic theory: *An Inquiry into the Nature and Causes of the Wealth of Nations* (usually known as *The Wealth of Nations*) by Adam Smith, and *Principles of Political Economy and Taxation* by David Ricardo. We have chosen to use these quotations because they, in a very basic way, describe how markets work. The fact that these books were written some 200 years ago is interesting because we argue that the transparent market arising from the development of electronic trade is closer in its way of functioning to the markets of classical economic theory than markets have ever been before.

> The produce of the earth – all that is derived from its surface by the united application of labor, machinery, and capital, is divided among three classes of the community, namely the proprietor of the land, the owner of the stock or capital necessary for its cultivation, and the laborers by whose industry it is cultivated.

> But in different stages of society, the proportions of the whole produce of the earth which will be allotted to each of these classes, under the names of rent, profit, and wages, will be essentially different; depending mainly on the actual fertility of the soil, on the accumulation of capital and population, and on the skill, ingenuity, and instruments employed in agriculture. (Ricardo, 1996)

The mission

Many writers of books and articles have predicted that we are about to enter a new age in which the old rules of business and society will no longer apply. We are convinced, however, that none of the writers and visionaries whose material we have read has envisioned the full impact of the changes that lie ahead of us.

We can think of four different approaches that would be possible for an author to take when trying to predict the future development of society. These could be called 'researching the future', 'the technical approach', 'the economist approach' and 'the management approach'. Although these approaches are, to a large extent, gross simplifications of the approaches of other writers, readers could easily find examples of each of these categories in modern literature and journalism discussing the future.

■ The approach of 'researching the future' means that we would make 'the future' our main area of interest. Our methodology would rest on two major building blocks, namely the study of trends and the reading of the books by other researchers into the future. Our main method would be to spot trends and to extrapolate these trends, one by one, to form a picture of how the future would look in each area. The sum of all these trends would create the picture of future society. In order not to overlook any important trends that we had missed ourselves, we would read the books of our colleagues and glean further ideas from them.

■ 'The technical approach' would involve describing present and future technological developments and what we could achieve with the help of new technologies. It is from writers and journalists who use this methodology that we get to know about innovations such as new multimedia techniques, fast, high-resolution computers and new high-speed networks. In using this approach, however, we would not be trying to create a picture of future society but would instead be content to present innovations. Examples of this can be found in the numerous magazines dealing with different aspects of technical development.

■ If we were to choose 'the economist approach', we would hold the belief that economic development is one of the most important aspects of the future and that the best way to know more about the future is to use economic analysing tools. We would describe the different factors that, from an economic perspective, would drive the predicted development and talk about economic peaks and troughs, the future of the Asian economies and the relationships between different currencies. We would also take into account technological developments and differences in factor costs between different countries, and look deeply into the long-term trends of the economy, analysing all the factors that are, from a historical perspective, known to have an impact on the economy. Examples can be found in the forecasts of future economic developments that are regularly published by banks, stockbrokers and governments.

■ Proponents of 'the management approach' regularly present new management tools that companies need to apply in order to cope with the future. If we were to choose this approach, we would hold the belief that most companies are in charge of their own destinies and that all business problems can be solved through the application of the right management techniques. One example of a book with this approach is *Mission Possible* (1996) by Blanchard *et al*.

Why is it that intelligent people with good motives do such a poor job at anticipating the future? (Barker, 1993)

In this book, we try to use all these four approaches side by side to view the whole spectrum of changes that may affect us in the future. Since we are interested in the future, we of course take trends into account, but we do not think that those which will have the largest impact on society have been visible for more than 2 or 3 years. The trend we are referring to is likely to bring a completely new logic to business and other aspects of society. Thus we are using the tools of the 'researching the future' approach.

In Chapter 4, we describe some important technological developments that form the foundation of the Internet development. This is our contribution to the technological approach. Throughout the book, particularly in the concluding chapters, we formulate our conclusions about what impact this development will have on our economy as a whole and on the business situations of many types of company. This means that we will use the perspectives of 'the economist approach' and 'the management approach', although we do not claim that it would be possible to solve all the problems that companies might encounter through this development even if managers were to apply the best management techniques. The reader will be the arbiter of whether we have been successful in our endeavour to synthesise these four approaches and whether we have managed to create a coherent and reasonable picture of the future society in a number of respects, including economic ones.

In our work as management consultants in the fields of IT and organisational and business change, what we have experienced gives us reason to believe that major changes are likely to come upon us, which authors in neither of these categories have been able to spot. The whole picture of the future we believe is starting to emerge has not, to our knowledge, been described in the literature.

One of the main reasons for this is that neither of the categories has realised the importance of the fastest growing technological innovation in history, namely the Internet, and the electronic trade that will arise on this medium ('Internet' is used throughout this book as the name of the new communication medium through which we can shop, interact, exchange information or be entertained. The Internet is the most probable future infrastructure for all these things, but there will be other media that could serve the same purpose.) The most likely reason behind the fact that authors seem to have missed the Internet's impact on the future economy and structures of society is that it is a very recent, although extremely rapidly growing, trend and has not yet had any major impact on anything important; this accounts for the fact that it has arrived almost unnoticed by those whose vocation it is to forecast the future.

This book is an attempt to make as comprehensive a description as possible of the extreme changes that the increasing use of the Internet as a platform for trade, information-sharing and communication is likely to produce in the near future. It is based on the assumption that one of the really big drivers of change will be the 'transparency' of all markets and the whole of society, that will be described in the first chapter.

Of course, the future is very difficult to forecast. We often talk about possibilities and opportunities rather than trying to make actual predictions. We know that the forces driving change in the direction we indicate are very strong. However, changes may be greater than we are able to predict. We base this belief on the assumption that change will not happen within the traditional boundaries of industries and markets. It will come from a new force that has proved to be very powerful: the access to information over a common worldwide communications platform, combined with tools that make this information accessible and possible for each one of us (that is, not just experts or people with money or power) to use.

> The Internet and information technology is fundamentally changing our whole society and it is no longer a case that some companies are IT oriented and others are not. Those who do not join the IT revolution 'will go to the wall' – and fast. (Percy Barnevik, chairman of Investor, the largest owner on the Stockholm stock exchange)

To those who, after reading this book, are still sceptical of the changes that we describe, we would like to address the following. As humans, it is natural for us to think that even if many things will change in the future, the overall picture of how society works will, to a large extent, remain the same. This means that we tend to think that citizens, customers, companies, governments and all the other major building blocks of society will act and think in largely the same way in the future as they do today. Customers will use the same criteria when they make purchases, largely the same factors will distinguish successful companies from less successful competitors, and we will have the same or a similar political system and a type of government similar to that which we have today.

The reason we believe this is because our brains work that way. We are not supposed to change our ways of thinking too easily. However, in his book *The Structure of Scientific Revolutions* (1996), Thomas Kuhn describes how 'paradigm shifts' remove the whole logic of how things currently work and replace this with a completely new logic. When this happens, companies that were successful under the old paradigm may be totally devastated if they do not manage to adapt to the new one.

A historical example of a major paradigm shift could be taken from the worldwide watch market. In the 1960s, a number of Swiss companies dominated the market for watches on a worldwide basis. The Swiss held some 70 per cent of the total world market. One of their competitive advantages was their command of fine mechanics.

In the late 1960s, a Swiss researcher invented the quartz mechanism, which allowed greater accuracy and lower production costs. When he introduced his invention to the managers of the watch companies, they argued that if Swiss companies adopted the quartz technology in their watches, it would mean the death of the whole industry, because a quartz watch is made without any fine mechanics.

The Swiss, however, showed the new invention at a trade fair, where the idea was picked up by some American and Japanese competitors (Seiko and Texas Instruments), who quickly became the new market leaders. In the late 1980s, Swiss watches enjoyed less than 10 per cent of the market, this loss of market share being mainly the result of the paradigm shift from fine mechanics to quartz technology.

A paradigm is a set of rules and regulations (written or unwritten) that does two things: (1) it establishes or defines boundaries; and (2) it tells you how to behave inside the boundaries in order to be successful.

When a paradigm shifts, everyone goes back to zero. (Barker, 1993)

When a new paradigm makes its way into an industry, experiences from within the old paradigm become almost worthless. It becomes impossible for the old market leaders to defend their position if they are not able to see the implications of the new opportunities. What happens is that the old players defend their market share in a rapidly shrinking market while new companies gain a large part of a new booming market.

A typical example of a new paradigm that is growing in importance is that of the retail industry. Figures relating to electronic shopping in Sweden show that this market was worth about $300m in 1997. In 1998, this is expected to grow to $900m and in 1999 to $2,700m. This is small compared with the $120,000m that the entire consumer market is worth. However, the electronic market is growing fast, and the old market will probably shrink. In some areas, Internet trade will grow more rapidly than in others.

Most paradigm shifts affect one industry or a few industries, or just a part of the production logic of a product, but they can have an extreme impact on those who are not quick enough to adapt. In this book, we describe a number of paradigm shifts that will together affect the whole of our society. And most of these changes have not yet made their impact on how we act and think. Those of our readers who read this book and try to challenge its content using arguments based on the present logic in society should consider that it is impossible to analyse the new paradigm with the help of experiences of past or present paradigms.

The ability to understand a paradigm shift and take it into account in forecasts of the future is vital when we analyse the implications of the development described in this book. The present paradigm includes a large number of rules of thought that are difficult to leave behind when we take the step into the future paradigm and a new type of society. It is extremely easy to end up in a debate that has its roots in the fact that people reason within different paradigms. One trick that can be used to get around this is to stop for a while and discuss which rules will apply and which will not. A discussion about the future labour market, for example, could be very contaminated if one person were convinced that people will always see a job from the perspective of 8 hours a day, 5 days a week, and that it should be performed in a traditional office or industry environment, while another sees work in the future as something entirely different that would also be organised and rewarded in ways different from those of today.

When we evaluate the argument put forward in this book, we should see it in the light of earlier paradigm shifts in history. We could, for example, think of the visionary who would argue about the importance of the coming Industrial Revolution in the late eighteenth century. He might suggest that the Industrial Revolution would make agriculture more efficient. He could say that agriculture in the future would be so efficient that only half of the total population would work in agriculture compared with the figure in 1790. That could, in any country, mean that the share of the population in agriculture would decrease from 70 to 35 per cent. Would anyone believe him? Probably, but not very many!

He would argue that the changes would need to be based on a development in which people moved from farm work in the countryside to factory work in the cities. The factories would produce technical equipment that would enable the increase in the efficiency of farming. Today, we know that it was possible to shrink the share of the population involved in farming, not to 35 per cent, but to less than 3 per cent, and still increase the volume of production.

There have been many large changes during the twentieth century, but when a change takes 20 years to complete and has only a small impact on one or a few industries, on one or two categories of worker, society has the time to adapt. The changes that will be described in this book could influence just about all industries and most other areas of society over the space of only a few years, so it then becomes more important for all of us to be prepared for the changes. Changes to the way in which we communicate between individuals and between companies could wipe out a number of industries that we think of as pillars of our economy and change other industries into completely new structures with new players. A number of such industries will be mentioned throughout the book.

Besides these massive changes, we also highlight all the opportunities for companies, individuals and society as a whole. We indicate the risks that we will encounter if changes are so quick that we are unable to adapt to them. This is truly a challenge for all of us. If we are right in our predictions, we need to mobilise the whole of society in order to be able to change it at the pace needed to take advantage of the opportunities encountered.

We are convinced that the development we describe will, in the long run, turn out to be a spectrum of opportunities. If we manage to take advantage of them, we will be able to create a society that could be both more efficient and much more humane than any of the societies that humanity has known so far. If we manage to use the opportunities to our advantage, we will work shorter hours, live our lives where we want to, have more time for the people around us, including our families, and improve other areas of our lives that we would like to change for the better.

The key issue, when it comes to the management of the change process of society as a whole, seems to be the ability to change both our way of thinking about key issues in society, and the systems of society and business accordingly, so that we can take advantage of opportunities while avoiding the problems that could arise from not managing the change. One example can be taken from our views on labour and unemployment. We argue that many jobs done today will not have to be done in the future. We could choose to treat this as a problem of unemployment or, looking at it another way, could see it as an opportunity.

The key to this perspective is that we may have to use fewer hours of work to produce the amount of goods and services that we produce today, but we will not be worse off from society's point of view. The fact that we will spend fewer hours on production does not mean that we really have a problem, but only that the people still employed in this production will be more productive than we are today. (The reasons behind this increase in productivity will be explained later in the book.) The result is that the people without employment and those who work fewer hours will represent a resource that we can use in another way.

Another conclusion we draw is that we may be in the midst of change in only 2 to 3 years, and we are definitely not prepared for it. Most of the systems on which we have built our present society were created for the industrial society. Now, many people argue that we have to change the way we run businesses, governments and authorities in order to build a knowledge-based society, but the conclusions that the experts have drawn so far are far too conservative in their nature. In order for businessmen, politicians and 'ordinary' individuals to prepare for the changes to come, we need an understanding of what will happen. There is no other way. In our predictions, we are convinced that more people must turn their attention to the analysis of this scenario. We ask readers to use the book both as an eye-opener and as a checklist, on which the developments that we will see in the next few years can be ticked off and where new predictions and conclusions about the future can be added by readers along the way.

When we present new possibilities that will arise from the use of new IT, we describe applications that can be created using existing technologies. This is important to notice and highlights the fact that we are not discussing how things might develop *if* a network like the Internet were built, *if* computers become 10 times faster or *if* a new type of software could be developed. The applications we describe are either already in existence or could be created at this very moment.

A quote from the *Investor Guide* summarises a large part of what we are saying:

> The internet is the biggest megatrend in history. It's fundamentally changing the way companies do business, and it will soon change the way people live. This convergence of personal computing and communications is a trillion-dollar business that's creating incredible synergies, allowing traditional things to be done better and allowing new things that couldn't be done at all before. Over the next 15 years, the internet will eat traditional communications (telephone, fax, post office, videoconferencing), entertainment (TV, video games, music), publishing (newspapers, magazines, books), client/server computing, commerce and transaction processing, research – the list goes on and on. (*Investor Guide,* www.investorguide.com)

The perspective

Although the changes described will affect the whole of society, they emanate from changes in the market driven by recent developments of IT. For this reason, we will use a business perspective throughout the book.

This does not mean that the book is interesting only to business people. On the contrary, everybody will need to understand the changes described because everybody will be affected by them. Not least, our politicians need to grasp these matters as soon as possible in order to start to adapt the basic systems of society, such as taxes, laws and education.

Many readers are likely to think that the development described in this book could be a reality in 20 or 30 years' time. The truth, however, is that the first signs of change may become visible tomorrow if only enough customers start to use the computers that they already have to buy products from already existing Internet-based companies. It is true that many Internet-based players still use existing distribution structures to serve their customers, but entirely new structures could arise rapidly if the volume of Internet trade grew quickly.

We can assume that a market share of Internet trade of 20 per cent of the total market in any industry would mean that some existing companies, especially companies in middleman positions, would face problems. This has already happened for the car companies in New York city, where 20 per cent of new car trade is done over the Internet. If a large number of industries did 20 per cent of their trade over the Internet, not only would existing companies be affected, but so too probably would real estate companies, who would face new demand patterns in, for example, city centres. By the time Internet trade reached 30 per cent, it would probably be difficult for many customers to find what they wanted in their local markets, especially in small towns, and the prices in traditional shops would have to increase substantially, whereas the prices from Internet-based outlets would be lower than they are today. Thus more and more people would be forced to do their shopping over the Internet. This argument will be substantiated throughout the book.

Finally, one of the basic assumptions that we make when we say there is a high probability that the Internet market will develop more rapidly than we would think, is:

> People and companies will continue to behave as they usually have done in the past.

This means that people tend to move purchases to suppliers that give them more value for their money, regardless of whether the new forms of trade are perceived as less personal. This has been the case in the transition from small specialised corner shops to large supermarkets and this trend is likely to promote electronic trade as well. Similarly it means that companies will continue to try to utilise new technologies to increase efficiency and customer service.

Part I
Observations

The starting point for this book is a set of observations of current market developments. These observations permeate the whole of society and turn up in different shapes in different places, but they emanate from the same technological innovations. We have given these trends the names 'the real-time society', 'disintermediation' and 'the innovation-based economy'. Different aspects of these trends are described in the first part of the book. Our argument is that, in order to understand these developments, we need a new paradigm through which we can see society, namely a paradigm of transparency, which is discussed first.

If we use the transparency paradigm when we analyse recent developments in society, it becomes very clear that we have left the industrial society behind us and are heading for another type of society never before seen.

2 The Transparent Marketplace

'Transparency' is a word that points to one of the most important characteristics of the emerging electronic marketplace. 'Transparency' refers to the fact that an object can be seen through (light can pass through it). In a more general sense, it also means 'open', 'frank' and 'clear'. In this book, the word is intended to indicate the fact that every aspect of a system or an object is visible to the viewer. The analogy is meant to stress a major difference between the marketplace of today, in which only a limited amount of information can be accessed, and the market of tomorrow, in which all relevant information on any subject could be accessed by anyone, anywhere.

One illustration of the concept of transparency that could turn out to be a whole new way of organising collective transport and freight is the samake (in Swedish 'samåka' means car-pool) site connected to the homepage www.vellinge.se, published by the municipality of Vellinge in southern Sweden. At this site, people who have free seats in their cars can advertise them, together with the date and time when they will drive to a certain destination; people who would like to go there at the same time can book these seats. This means that people who want to go from Vellinge to the nearby city of Malmö could choose this alternative means of transport instead of using a bus or taxi. Of course, the site could be used by people from Vellinge regardless of where they would like to go, whether it be Stockholm, Copenhagen or Munich instead of Malmö.

Furthermore, anybody anywhere could in practice use it. If people in Barcelona understood enough Swedish to enter their places of departure and where they would like to go, for example from the centre of Barcelona to one of its suburbs, they could also do so and hope that people in Barcelona with free seats would list them on this homepage.

At present, there is no formalised way of setting a price on the seats that people book, but people could, of course, informally develop the custom of paying each other for the services. In the future, however, any site for booking travel could be equipped with a field where sellers could enter prices. This pricing system could be designed in a number of different ways. One way could be to allow the provider of seats to suggest a price and allow the buyer similarly to make an offer of how much he or she would like to pay for the service. In this manner, all participants in the market could see the current market price for transports between any two towns or cities or for local transport within a city.

Such a system could be operated either as a tool for advance booking or as a way of finding transport in real-time, like any of the present taxi systems. The providers of transport services could be professional drivers, people with private cars who simply had free seats or a mixture of both. The system could also be extended to encompass bookings of freight space with professional transportation companies or with owners of private cars who happen to have some free luggage space when they drive between two specific points.

This example illustrates the meaning of transparency. Through this type of tool, it is possible for the sellers of transportation to see at any time the total need for transport; these sellers could then allocate their transportation resources in the form of cars, buses, trucks or even planes and trains to the routes where they could make the biggest profit. At the same time, buyers of transportation could see the prices of different types of transportation for any desired trip, be it long or short, and choose the most advantageous means of transportation depending on the market price. Over time, the price fluctuations in such a market would diminish, and the market price for any particular trip would become reasonably stable.

For readers who know basic economics, it may be obvious how this type of market becomes more similar to the 'perfect market' described in classical economic theory than to the present market for transportation. One prerequisite for a 'perfect market' is that all players in a market have complete information both about all transactions in the market, and about the current offers of all buyers and sellers. In this type of market, all the conclusions of classical economic theory that are made for such a market could be realised.

The effects of this development on the structure of different industries and on the structure of society as a whole will be described throughout the book. Transparency is the key in all the developments that are discussed.

At the crossroads

Efficient communications are key to the overall efficiency of most systems in society. This is not a statement to be taken lightly. On the contrary, the increasing access to information will change the way in which we organise societies, companies and our daily lives. In this chapter, we will describe what transparency means and also describe the effects that it will have on costs, industry structures and competition on a high level. Our message is that we are now at a crossroads in history, where our previous investments in IT could very rapidly begin to increase the overall efficiency of society.

If we look back in history, we find that trade has gradually overcome a number of difficulties connected to the geographical distances between people. In a typical agricultural society before the Industrial Revolution, production units, whether farms or artisans' shops, met little competition because the most efficient producers were unable to trade their products over long distances, transportation being both dangerous and very costly. Only the most wealthy were able to buy spices and other imported products. This meant that the market for such goods was very small. The lack of efficient communications obviously played a role here.

One of the drivers behind the Industrial Revolution was the invention of the steam engine, key to the birth of mass production. This machine made it possible not only to start factories that were equipped with steam-driven machines, but also to build railways and other means of transportation that helped in the creation of markets that were, from a geographical perspective, larger. As this and other inventions, such as the telegraph, made it possible to move goods and information over large distances, trade gradually grew. This growth has continued now for more than 200 years and has gradually changed society from an agricultural to an industrial society, and more recently to what some researchers call a 'knowledge-based society'.

There was one major paradigm shift as the agricultural economy was turned into an economy based on industrial production. Many authors have said that we are in the midst of a second paradigm shift, one which will fulfil the change from the industrial society into a knowledge-based or an information-based society. We agree that we are entering a new era. We would say, however, that most of us still do not see the full implications of the new society, on whose threshold we currently stand.

This development is well described in another quote from the *Investor Guide*:

> Shortly after motion pictures were invented, it was thought that their main applications would be training films and travelogues. Well, the applications listed above, the ones you're seeing today on the internet, are the equivalent of training films and travelogues. Thousands of other uses lie waiting for creative individuals to discover. (*Investor Guide*)

The first signs of transparency

To better understand what the early signs of increasing transparency are like, we would like to start with some simple examples. Take, for instance, a person who wants to buy a CD. This person will be able to find out which supplier in the world will be able to deliver it at the most competitive price, all extra costs being taken account of. This also means that a person who has a complicated problem to solve will be able to find others who are willing and able to offer their competencies to solve some of its particular areas. Over the Internet, any person, regardless of the position he or she has in society, will be able to find the best information available on any subject. Therefore, we would like to make our readers think along new lines, by taking a simple example from the car industry showing how transparency could change some important aspects of this industry. We may note, however, that we will be able to see many more possible changes to this particular industry, but we have to start somewhere...

When we buy a new car, we are used to going to a car dealer in order to learn about different models and the exact price of each model. Although we know that prices differ between dealers in different cities, most of us do not undertake the task of finding the lowest price of a certain model in the region where we live. Instead, we compare cars of different makes that are available locally and try to figure out which car offers the best value for money from a number of different perspectives. When we have settled for the car that we want to buy, we go to the local dealer to make the purchase.

Today, it is already possible to get information about each type of car directly from the producer. By entering the homepage of any producer, the customer can find more detailed information than he or she could expect to get at a local dealer's. This is true because a producer can make all information available on the Internet. The equivalent would be very expensive if information had to be distributed physically. Besides the actual product information issued by the producer, the results of all the tests of all types of function of a car can easily be accessed over the Internet. It would be an interesting business opportunity for some future company to structure the information from a number of tests of different aspects of cars of all makes for customers to buy for a small price. Since the market for such a service would be worldwide, the cost for each customer wanting to buy the service could be very low. With access to such information, consumers could make their decisions based on a solid platform of objective information. They could then weigh advertising information from different producers against test results of all kinds and choose which type of information to base their decision on.

At present, we still have to visit our local dealer in order to buy the car, but it can be expected that current car manufacturers will receive competition from producers without regular dealer networks who market their cars only over the Internet. Cars sold in this way will be less expensive than cars sold by local dealers, since a large part of the dealer's cost will be taken off the price tag. This would make it less expensive to buy a car in the future than it is today. After the decision to buy a car from a future Internet distributor, the car could be delivered directly from a storage facility. Thus the major part of the cost of the distribution system could be eliminated.

At the end of 1997, 20 per cent of all car deals made in New York city were made over the Internet. Microsoft provides the marketplace in which these cars are traded, making it possible for potential customers and car dealers to meet electronically.

Distribution structures have not yet been aligned to the opportunities offered by the electronic market. This means that we still have to wait for the effects of this development on the labour market, on price levels and on the distribution structure.

Other changes in this market are already known among car dealers. Through the use of the Internet as a first step, customers are better prepared when they enter a shop and start to talk to a salesperson. Customers today often know exactly what they want and just use the shop as a place to order the car rather than to get information. This makes it more difficult for salespersons to influence the choice.

It is important to remember that the new electronic marketplace is not only about the consumer market: it is just as much about the business-to-business market. So, the next step in our example would be for car manufacturers to make purchases of parts from suppliers over the Internet. The technical specifications for each part, for example a brake system, could be made available over the Internet. Then any producer with the right competence could calculate the cost for the production of such parts, and each possible supplier of brakes could make an offer to any of the car manufacturers. At each point of purchase, the car manufacturer could buy brake systems from the supplier who could offer the best price. The reason why this way of purchasing is not practised to any great extent today is that transaction costs are higher in the present system than they will be in the future, and it is therefore more economical to stick to the same supplier for a long time since this strategy reduces transaction costs.

This way of purchasing will, of course, be much easier to apply for a manufacturer that uses purely standardised parts in its production, than for a car manufacturer developing special solutions. This means that the procedure may be easier to apply for the producer of brake systems in the purchasing of parts for these systems than for the manufacturer of cars in the purchasing of brake systems. Over time, however, we would expect manufacturers of cars to be able to use standardised systems to a greater and greater extent in order to be competitive. For a customer, it will be easy to see, from a number of tests available over the Internet, whether the extra cost of specialised parts results in better performance for the car in the relevant respects.

Radically increasing efficiency in value chains will have a large impact not only (as was discussed in the example above) on the price of cars, but also on the structure of whole industries, including systems of suppliers. In order to be able to take advantage of the opportunities that this development offers, and not to be struck by its seemingly negative consequences, we ought to investigate what the effects on society of this development will really be.

Transparency is not only valid in the direction from customers towards suppliers in the market. It is equally important for companies that want to get a quick view of demand. Individuals or companies that want to enter the market by starting production in an industry will be able to communicate this to all possible customers at the same time. It is also possible to see the current demands in the market and control production and packaging based on that information. This will lead to increasing customisation and production 'on demand'.

The ability to distribute and access all the necessary information about the market is one thing; making practical use of it is another. Therefore the foundation of this new market environment is not just communication but information management as well. Without this, information will be useless and we will drown in it (or at least give up our search for information). This is important to remember when we step into this new 'transparent marketplace'. When we say 'information management', we mean all the tools and technologies that help us to use the information around us. This could be better user interfaces, better ways to collect, structure and view information, search engines, pictures, graphs, sound, animation or even advanced decision support systems.

Transparency will have huge consequences in many other respects too. Changes in the way in which companies compete and in the way they organise work will have an impact on how we do business, how we travel, how we plan our cities, how, and how much, we are paid and so on.

Furthermore, the transparency and the flexibility of the market are not the only changes that are driven by IT. Today, the limits to how we could apply technology to solve problems of all kinds are no longer set by technology in itself. They are to a greater extent set by our imagination and our ability to combine competencies so that we can find the most successful solutions.

Available information on the Internet is growing fast

Currently, only a small amount of information is available on the Internet. The development started only a few years ago, and in the beginning some companies felt that they had to create a presence in the new electronic marketplace, although there was uncertainty about which opportunities the new market would create. It was obvious that it could turn out to be a powerful medium through which market products and services, which led many companies to create an electronic 'shop window' that showed a nice picture of the company itself and some offerings.

Nowadays, it has become clear that this medium will become more powerful than a simple shop window, and the pace at which companies are trying to become leaders in this area is incredible. It means that enormous amounts of information are made available on the Internet every day, not just by new pages in HTML (the computing language behind web pages) but, more importantly, by adding web interfaces to more and more systems and appliances. Information that has been unobtainable and isolated in systems that only a few 'experts' could reach is now starting to become accessible to anyone who needs it, independent of location. A more in-depth discussion of this can be found in Chapter 4.

This development has now started within most companies, and it creates a powerful information environment within the company. Even if the advantages of these 'intranets' (Internet technology used within a company) are huge, the real changes and opportunities will come when a large portion of this information is opened up to the rest of the world. Many companies try out new services internally before they give customers or suppliers access to them. They often argue that this is for security reasons, but it is possible to manage the important aspects of security. Another reason could be that they need time to prepare for the major changes in the way in which they organise work that this will lead to. The effects of transparency are likely to be overwhelming for many companies!

Cost-efficiency and improved services will be the main drivers

The main factor that drives the development of the use of information technology is the striving for the greater cost-efficiency and improved service of all systems in society. Many people who doubt that IT will ever have a large impact on how we organise work argue from the standpoint that we will want to work in the same manner as we are used to. Others will argue that IT will never have any substantial impact on the costs of production of goods or services since it cannot be proved that it has had any significant impact in the past.

Our argument was mentioned above. We are now at a crossroads, having built our information infrastructure and competence to use this to a level at which we can finally benefit from this development. The ensuing paradigm shifts are built on the basis that there has been a gradual change to our way of working and to our way of doing business that is now gaining momentum through the fact that information systems are no longer stand-alone systems. That more and more systems in the world are now tied together by the Internet and by other means of communication creates the transparency in society that makes it possible to make optimal use of our resources for production and distribution.

The development of the Internet is the technological innovation in history for which we have experienced the most rapid market penetration on a worldwide basis. James Gosling, the vice president of Sun Microsystems (the company behind the Internet programming language Java), describes it as: 'Internet runs on dog years', which means that the pace in this area is at least seven times faster than that in a traditional industry.

The number of Internet users currently doubles every fifth month, and there are no signs indicating that this will slow down in the near future. This means that there will soon be around 100 million Internet users. We also see how innovations, such as the introduction of new ways to create advanced Internet solutions and electronic commerce concepts that make Internet trade more efficient and attractive, happen virtually every day.

One of the main reasons behind this very rapid development is that each new piece of information and each new service that is introduced can be accessed by all Internet users immediately. Historically, new business concepts had to be spread physically over the globe, with substantial investments in dealer networks and market communication as a prerequisite for success. Today, with a comparatively very small investment, a company can spread its new products or concepts to the whole market at once, and this holds true for physical products as well as information.

> One example of this is the web site www.amazon.com, which will be described in more detail later. This book dealer can sell books (which are obviously physical products, even if they mainly contain information) all over the world by using the same site on the Internet for all markets. It needs no investments in shops and very few staff. Amazon.com is not a totally transformed company, using all new opportunities in the transparent marketplace. It still carries high costs of warehousing and transport. However, the investments that the company has made in programming and computer capacity can be used for an almost unlimited number of customers daily with only small additional costs in extra capacity as the Internet market for books increases. At present, this company claims to be growing at a rate of 30 per cent a month in volume, and in late 1997 it served its millionth customer. It is, however, worth mentioning that the company has made no profit in the first years of operation owing to the fact that, in many parts of its value chain, its costs are the same as they are in traditional bookshops.

The consequence of transparency is that buyers in all markets will have an enormously powerful weapon in their hands. Customers who want to buy the same products that they buy today, but at lower prices, should do as large a share of their purchases as possible over the Internet. This is because existing companies with less efficient production and distribution structures than those possible using the Internet will try to resist major changes to their ways of doing business. They want to see the Internet as a tool to improve their profitability but not as a tool for customers to force producers and distributors to rapidly decrease cost. If customers want to drive these changes, there is nothing that existing companies can do to stop this, if only there are enough efficient alternatives available on the Internet.

Transparency has the power to be an overwhelming experience for customers. The amount of information available in some situations can be far larger than today. When we select products in a food store, for example, the available information about different alternatives is limited to the amount of text that there is room for on a normal package. This reduces the available buying criteria to a minimum (the customer either has to go by the information on the package or bring his or her own information to the point of purchase, either on paper or in memory), which makes brand names and commercials very important ways of influencing customer decisions. In the transparent marketplace, customers will have access to a full picture of all products in a market where things such as production methods, health matters, environmental care and so on can be taken into account at the point of purchase. This may become such a breathtaking experience that many customers will stick to old buying habits because of the risk of drowning in information. However, we will soon learn to use the new opportunities and see them as positive and natural. Special interest can guide the choice to a larger extent than today.

Today, the search engines that help users to retrieve information from the Internet are quite basic in their nature. It is difficult to get well-structured information that can provide an overview of the market situation in a whole industry on a global basis unless there is a company that provides the whole picture on their homepage, as Amazon, mentioned above, does for the book market for readers of English. This is, of course, because such search engines have been developed only in the past few years. As these are further developed, they will become more and more accurate, and it will become easier to find exactly the information that is needed. As this process goes on, companies that sell on the Internet will also provide more and more information as it becomes clear that it is vital in competitive terms to have a strong presence on the Internet.

During this process, many companies may find that they will have to publish information on the Internet that they would never dream of making public in the physical market. This could mean that companies that make it their business idea to compete on the Internet start to publish information about their total capacity situation, different price levels and perhaps even how they calculate their prices. As buyers find it convenient to buy from such companies, competitors will have to follow suit, which in turn means that it will be very difficult for one company to charge higher prices than another if it cannot be shown that it actually adds more value to customers than do the least expensive suppliers.

Implications for competition

In different types of system in the market, different types of competition will evolve. In an agricultural system, we could assume that there would be limited competition, since production units would not have access to markets big enough to increase volumes above the local demand, and there would be little inflow of goods from other villages, towns or regions. We could think of a typical agricultural society as an example, most of the production being done for the single household. In each village, there would be a blacksmith, a stonemason and a carpenter, but they would not compete very much against their equivalents in other villages.

In a production system where there are transportation links between production units, competition will increase. The level of competition will depend on how advanced the methods of communication there are. As transportation and communications via telephone or fax get better, competition in the system will increase, since the most efficient producers will be able to sell their products to a larger and larger market base. Our own society 10 years ago represents a good example of a system in which competition had increased to a high level in many industries largely because of these factors. Another factor that has increased competition in recent years is the deregulation of many industries and sectors of society, which has made it possible for companies to get access to larger markets and combine services more freely.

In the third type of system, where transparency is complete, competition will increase even more. Customers are able to compare value for money on a worldwide market without leaving their desk or sofa. This will increase the pressure on all players in the market to become efficient. The competitive edge will move even further towards adding value rather than reducing cost (as low cost will be taken for granted). To be successful, organisations need to stimulate creativity and be better at turning ideas into solutions.

New entrants in each industry will either have to be more efficient, or at least as efficient, as the existing producers or offer better services than existing competitors in order to survive their first day in the market. This is likely to be the reality in the future. There is, however, another side to this issue. Owing to the global nature of competition, it will not take long in this environment until some companies have arrived at a level of efficiency at which it will be difficult to increase efficiency further. These companies will then have used all the opportunities to decrease cost that present information technologies can offer. In this situation, it will become rather easy, since the service concepts of these companies and the prices will be known to everybody through the Internet, to copy these concepts and arrive at a similar cost position. Each company will then have an advantage in its regional or local market, since the remaining difference in cost will be the cost of transporting the products from producer to customer. This could, in many industries, result in a situation in which many companies worldwide used similar concepts and each company would have a remaining competitive advantage in its own neighbourhood. Only in markets where transportation costs were close to zero would it be possible to have global competition. The reasoning behind this vision will be substantiated throughout the book.

3 Three Main Trends

S o far, we have discussed the development towards transparency driven by the development of the new electronic marketplace on the Internet. To be able to get a good position in this new market, it is necessary to know more about this development and to try to structure this knowledge into a firm picture of the market that is emerging. This chapter will start the journey into the future market by taking a close look at some of today's trends.

We will describe three observations that, taken together, indicate that life in the future will be different from the life that we have led so far. It is obvious that the changes we describe here started a long time ago. The point is that the latest developments of IT have the power to enhance the speed at which these trends are assailing us, so that we may find ourselves in the midst of changes we do not understand sooner than we expect.

In his description of paradigm shifts in his book *Paradigms* (1993), Joel Arthur Barker noticed that people tend to interpret their observations from the perspective of their old paradigms even if the same observations are signs of a new paradigm that is coming. This means that even the most open-minded people tend to hang on to old ways of looking at the world longer than they should because they tend to apply old paradigm solutions to problems that would be more accurately analysed from the point of view of a new paradigm.

Politicians look back at the solutions that solved unemployment problems 10 or 20 years ago even though unemployment today may have causes that call for new solutions. We also see how companies, faced with the problem of employees who spend working hours surfing the Internet, calculate the cost of the time lost in this way and decide not to use the Internet for professional purposes in order to keep employees from spending time on unproductive activities.

These are symptoms indicating that there are limits to how well our present paradigms could help us to understand the world of tomorrow. Below, we will describe our observations of three trends that we can see in society at present. We have named these trends 'the real-time society', 'disintermediation' and 'the innovation-based economy'. These three trends form the basic understanding of the new paradigm that will be further analysed in the rest of the book.

The first trend: the real-time society

Real-time is a technical term describing the fact that a process is fast enough to follow a course of events as they happen. The term is widely used in the field of computing, where it indicates that a program can work on data from the outside without delays and present the result immediately it is ready. In this book, the term is used to stress that the requirement to be able to order goods when we would like to and to get all kinds of services immediately we need them will be the main driver of new services and solutions.

The rush for real-time solutions is currently influencing many areas of society. Everybody who uses IT is involved in this change, helping to drive it forward. The trend is slowly, but irreversibly, taking a central place in our minds. Most of us have probably not thought about it, but we will see the effects in the coming few years. The trend can be characterised by one simple word: NOW. In more and more situations in our daily lives, we expect immediate actions. When we can have what we request immediately, we will never settle for less. Technology and new ways of working make this a reality in an increasing number of situations. As activities take less time to perform, we suddenly realise that it will lead to more fundamental consequences than we can imagine. It will also change the demands on internal processes within companies, and it will change the way in which business strategies are developed.

An example from our daily lives is probably the best way to start to show what the effects of the real-time society can be. When we buy products or services, we expect after-sales support if we run into problems. These problems can turn up at any time, and we need instant help. Traditionally, it was enough for a company to offer support during office hours, 5 days a week. Of course, it was inconvenient for us as customers to wait, to plan for how to get a couple of minutes free during work and to start to deal with the problem that had occurred a day or two before. Today, the situation is different. Many companies, especially in different fields of IT, offer 24-hour support to increase their competitiveness, and it is now possible to deal with many problems immediately they occur. This is often a much better solution for customers because they can deal with tasks in real-time rather than putting them on a waiting list and coming back to them later. One such example is ordering goods over the Internet and dropping this from the 'to-do' list until they turn up in the mail or are delivered at home.

Another example of this trend is that companies on the Internet offer customer support that can be used at all times during the week. Microsoft is perhaps one of the most prominent examples (which will be described in more detail later in the book).

On-line and Internet banking is a way for banks to enter the real-time market by offering 24-hour banking services. These alternatives offer the same types of service as an ordinary branch office.

To get deeper into the nature of the real-time society, it is necessary to look at the causes behind the change. There are at least two reasons behind the fact that everything has taken time in the past:

1. Communication in the physical world takes time, and tasks that require a large volume of information in order to be able to make the right decisions take time. This is because a large amount of information from different sources has to be collected, with lead times for the delivery of each item.
2. The management of different kinds of information, which includes keeping updated versions of price lists, catalogues and other product information, also takes time. One reason for delays is that other people are involved in a process carrying out various tasks, and it is easy to blame others. People often say that their tasks take time because they have to communicate with a number of others, and this reason often has to be accepted.

Let us stop briefly and think about what would happen if most tasks did not take time. What would it mean to overall performance and lead times? Would lead times approach zero and performance increase dramatically, or would there be other factors slowing down the process?

The answer is that communication does not have to take time, and information can be made available in the right form whenever it is needed. This fact leads to more far-reaching consequences than most of us can imagine. It will change the concept of time in all parts of the business environment. When things no longer take time to perform, many industries will change shape. This development has, of course, been going on for a long time, with shorter and shorter lead times as a consequence, but so far it has had little effect on the way in which we organise work.

To understand what this trend can lead to in the long run, the following example can be used to bring some thoughts to mind. Imagine a board room in a large corporation that sells products over the Internet. Let us assume that they sell books. In the room, the entire management team has gathered to discuss a new approach to the pricing of books in one of their market segments. They discuss what the effects may be and try to forecast future sales. In present society, they would have presented the idea, discussed it for a couple of hours and then ended the meeting by assigning tasks to some of the members to analyse the matter, perhaps ordering a market study. As we all know, this would take a couple of weeks. After that, the team would meet again and (with a little luck) determine whether the idea was good and whether the website should be re-programmed and changed to reflect the new pricing ideas.

However, this is not the way it would be handled in real-time society. Here, all the opportunities of new technology are used to deal with this in a totally new way. The management team still meets but not necessarily at the same geographical location – they may have an Internet meeting and save time, money and environmental resources by avoiding travelling. After the presentation of the new pricing ideas, they change the website in real-time and offer the new concepts directly to the market. They deal with other matters for a while and come back to the changes in pricing to evaluate the direct effects after an hour of its use.

By monitoring changes in customer usage, they can get a good statistical and economic picture of the consequences (in a world market, perhaps thousands of customers have already ordered goods using the new offer during the management team's meeting). Before the end of the meeting, they can decide whether it is a good idea to continue with the offer, whether it has to be changed or whether the old pricing should be brought back again. Such a test may cost some money in lost revenues if it does not work out well, but there is always the opportunity for the company to run both concepts (the old and the new) in parallel during the meeting in order to see which of the alternatives seems to be most attractive to customers.

Some conclusions can be drawn from this example. In the real-time society, there is never a 'later' or a 'tomorrow', only a NOW! Many things that we now have to plan, analyse and use several hours of work to finalise can be achieved immediately.

Another interesting aspect of this example is the fact that customers today may be confused by frequent changes to an offer. They may feel unsure if an offer changes several times during a day. However, customers in the real-time society would expect this because this would be a normal procedure and it would be to their advantage. They shop for the best solution in the world market with instant access to all prices and all alternatives, so they will not need the safe haven of a well-known bookshop on the Internet where they always go. Instead, customers would look upon most markets in the same way as we look upon the stock market or the currency market today. We see frequent changes in the prices of stocks as a sign of a healthy and well-functioning market, and nobody is surprised that a price one day alters the next.

> An example of a company that has started to see the effects and opportunities of the real-time trend is the Swedish training company CEI (Continuous Education Institute, www.cei.se). They formerly published descriptions of their training courses in brochures that were updated once or twice a year. These long periods between different versions made it difficult (or even impossible) to experiment with different alternatives and test new options. By publishing new courses on the Internet, it is possible to offer a new course, evaluate interest after a few weeks or months and then decide whether to give the course or withdraw it.

We will now start to look more closely at the real-time society from three different aspects: how to get information quickly, how to communicate in real-time and how to make sure that customers get their products and services instantly.

Direct access to information

It is possible to find a number of ordinary daily situations in which the real-time society has started to become visible. Let us look at how we now can find the information that we need about all kinds of issues we have to deal with on a daily basis, both in business and at leisure. When we face a new task at work for which we need to find a piece of information or collect information from several sources, the procedures are handled very differently from the traditional route. The methods and media can, of course, differ depending on what we do and where we are, but the common aspect is that in many situations we now start with the assumption that we can find information instantly. We think about the Internet, various on-line services, text-TV and other instant media. We know that they have the power to offer information 'at our fingertips'. The interesting factor that relates back to the trend we are trying to describe is that we want to conclude the information search as quickly as possible in order to go on with the real task we are facing. Let us look at an example.

Assume that, at short notice, you have to get to an important meeting in London early the next morning. Since you live in Birmingham, you need to make travel arrangements for early next day. You want to conclude the task immediately so that you can continue with the next thing on your day's agenda. What do you do? Tradition tells us that a travel agency, or a secretary, needs to be contacted, but that takes time and may require time-consuming communication. Instead, you quickly switch over to a travel site on the Internet and enter your request there. You will get a direct answer about alternative ways to get to London, what it will cost and whether there are any seats left. This will make it possible to conclude everything and confirm your booking. Several such sites are present on the Internet today, some 'complete' with booking and confirmation facilities (for example www.sas.se and British Midland's CyberSeat service, www.iflybritishmidland.com).

Another example from the Internet showing how time can be reduced is when we search for information about products to buy. This has traditionally been a rather tedious task requiring several telephone calls: to ask for those with knowledge about the products, to ask for brochures to be sent and to wait for this information to arrive or go to conferences and exhibitions. We then contact the company and ask for product samples, wait for them and test them upon arrival. A piece of work like this could take weeks or months. Nobody thinks about how much time is spent on this, the most important thing is, after all, to get the best possible product.

Today, this task could be done in a totally different manner. Several sites on the Internet offer comprehensive information about products, with information, references and news collected in one place. A typical example is the Internet Product Watch site (ipw.internet.com). Here several hundreds of products are made searchable, and it is easy to get an overview of the total market for a certain type of product in only a few minutes. When interesting products have been identified, more information, together with demos and evaluation copies, can be downloaded directly from the suppliers in a matter of minutes. It is easy to see how this can be extended to include buying and paying for these products as well. The result of this is that a process that once took weeks takes only a couple of minutes, which is a good example of immediacy, leading not only to lower costs in this area, but also to more frequent product evaluations in many industries.

If information is not accessible in real-time, the activity will suffer. We have to stop the process, wait until the information has been collected and start the process all over again at a later stage. In the travel example, we could spend a large part of the afternoon waiting for the secretary to come back only to find out that the preferred departure is fully booked and that we will have to go for an alternative. This behaviour is the same in our private lives. Many of us have equipped our homes with information channels that make it possible to find what we are looking for: the weekend weather, the latest news, the latest sports results or the availability of seats at the local theatre. We are only at the very beginning of this era of free access to information at any time. Now we are trying the concepts in a limited number of situations, but when we get used to what the new media can offer us, we will see more advanced and thrilling examples of information immediacy in the world around us.

Some obvious signs of this type of society are 24-hour weather channels and news channels on television for those who cannot wait until the next hour or the next evening. News on the Internet is also a good example.

Information that was very difficult or impossible to obtain only a few years ago can now be accessed directly over the Internet. A Swedish musical, written by two former pop stars of the group ABBA, Benny Andersson and Björn Ulvaeus, has been running at different Swedish theatres during the past few years. Many newspaper articles have been written about all aspects of the musical, but this type of information has been very difficult to obtain when it was needed. Now, a person with a special interest in this musical has collected a large amount of information on a homepage on the Internet, where it is available free of charge to anyone who is interested. More than 55,000 people have visited the homepage in the few months that it has been available. The response from the company responsible for the official information about this musical to the question why they had not done the same thing before was the laconic: 'There is no need for it.'

If we look at what instant access to the right information really means, we will find far-reaching consequences in many areas, not least in our working lives. Here we have become used to so many delays owing to problems of accessing information that we have forgotten that it is largely because of this that we cannot use our time more efficiently.

Because of the fact that it is very difficult and time-consuming today to evaluate the entire market each time a product or service has to be bought, most companies and customers have used long-term contracts and agreements to make it easier. These arrangements have made it easy for the customer to buy products, and it has given suppliers some time and stability to be able to plan production. However, this situation is now changing rapidly as more and more people experience the benefits of the real-time society.

It is now possible for purchasers to change suppliers every time a product is needed instead of making long-term contracts with one supplier. This will work in the same way as when somebody trades on the stock exchange today. Products will, to a large extent, be bought on demand. Information about different suppliers, their products and qualities will be available from different sources, just as information about the qualities of wines and the records and capacities of different wineries is available on the Internet today. One of the technological developments that will make this scenario possible is the development of 'electronic agents' that will help people, for example purchasers, to scan the Internet continuously for new offers in a particular field of interest. These agents will be described in Chapter 4.

Instant communication

Another area in which the real-time society is very visible is the field of communication. In the old world of communication, built on physical meetings, telephone calls and letters, almost no information could be accessed in real-time. With a little luck, it is possible to get in touch with a person directly over the telephone, but more often it takes several attempts. Today, we have become used to a completely different way of communicating, and we often want an immediate answer. For practical reasons, it is not possible to get hold of a person at all times, but there are other means that help us to stay in the real-time society. Mobile telephones are the most obvious equipment to increase the possibility of getting instant access to people. The penetration of these new gadgets has reached a level that nobody could dream of a couple of years ago. In the Nordic countries, the penetration has passed 30 per cent of the population. However, it is easy to say that this should mean that we have a very high probability of getting hold of a person at any time, but this is, as we all know, not the case, because telephones are, for one reason or another, often kept switched off.

However, the real-time society has started to make us all impatient, and new means of solving this problem have been introduced. There are two basic approaches to this: we go either for a real-time solution or another more traditional one, which could be some type of voice mail system guaranteeing that we can conclude the task later (at least it is possible to transfer the task and drop it from our own agenda). The alternative real-time solution is different. Our message or call may be switched to the best person currently available to take care of our problem (instead of to a specific person who is not available). This will add efficiency to the economy and decrease costs to society, but it may in the eyes of many people seem to make society less personal. New IT solutions can help this re-routing of messages and calls with a high degree of efficiency.

> A product that has taken the lead in the area of providing instant and professional access to people in an organisation is Wildfire. This is an intelligent electronic assistant, with an arsenal of agents that it deploys as needed. It manages telephone calls, contact lists, voice messages, whereabouts and reminders for work groups. Each person in a work group has a dedicated 24-hour voice assistant.
>
> Wildfire is the brainchild of a Lexington, Massachusetts start-up company and is operated by voice commands, although it can also be operated by the telephone keypad in case a telephone connection is so poor that voice recognition fails. A user engages in spoken interaction with the Wildfire assistant, which is represented by a female voice with a sense of humour. A Wildfire session is initiated by the user dialling Wildfire or by Wildfire calling the user with a call or a reminder. During the session, the user can listen to messages, place calls, handle incoming calls, put the current call on hold, listen to, record and schedule reminders, create or update contacts, ask the time, redirect phone calls to a different place (for example home or car), ask the assistant to take messages for all but important contacts, or ask for messages to be taken for all calls until a specified time.

Instant communication is a vital part of business life and also a vital part of providing excellent service and support to customers. Here it is necessary for any company that wants to stay competitive to take a step into the real-time society and provide better channels into the organisation. Twenty-four-hour support lines and sales slips on the Internet are typical examples of this. Why let the customer wait until the next day when he or she is willing to buy the product NOW? This is particularly important when products are marketed over media such as television or the Internet. If customers are not offered the opportunity to buy the product directly, the number of people who buy products becomes much smaller. Therefore, companies often provide customers with opportunities to do on-line shopping or to use 24-hour telephone services.

Rapid delivery

When a customer has ordered a product, the time to deliver it will decrease in the future, not only for products that can be delivered over the network, but also for products that have to be delivered physically.

> An example of the development towards the real-time society, when it comes to transportation, is the new service from UPS: guaranteed delivery before 8.30 am the next day to a number of locations. The basic service is to get a package delivered before 10.30 am, but that is not enough in the real-time society. At 10.30 am people have already been working for some hours by the time the package is delivered, and that delay incurs a cost for the company. So now we only have to pay a small extra sum and get it delivered when we arrive at work in the morning (or when we start to work in our home office).

Getting a glimpse of the real-time society

Since every step of a process takes time, there is no real driver today radically to reduce the time of a particular step. Therefore, we have great problems imagining what it would mean to leave this deeply rooted way of thinking about constant delays in everything we do. Many people will probably argue that time compression programmes in industry are not new and that they have already gone a long way in many organisations, with reduced lead times as a consequence. We are not saying that these will stop or take another shape. On the contrary, they are important initiatives that have to continue, but the opportunities of achieving dramatic reductions in lead times will increase in many industries. When these reductions have reached a certain limit, we will see changes to the whole value chain in many industries that we would

The real-time society may seem like a small change to the way in which we work and perform our daily tasks, but it is not. This development could lead to major changes in the way in which we organise work. The first time we come across the new opportunities, we will probably feel good and be happy that a task that has previously taken several days can now be finished in one session. We may, however, also realise that we now only have ourselves to blame when we do not manage to do what we have set out to accomplish.

Figure 3.1 shows the effects to a typical work environment in which jobs have lead times for the collection of information before they can be concluded, and another environment in which such lead times do not exist. In the first case, we start Task 1 and, when we need to gather information or order services, we have to wait until we have received the information or until the services have been delivered. During that time, we may start a second task. So far so good, but when we need input from others or gather information this time, we cannot progress. Then suddenly, Task 3 turns up and we start to deal with that. After some time, we get the input that is needed to conclude Task 1 and we decide to go back and finalise that before it is too late, which we cannot… (and so on).

In the real-time society, this will not happen. We will always be able to conclude the tasks we are dealing with without delays. Therefore, we start to do tasks in a straight series and end all the three tasks in less time than it took to do the first task in the former example. In order to do our job, we have to take advantage of the opportunities of the new society. Otherwise, we may not be as competitive as we could have been, and we may eventually lose our job.

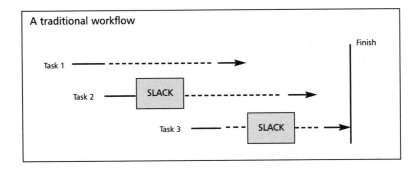

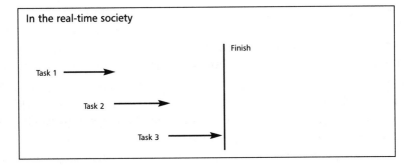

Figure 3.1   Implications for work in the real-time society

not expect, since we are used to thinking of time from the perspective of our present situation. When time is reduced in key business activities, it will lead not only to business as usual (albeit more quickly) but also to completely new ways of doing business, which we will describe in Chapter 7. We are moving into a society where we can always finish what we start before we do the next task. In the new society, we tend to do tasks in a series instead of starting a number of activities that cannot be finished and keep most of them in an idle state at any time.

This is a fundamental change to the way in which we will work, and it will have a number of effects:

- In the old world, we all had time to think and plan. This was seen as natural, because activities took a certain time to perform and we could use that time to have second thoughts about different alternatives and to discuss them. When activities do not have these natural breaks, we face a new challenge: how to organise work to ensure that the right decisions are taken at the right time. To be able to do this in the real-time society, a number of changes are required to how we act in the market and how we organise work internally.
- In the old world, companies could have a large number of people involved in activities not based on real-time communication, such as getting information, trying to communicate and waiting for things to be implemented and delivered. For some people, it may have been a pleasant working life, but it has perhaps not been so advantageous for customers, who have had to pay for these inefficiencies.

How far can real-time go?

We have already noted that it will be possible to reduce waiting times and interruptions in processes by applying real-time communication alternatives more often. In many cases, real-time services will require computerised service concepts, but it will also be possible to increase the availability of human expertise through networks where calls are routed to the person in the network who is available at any given moment. The question now arises of whether there is a limit to how far we can take real-time communication.

Measured by how it works within our present paradigm, we would expect there to be limits both to which issues can be solved through real-time solutions, and to our willingness to be served by computers, if that were the only alternative. The first of these problems, the assumption that some issues cannot be handled in real-time, must be rejected on the grounds that we know very little about which future solutions could be applied to solve specific problems. Our willingness to be served by computers would probably increase over time if we saw that there would be more advantages than disadvantages from this development.

If all of us could work shorter hours and work closer to our homes, if not at home, and if we could use our increased spare time to do things we really value, we might be willing to accept that we did not have to go on our daily shopping excursions and meet shop assistants with whom we only exchange a few words as we pay our bill.

Real-time solutions, be they in the form of human or computerised services, will seem more attractive as we can measure the results of this development. These measurements will also probably increase our creativity in the development of new solutions. This increased creativity will come both from our improved understanding of the opportunities and from the probability that more people will turn their attention to the development of new solutions as the demand for this type of services grows.

The second trend: disintermediation

The second trend is about new communication paths in the market and in organisations. It is often called disintermediation. The idea is that middleman functions between producers and consumers are eliminated through information networks that can increase the transparency of the market and make middleman functions obsolete.

Wholesaling and retailing are examples of typical middleman functions. The reason why the present distribution structure of many industries has developed is because it has been impossible in most markets for producers to communicate with all end customers themselves. Since each market has been local, there has been a need for national or regional wholesalers to buy large volumes of goods, store them for the national or regional market and sell them in smaller quantities to retailers in direct contact with customers. This structure has been necessary for production to reach the advantages of scale from which we are profiting today. The distribution structure of the industrial society comprises everything from market communication, including customer contacts and customer support, to the final delivery of the product. One of the purposes of this book is to describe how this chain may change as the use of the electronic market spreads.

In the future, it will become possible for each producer to communicate directly with all end customers over the Internet. Customers can get information about all the products that are available on the homepage of each producer and can, within seconds, compare the offerings of all the producers without having to spend weeks roaming the shops in order to find the best product at the most advantageous price. In this situation, customers can get better and more accurate information about products than they can in their shops today, since producers can always offer updated information about the products, delivery times and prices on their homepages. It will be possible to ask questions either of a computer with predefined answers or, if necessary, of a person who we will be able to see as we talk to them in front of the computer.

When customers have made their decisions, the products ordered will be delivered to their homes or to a storage facility in the neighbourhood from where it can be fetched. This means that a large part of the cost for the wholesaling and the retailing parts of the present value chain would disappear. It may even be possible to decrease production costs since producers can produce more of their products to order to keep their stocks of goods at a minimum. In many industries, 'distribution costs', meaning the costs of the wholesaler and retailer networks, amount to 50 per cent of what the customer pays for the product. This indicates that the disintermediation trend could save consumers substantial amounts of money.

Disintermediation is about changing the signalling pattern. Consumer goods producers will not need wholesalers or supermarkets when customers can replenish supplies weekly by accumulating entries in their shopping list database and take delivery at home. Hotels will not need travel agents to execute booking transactions when everything can be done by would-be travellers 'helicoptering' in a geographical information system over their destination city.

Middlemen exist both as separate companies in the market and as departments and people within an organisation who are focal points for processes and information flows. One example of an organisational middleman is the middle manager. People who have followed the development in business in the past decade know that the number of middle managers is steadily decreasing.

Elimination of middleman functions

One example of changing information patterns in a large organisation can be seen in processes such as product development, which is often called 'time-to-market'. This process is focused on the introduction of new products in the market. Many parts of the organisation are involved in it. Information and decisions have to travel through many middlemen before they reach the person or function who needs them. Some examples of this are:

- direct access to customer and market information in the design of new products and services;
- the direct communication of order information to people who package and customise products and perform services;
- direct access to supplier information when external products and services are purchased;
- direct access to product and service information when solutions are sold to customers.

Today, a large part of this information stays with the middlemen, so that producers never get access to the most interesting and most accurate data about customer needs. The disintermediation trend means, therefore, not only that costs can decrease substantially, but also that the whole system can function more efficiently, through transparency, since more accurate information for producers also means that they can satisfy more of their customers' needs.

Another example of disintermediation in society today is the way in which purchases of products and services are made. What we see in the development of trade on the Internet is that buyers will be able to compare products from all equivalent (or semi-equivalent) producers against each other at each point of purchase and always buy from the producer that offers the best quality at the most competitive price. This will be true regardless of which type of product we are discussing. The only difference will be that the transportation cost between supplier and buyer will in some cases be higher than the saving made on an advantageous price, which means that the market will in some cases be restricted to a smaller geographical area than in others. We might expect, however, this practice to increase competition substantially in most industries.

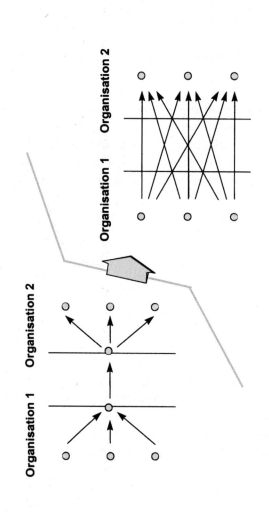

Changing patterns of communication create new signalling patterns in many of society's systems. In the present society, with our old ways of communication, we have been forced to organise in a way that simplifies communication. In many situations, we have created roles where people or organisations have existed for the sole reason of being a communication node through which information and/or goods have been channelled to one or a number of receivers or buyers. We could mention a number of such roles, which we often call 'middleman functions':

1. Wholesalers and retailers act as middlemen between the producer and the end customer.
2. Newspapers function as middlemen between journalists and their readers.
3. Middle managers work as middlemen between top management and the front-end staff.
4. Top managers are middlemen between the market and the organisation, one of their main tasks being to interpret signals from the market and turn them into actions or changes of the organisation.

Through the opportunity to create new information patterns, many of these functions will be eliminated. It may be surprising to find that new information technologies could make it possible to take away middleman functions that seem to have as their primary purpose to distribute goods, but if we look more closely at the situation, we find that wholesalers and retailers exist mainly for information reasons. Not even in the existing society would it be very difficult physically to send all types of goods directly from producers to customers. The problem at present seems to be keeping customers informed about existing alternatives and keeping costs down without using networks of retailers and wholesalers.

This trend of 'disintermediation' may have a different level of impact on different industries and types of function. In many industries, the main function of the retailer is to show products to the customer, who buys such products infrequently and one or a few at a time, as is the situation with white goods, hi-fi and furniture. In such cases, the whole function of the middleman may be eliminated. In other industries, such as groceries, two of the main functions of the wholesaler and the retailer are to break bulk and to store products from a number of different producers. In these cases, the function may only be changed dramatically rather than eliminated altogether.

In the case of organisational middleman functions, such as middle managers and top managers, elimination of these functions may proceed at different speeds depending on how much competition existing companies meet from new Internet-based competitors. In industries where competition will soon be fierce, such as many types of retailing, existing companies will have to cut costs through eliminating organisational middlemen such as middle managers. Over time, many Internet-based companies may find that even the number of top managers will have to be reduced as other forces, such as 'network intelligence' (see Chapter 5), take their toll.

Figure 3.2   Disintermediation (see Figure 3.1)

There is already evidence that large organisations see extensive potential savings in this type of purchasing. In Sweden, with only 9 million inhabitants, the authorities have started a project whereby electronic trade is promoted, which they estimate will reduce the workforce by some 40,000 people in the Swedish public sector alone. A Swedish organisation that represents the managers of all the Swedish county councils, municipalities and state organisations has written contracts with industrial groups of providers of software and communications solutions for electronic trade packages. These three groups of large companies in the communications and IT sectors are asked to compete with each other in the sale of electronic trade solutions to the Swedish public sector.

In the plans for this project, the objective was to decrease administration costs, but it should also be taken into account that the new purchasing procedure could, as a next step, substantially increase competition between all companies supplying the Swedish public sector. It is likely that the savings from this increased competition would be as large as the estimated savings on administration and that another 40,000 jobs would disappear in this part of the value chain. These two figures taken together ($2 \times 40,000$) would amount to 1.5–2.0 per cent of the total Swedish workforce.

This also means that the opportunities of large companies to influence consumers to buy their products decrease. Any customer wanting to could make a database of equivalent products in terms of different features, so that buyers could always choose the least expensive of the equivalent products. If any person, or couple of people, were to analyse the situation from a perspective of the cost of production, they would find that they could produce at a lower cost than the most efficient present competitor, just add their offer to the list and send out product samples to the largest customers, without the high sales costs that are there in today's system.

In our work as consultants, we have come across several companies acting only as middlemen. Their entire businesses consist of buying from producers and selling to end users. These companies are often struggling very hard to convince themselves and the rest of the world that they really add value to the value chain, but this will hardly be true in the future. When we penetrate the issue of how they add value, we often find that they collect information about products from a number of sources (mainly producers of goods) and compile a catalogue, which they publish in their customers' language. This has been a substantial added value in the past, but that will no longer be true in the electronic market. In many cases, the only value left for these companies to add will be that they can translate product information into other languages and make it easier for local companies to buy products that have been produced abroad. However, even this added value can be wiped away as new software becomes available that provides functions for automatic translation.

The third trend: the innovation-based economy

There is a trend in society that could be interpreted as if we are moving towards an innovation-based economy, in which innovative products, services and ideas are the key to success. This has been true for a long time in industries where the pace of innovation has been high, but we can see that it is starting to become more and more true even in industries where competition and the rate of innovation have traditionally been low, for example telecommunications (both hardware and software) and utilities.

One reason behind this is that many industries whose markets have been largely domestic through natural monopolies or regulations are experiencing a trend towards competition and internationalisation. On the other hand, we can see that new technologies are opening up new opportunities for innovative competitors who want to have a share of the market. Another reason behind the high pace of innovation is that IT has enabled many previously impossible innovations because of the lack of potent enough information-processing tools.

One example of this is the rapid increase in Internet marketing, which makes it possible to reach a global market with very niche-orientated sales approaches. Marketing people who work in this market are now talking about a possible market segmentation down to segments (or perhaps fragments) of some 50 or fewer people at whom an offer on the network market could be aimed while still having the potential to be profitable. Some even say that all companies will have to aim at these small segments in future; they speak of the obsolescence of mass marketing. The prerequisite for this is that producers can communicate directly with consumers to a larger extent than today, so that they get a better understanding of the real requirements of consumers in terms of the basic features of products and service concepts.

This is becoming clear to product planners, strategists, engineers, developers and managers in many industries. A company that has just developed a great product or service has to develop a better one that will make the first one obsolete before somebody else does. This will have a direct effect on how companies earn their money on products and services. Twenty years ago, an innovation often led to several years of revenue before it was time to develop the next generation of products to replace the old ones.

In industries where a large share of development is driven by developments in IT, there is a tendency for product life-cycles to become shorter and shorter. There are, however, other industries in which this is the case. In the field of cars and other types of product, the same is true, and in these industries IT has played only a secondary role behind the increasing speed of development. Instead, the driving forces here are related to the increasing level of global competition and service proliferation.

This development towards shorter and shorter product life-cycles means that companies have to become more and more efficient in order to be able to get a pay-back on their investment over fewer years than before. An alternative could be to increase their markets, so that investments in development could be repaid through selling to a larger customer base than before. The best way to achieve this is to use all the power of new tools to build new products and develop services through the utilisation of fewer resources. The use of old methods and tools would lead to costs that were too high. Launching products more quickly (even if they are only pre-releases) could lead to a more rapid increase in market share, earnings and return on investment.

The most obvious example of the planned obsolescence of a company's own products is the steady flow of new versions in the computer software market. In order to be the first company in the market with a new software application and to make the new product an industry standard, a company releases a first version with only the basic features that customers would like to have. As the first version is released, the company is already working on the second version and may be in the process of deciding on the contents of the third. This has a number of advantages, one of the biggest ones being that it makes the company's application the preferred solution of many customers and makes it possible to earn money on the early versions as the new ones are being developed. Still, everyone knows that the program they buy today will be replaced by a better version in only a year's time.

Creation of new markets

Although IT has been used as a tool in business for some decades, the results in terms of increased efficiency have not been as good as many people expected. Benefits have been limited owing to the fact that technology has been used to support and automate existing tasks and activities. In other words, technology has been introduced to do things in the same way that people did them when they were carrying out manual tasks. For example, control systems in the process industry have replaced people who read meters and turn valves, network management systems in the telecom industry have replaced people who physically managed networks, and financial systems have replaced people who did calculations and plotted graphs. This way of introducing IT has seldom led to any significant improvements in productivity or increased revenue. The development has also been slow, which has made it possible for all competitors in an industry to reach almost the same degree of technology, that is, positioning them in almost the same position in the market as before, with similar products and service offerings.

New solutions have been developed with traditional requirements in mind, and when they were ready, IT was brought in to support some part of the solution. This has been the case for a long time because of the lack of really powerful technologies that could be used to realise completely new solutions, but the technologies available for information-processing and communications are becoming more powerful in a number of respects. IT is becoming an enabler that makes entirely new solutions come to life in a number of industries.

In the innovation-based economy, human imagination is the main source of value creation. The critical challenge for any company is to create a climate in which innovation is prized, rewarded and encouraged. Every company needs an innovative culture and an organisation that fosters creativity. Growth in the innovation economy comes from small and medium-sized businesses rather than large corporations or state-owned companies.

Product and service leadership is crucial in the innovation economy, but it is not enough to understand customers and their concerns and desires. Given the pace of change and the complexity of markets, customers often cannot articulate their needs. In this field of opportunities, companies must innovate beyond what their customers can imagine. In other words, companies have the opportunity to create new markets at the same time as they compete for a market share in the existing ones. Even companies that are not at present very innovative will need new routines for product development and introduction, and companies that already think of themselves as innovative are likely to need to upgrade their methods in order to stay competitive.

In this respect, the innovation-based economy could be described as a new land that will have to be conquered. To give an analogy, we could think of the colonisation of the United States. The first people who arrived and the most courageous were able to secure the best land for themselves. When people had settled down, it became more difficult for those who arrived after them to own a farm of their own. They either had to steal land or raise money to be able to buy it. When we think about the network market using this analogy, we should expect some of the companies that arrive first in the market to be able to secure a share of the market for themselves. All in all, it will be companies with an innovation-friendly climate that have the best possibilities of succeeding.

It may sound simple to say that companies must create new markets to become successful, but what does it really mean? How should they find these new and unconquered parts of the market where it is possible to start to build new products and services without having to think about existing neighbours (that is, competitors)? The most important starting point is to have a vision of new needs and patterns of life, or methods of work that still have not been discovered and satisfied. The digital revolution that started when the microchip was invented still provides an amazing *smörgåsbord* of new opportunities and possibilities. Here we often find the basis for new inventions and new markets.

Our imagination today, rather than technological boundaries, sets the limits to what can be created, but companies also need a thorough understanding of the new technologies that we present later in this book. Despite a general view of the technologies themselves, companies will also need to analyse how different technologies could be applied to improve customer service and cost-efficiency in their own industries.

The Internet is a typical example of a location where new markets can be created. Web hotels are such an example. To create a presence on the Internet, it is necessary to have a web-server constantly connected to the network. The costs of arranging this are often too large for small companies and organisations. When the popularity of the Internet grew a few years ago, it became increasingly important to find other ways of reaching the net. Here some companies saw the opportunity to create a completely new market: web hotels. These provide a web-server with access to the Internet and all the necessary services to keep it in operation 24 hours a day. Costs for servers, communications and maintenance can now be shared among a number of users, and the barrier to entry to the new electronic market has been significantly reduced.

Other markets that have been created in the early days of the Internet and the World Wide Web (WWW) are those for search engines (for example www.altavista.digital.com and www.yahoo.com) and providers of Internet marketplaces where services and products can be offered. Many of these conquerors of the Internet market have rendered huge interest from investors of various kinds. Yahoo, for example, was introduced on to the New York stock exchange in 1995. It was, and still is, a relatively small company in a market with almost no track record or 'safe profits'. However, the stock value of its first day in the market exceeded by 1,000 times the revenue per year at this time. This shows that a company conquering a new market has the potential to become extremely valuable, but many of them will turn out to be very risky investments.

> One example of a company that has adopted the idea of creating new markets is Microsoft. Many people would argue that they are in the well-known software development market, but Microsoft instead talks about software publishing, to stress the fact that software should in the future be handled in the same way as other media. Their view of future business is based on the creation of new markets as a competitive weapon of increasing importance. They look at possibilities such as markets for on-line services (their recent operating systems also contain more communications software than earlier versions), electronic commerce and even markets for children's edutainment (entertaining education). This latter market can be formed out of the increasing use of computers among children and the possibility of moving from purely game-orientated software to software that will educate and entertain children at the same time.

The creation of new markets can be positive in more than one aspect. The very fact that a new market is not well defined and well known leads to a process by which companies try to describe and understand the nature of the needs that the new market will address. Innovators and strategists as well as marketers and designers will have to make offers as concrete as possible. By doing this, the company will generate ideas for new products and services. This innovation process is important and could, in many cases, be more beneficial than even the discovery of the new market. Managers at different levels can use this to release the creative power of the organisation and make people think along certain lines that can lead to a more creative company climate.

There are several examples of this. Marc Porat, former Chief Executive Officer of General Magic, was using this approach to drive the development of intelligent agent software in the company. By describing how personal assistants, accessed on palmtop computers, can help people to find products and services they need without knowing exactly where and how to find them, he has created the foundation for great inventions in completely new markets. James Gosling has used the same techniques to push Sun Microsystems into the area of Internet technologies, based on the Java programming languages. Microsoft and Bill Gates have also used this approach to develop Microsoft from a traditional software position into new and unexplored markets.

Even companies in rather slow and stable markets have found that they cannot expect to be left outside this development. Even if the industry is built on products and services that are not directly in the media, IT, computer or Internet business, innovation and creativity must be taken seriously. Even if the market for the basic product is quite stable, such as with electricity, telephony, books or groceries, a number of opportunities could be found in the packaging of these services and in serving customers. Electricity companies have started to look at the concept of intelligent buildings to help customers manage energy costs by more information about the use of energy and the remote and automatic control of household appliances. By doing this, these companies move into new areas where they may find new ways to earn money.

Unlimited advantages of scale

One other interesting development that companies will try to take advantage of in the future is the tendency for the new distribution channels on the Internet to give companies that develop new products almost unlimited advantages of scale. Even though this development seems most clear in IT-based industries where products are delivered over the Internet, it is becoming obvious that new materials and production technologies, even in markets where physical products are traded, make production so relatively inexpensive that the cost of product development is the main outstanding item.

Examples can be taken from the field of mobile telephones, in which a telephone takes only about 10 minutes to produce, which means that the cost of production is so low that development costs comprise the major share of the price to the customer. This also allows for international producers in the field of mobile telephones to make large profits on their products, because the product itself is relatively inexpensive and companies have a world market to sell to.

Another example is Microsoft, described elsewhere in this text. With their office package, they are now almost unchallenged in the market and manage to sell each new version that is released to a large percentage of their professional users worldwide.

This indicates a situation in which the winner takes almost all. We can see how companies such as Netscape and Microsoft, which have been among the first to enter their markets, have the opportunity to take a leading position in an industry, from where they are in a good position to defend themselves against new entrants. The major threat to these businesses is the possibility of a technological paradigm shift in which a new technological solution becomes the preferred alternative.

There are arguably many industries in which production costs are brought down to a level at which advantages of scale become almost indefinite, at least as long as the market leaders are able to keep the pace of product development and outperform copying companies.

> Luckily, however, many industries, such as the car industry, still use the same old-fashioned techniques and old materials that make the market for cars fairly stable. Recently, however, Chrysler presented their new invention, the PET car (made of PET plastic). Their future car, the Composite Concept Vehicle, is made from the plastic from 2,132 recycled 1 litre PET bottles. They could gear production up to full-scale volumes within 3 years and believe that the safety aspects of the car that still need to be solved could be handled by then. The company expects that this new type of car would cost approximately $6,000. The low price is due to several savings from the new technology, including the relatively inexpensive material, fewer parts in the car as a whole and a lack of need to paint it. Other car producers are reported to be experimenting with the same type of technology, which seems to be one of the future lines of development in the car industry.

The opportunity boom

The innovation-based economy is built on the assumption that technology will evolve quickly enough to stay ahead of imagination and creativity. The major developments over the past couple of years in the Internet and the flood of tools and techniques that surround it, together with technologies such as workflow, groupware and data warehousing, provide the basis for a new era in many industries: the era of push technology. Today, it is our imagination that sets the limits to what we can

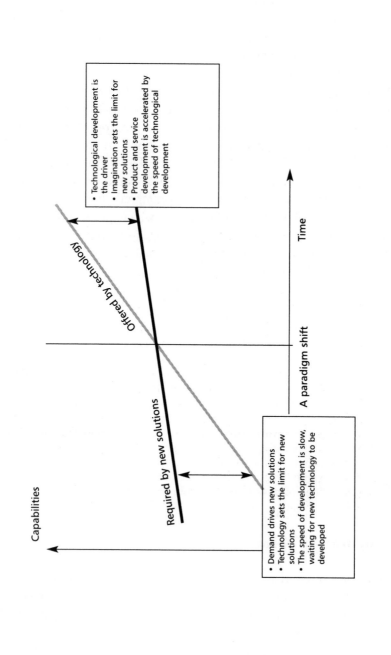

Capabilities

Offered by technology

Required by new solutions

- Technological development is the driver
- Imagination sets the limit for new solutions
- Product and service development is accelerated by the speed of technological development

- Demand drives new solutions
- Technology sets the limit for new solutions
- The speed of development is slow, waiting for new technology to be developed

A paradigm shift

Time

Historically, technology has always been the main limiting factor in the process of developing new products and services. This seems no longer to be the case. There are a number of recent developments indicating that the present situation is one in which the main limitation to development is our ability as human beings to make creative use of the technologies that have been developed during the 1990s.

The main reasons behind the booming opportunities are as follows:

■ Computing capacity, or the price of such capacity, is no longer a limiting factor, either in terms of memory capacity or when it comes to actual processing capacity.

■ There is coupling of the above-mentioned development to a steady decrease in the price of such capacity. It is no longer too expensive to handle extreme volumes of data. The American retailer Wal-Mart runs a data warehouse with a memory capacity of 70 terabytes, which is more than anyone could even conceive of 10 years ago.

■ The development of new types of application have made it possible drastically to extend the realm of what can be achieved with the help of computers.

■ Communication over the Internet has created opportunities through the combination of data that would have been impossible in a society of stand-alone systems. The opportunities that are created by the Internet would never have been possible had systems not been able to communicate with each other.

■ Many developments outside the field of IT, such as the development of new materials, have also been key in this development.

Figure 3.3   The opportunity boom

achieve with the help of technology. The shift was probably not noticed by many people, but the increasing gap between what could be achieved in new solutions and the ideas of how to build them is difficult to ignore. In order to close this gap, we need to organise in new ways so that the imagination and competence of people can flow freely inside and outside organisations, ways that try to combine those with the imagination and competence of people who want to work on a particular type of problem. Deep knowledge of the opportunities, rather than a deep knowledge of technology, is required.

Companies that refuse to take this challenge are likely soon to find themselves far behind the leaders in their market. To learn more about the roots of this development, we have to look at what technology can offer us today and what is waiting just around the corner, which we will do in the next chapter.

To show what we mean by the opportunity boom, we will try to exemplify the technological obstacles that have been removed and how these new opportunities can be used. Let us look at a typical office in a company. In the distant past (which in this case is only a couple of decades ago), the focus was mainly on the local environment where people were working. Just think about the tools that were common: typewriters, calculators, drawing boards, meters. Today, this is history; the office in many respects has been opened up to the rest of the world. However, managers and work descriptions still manage work in many companies in a detailed and very inflexible way. Processes can be managed and monitored by workflow and process management tools that can be redesigned in almost real-time, but many companies still have not taken that step. Yesterday, a limited portion of information was managed electronically, the rest residing on bookshelves and in people's brains. Today, all company information can be managed electronically, and by using advanced tools, anyone can get the right information at the right time. Yesterday, tools at the local workplace were static, and any change required extensive work. Today, tools can be offered over the network from any place in the company, which means that the right tools are always within reach and can be changed as soon as conditions change. Does this sound like science fiction or a good description of your office? The fact is that technology provides all this today, but very few companies and people have realised what this implies. This is one part of the development that we may call the opportunity boom.

Only a small number of companies feel the shock waves of the opportunity boom today; very few people have felt its real power. We can take an example that shows what we mean.

Federal Express is a global distribution company of mail and packages. The company defined its key quality measurements a few of years ago and found that too many deliveries went wrong, with delays, extra costs and complaints as a consequence. To cut a long story short, the staff found a way to deal with this. They introduced a distribution management system that made it possible to scan every package up to 9 or 10 times on its way from sender to receiver. They collected all this information in order to be able to discover problems as early as possible (at least before the customers did) and take action, or at least inform customers of new delivery times as early as possible.

This may seem like an ordinary IT system, but it has turned out to be much more. The information that is collected and stored in this system is a good example of an opportunity boom. Many new applications have been spawned from it. Customers can get information of where their packages are in real-time over the Internet, customer support personnel always have the latest information on packages, each delivery can be evaluated to see whether it has been profitable, whether the costs were too high or whether problems have arisen. This knowledge base is extended day by day and can be used to optimise transportation and quality. The list will become longer and longer as Federal Express uses its creativity and extends the concept to more areas.

Other typical examples relating to the opportunity boom are electronic trade solutions. When a company decides to go for electronic trade over, for example, the Internet, it can mean much more than just another medium over which to send orders or receive bills. These solutions are usually implemented without too much thinking through of what they really could mean to productivity. The usual procedures are employed, the usual partners are involved, and the usual people within the organisation handle it. We could, however, consider the real potential of this type of solution. What would happen if one company managed to implement structures and systems that made it possible to realise the full savings potential and potential increase in productivity of this new way of working? What would happen to the entire purchasing process? Would such a company find the best supplier at each moment rather than having long-term contracts? Questions like these are relevant and will lead to the introduction of new concepts making use of the opportunities created by the opportunity boom.

There must be limits to development and innovation

Based on the reasoning concerning unlimited advantages of scale, we can claim that there may be a limit to the technological development of each particular functionality that could be taken care of by machinery. We base this statement on the analysis that there ought to be a point at which further development, by definition, is not viable from an economic point of view. People tend to think of technological development as boundless in terms of opportunities, but it seems more and more likely that we will soon discover that there are fixed boundaries that development cannot surpass. We do not, however, say that new functionality could not be developed or that more value could not be added to the customer.

Our basic argument is that when something can be done with the use of zero resources, we can assume that further development in terms of increasing efficiency becomes difficult. We can see, of course, that new functionality could be added, which would increase or enhance the functionality of a product. Nevertheless, a situation in which something could be achieved with zero, or close to zero, resources is much more problematic from a perspective of improvement than is a situation in which efficiency in terms of resource utilisation is the problem waiting to be solved.

In many areas, we are coming closer to a situation in which a large amount of work can be done with a resource utilisation close to zero. As we have shown, in many industries we are now coming closer and closer to a situation in which there are almost unlimited advantages of scale, both in many product categories, where production costs are low compared with the costs of research and development, and even more so in information-based areas where products can be reproduced and distributed over the Internet in the future.

We could use the travel industry as an example. Until recently, booking a ticket for a flight has in most situations required three people. First, the customer (person no. 1) called the travel agency. Somebody at the agency (person no. 2) answered the call and, in turn, called some-body at the airline office (person no. 3) in order to make the reservation. A few years ago, large travel agencies became able to make on-line bookings in the databases of the airline companies, which eliminated one person in the chain (person no. 3). Now, it is quickly becoming possible for customers to book their own tickets directly from the airline's or the railway company's computer systems over the Internet. This means that there will no longer be any paid labour involved on the travel industry's side. Instead, one programmer, or a team of programmers, might spend a couple of months creating the IT solution that eliminates the work of one person for every ticket that is booked. The Swedish national railway company, SJ, is the first Swedish company to publish on-line services on the Internet for all transactions from booking to payment (www.sj.se).

In such cases, the work of the programmers who have developed these on-line booking services can be copied all over the world, so all airlines and railway companies could theoretically share the cost of the programming between them. Furthermore, the programs could be used for 5, 10 or 100 years, and new functionality could be added as the need arose.

This means that, instead of paying a few pounds for the personal booking service each time a ticket is booked, the cost of booking a ticket decreases to a level where it comes close to zero as more and more tickets are booked through the system. Even if there are several systems competing in the market, the total cost for society for booking a ticket would come close to zero over time.

This is an example of a situation in which the advantages of scale are almost unlimited, and it shows that in this example society is coming close to a situation in which it becomes more and more difficult to create a new system that could compete with the best one already in the market. If the one in use here is lacking in functionality, there will be an opportunity for a competitor, but from a cost perspective it seems more efficient to add new functionality to existing systems than to create new ones all the time. It also means that the need for more advanced hardware decreases if the present machines can handle the required number of bookings, even at peak, without too much waiting time. Even if there is a company that is willing to develop a totally new competing system, it must think twice, since existing competitors will have an advantage because they have already paid the costs of developing their systems. They can thus offer systems at a discount to new customers in order to keep new entrants out of the market.

This is one of the reasons why many software companies are highly profitable. The most profitable are market leaders in industries or market niches that cater to high-volume markets, for example Microsoft. They have an advantage over new entrants in that they already have programs or systems that have been paid for by previous customers, but new customers do not have the bargaining power, because of the lack of competition, to negotiate prices down to the level of the cost for the software company of programming and selling the next version of the programme. Instead, programming companies are able to make large profits on the reduction in resource utilisation that they offer society. Each new customer adds very little cost to the company, since a new copy of a program can be distributed at almost zero cost, but the new customer has to pay the same amount of money for the program as the first customer did, regardless of whether all the costs of development have already been covered.

> Another example of how something that earlier required a large amount of resources, could now be done with a resource utilisation coming close to zero is a new offer from Federal Express. This company offers its customers the service of establishing a worldwide retail network over the Internet at no cost, provided that customers promise to send their goods through the FedEx distribution network.
>
> Historically, it has cost companies enormous sums of money to establish worldwide retail networks. Through this service, Federal Express takes this cost away and makes it possible even for start-up companies to establish a worldwide sales organisation (in electronic form) from day 1. Even if there were customer needs or wishes that would not be satisfied using this way of retailing, it would be difficult to argue that customers who would be content with this type of service could be served in a more efficient manner. It could also be assumed that it might be possible to satisfy several needs of customers in segments that were not content with the services offered through the Federal Express solution using other types of electronic trade service, and that each one of these, when they were developed, would be difficult to surpass in terms of efficiency. As more and more electronic trade solutions are developed, it will become increasingly difficult to find customer needs that can be profitably satisfied with the help of non-electronic solutions, simply because there will be fewer and fewer customers left who want to shop in the physical market and because physical shops require substantial local customer bases in order to be viable.

Basically, the work of the programmer can be copied as many times as needed, without any additional cost when programs are distributed over the Internet. Historically, new programs were developed all the time because new hardware made it possible to add many new features to each new program generation, and a multitude of technical platforms increased the need for a number of systems that could do the same job.

One example of this has been the transition from mainframes to minicomputers and server-based systems, where the programs that have been developed for mainframes have become obsolete as minicomputers have offered more capacity and lower maintenance and development costs.

Minicomputers offer more capacity than mainframes ever did, and this also makes it possible to develop systems that have more functionality. Additionally it becomes easier to make systems communicate with each other, which means that the need to increase the capacity of every single computer diminishes. In a network of computers, the need to increase the capacity of each computer decreases.

As we come closer and closer to the point at which each new feature brings less and less value to the customer, fewer customers will be prepared to pay for the next version of a program or a completely new program at that. When we as customers can do what we want to do at close to zero cost in the computer system of one of our suppliers, few of these suppliers will feel the need to invest in new hardware or software. We must also remember that computers do not wear out in the same way as mechanical hardware does, which means that computers will in the future be able to run for much longer periods of time with the same software than they do today. We have already seen a trend towards using the web-browser as the only software to use on the PC. Through this interface, all kinds of services and programs can be reached, and the network (the Internet) becomes the real computer.

However, we will see a development towards more advanced ways of interacting with computers, using the concept of virtual reality. This has the power to turn interaction with computers into a whole new experience. We will be able to enter environments where we can shop, visit foreign places, undergo training, meet other people or be entertained. All senses are in focus in this development. Three-dimensionality and sound are a natural focus, as is feeling through the use of special 'clothes'.

Another aspect of the computer development is that a larger and larger share of the value of mechanical products is represented by embedded software. The same line of argument is valid for these applications. There will always be a piece of hardware to pay for, even if the cost of the software contained came close to zero as aggregated volumes increased over time. However, we see from the example of mobile telephones that new materials and production technologies make it possible to produce at cost levels that make production a relatively small part of an item's total cost.

General appliances

One trend that will lead in this direction is the striving to make appliances of various kinds more general in order to cope with different tasks and to function as the front end of various services. Traditionally, services have been tightly related to a specific appliance. We are so used to this fact that we usually think about a service in the form of an appliance and vice versa. Take, for example, a telephone and the service of telephony. The telephone is built especially to function as the front end of this service. All the components are linked to each other, and it is difficult to take the two things apart. When new services were developed based on the same basic service, a new appliance had to be developed (like the fax service and fax machine). As the development of services becomes more rapid, it becomes more and more difficult continually to develop new appliances because the company that could satisfy the same need with the help of existing appliances will have an advantage. It is not only expensive, but also takes a long time before customers have access to the new appliance and can start to use new services.

In the area of the electronic marketplace and the Internet, there is a battle going on between companies to be the one developing a general appliance that could become the front end of any service in this area. One of the main battles at the moment stands between the television set and the PC. The PC has won the first round, establishing itself as the main interface to the Internet, but cable television companies and producers of set-top boxes that could turn the television set into a general appliance are struggling to offer broadband services over terrestrial, satellite or cable television networks to conquer the market for more demanding services over the Internet. There are now appliances in the market that make it possible to access the Internet via a television set. The price of such an appliance is currently as low as £200. However, the resolution of the television screen is not as good as a computer screen, so the question remains of how successful this attempt will be.

The CD is also an example of a medium that has become more and more general. Today, the same CD can be used to store information, pictures, music and software.

The companies that win this battle have a golden opportunity to sell a large number of appliances and connection services to companies and to the home user market. Many telecommunications companies have waited for a 'killer application' to come along that will stimulate the use of digital services and especially broadband services. The Internet is definitely a good candidate for this application, and many service providers are offering high-speed Internet services to the home (for example to connect a PC to intranets for home-working purposes).

Another example of the battle to conquer the market for general appliances is the new combined mobile telephone and palmtop PC recently introduced by Nokia, Ericsson and others. This computer can communicate with the Internet and company intranets over a mobile telecommunications network. This improves the mobility of users, and makes the use of computers even more flexible than with the present types of laptop.

One of the most interesting parts of this development, however, is that this appliance has a mobile telephone connected to it. This development indicates that mobile telecommunications companies are trying to enter the market for PCs from their position as leaders in a communications industry. In the future, we can assume that these appliances will not have a telephone connected to them. Instead, we will be able to speak through the computer with the help of a 'headset' that is already provided by producers of mobile telephones as a simple form of 'hands-free equipment'. These sets include a microphone and a small earphone that make it possible to talk through the telephone with the appliance in the pocket.

It is probable that there will be a practical limit to how far any type of machine can be developed, even if it seems more difficult to determine where this limit is in the machine example than in the example of information-processing, because of the larger number of variables that are involved in the case of the hardware. In a way, the development towards general appliances underscores this since it seems as if producers of mobile telephones, for example, see new opportunities in entering the PC market. The risk that the market for mobile telephones may altogether disappear in the process, as we started to use computers as a general communications appliance, seems to be a small risk compared with the advantages that this development offers. For customers, it could become less expensive to buy a television, a telephone and a PC in the form of one unit instead of buying them all as separate appliances. The combination, of course, also offers a number of interesting new opportunities in itself.

4 What is Possible Today at the Forefront of Technology?

The paradigm shifts that are discussed in this book are based on the idea that new technologies in the field of IT, media and telecommunications will become the key drivers that have the power to change the entire structure of many industries and markets. Many people would argue that this is not new. Over the past 20 years new advanced technologies have emerged continuously that have had the power to revolutionise industries but have failed to do so. For example, large investments have been made in new computer systems for the past two decades without any significant benefits in terms of efficiency. This argument was already one of the foundations of the process re-engineering trend that started in the early 1990s. However, this trend has not had the extreme impact on companies that its proponents expected.

The development of worldwide communication has had the same impact on the use of computers as the development of roads and railroads did in the early days of industrialisation. Imagine what production would be like if there were no way to transport goods from factories to customers all over the country or the world. Without these means of communication, production could only be local and the number of potential customers extremely small. Had this been the case, factories would not have been able to go for mass production.

However, many people argue that there is too much talk about the supernatural power of these new technologies. Is it not true that many people argued that the birth of artificial intelligence and expert systems in the 1980s was going to change the world and replace not just routine work, but also experts, through new computer systems that could handle complex tasks and even learn to adapt themselves to new situations?

These past examples are, of course, a reality and cannot be neglected when we look at development over the next few years. However, there are some differences in these changes, compared with the others mentioned, which we think will make all the difference and make this new wave of technology succeed. The main differences can be summarised as follows:

- The technologies driving today's development are based on communication that creates transparency in companies and in society as a whole.
- Computer technology will develop affordable machines that have the power to offer a user-friendly interface and that are already applied in the form of embedded software in all kinds of machine and appliance (your car, dishwasher and CD player, for example)
- There must be an understanding that technology has to be developed in parallel and in concert with organisations and businesses if we want to realise the advantages that these technologies promise.
- Investments in IT will be cumulative over the years, which could now begin to pay off very rapidly for society as a whole.

In this chapter, we will describe the most recent technological developments in the hope that the reader will see the opportunities that are created by all these developments taken together. We should note that the economic potential of some of these technologies has begun to show, but many of them are still in their infancy. This means that we will see the cumulative effects of all these developments in just a couple of years.

Telecommunications

Telecommunications are the foundation of all the developments that are described in this book. Without communication over a worldwide network, it would not be possible to build the Internet (or any other communications platform) and the new market that depends on it. Traditionally, telecommunications were the same as telephony services and some simple services related to computer communications. Communication over long distances has always been associated with narrow bandwidth and poor quality. Over short distances, it was possible to run more advanced applications that required high-resolution graphics and a lot of information. This meant that communication within a company (in the same building) could be fast and with a wide range of applications, but when we enter the outside world, applications had to be very simple and narrowly banded (like text-based e-mail and telephone calls). In recent years, this situation has changed dramatically as a result of two new concepts that make cheap, wide-area broadband communication possible: the new communication infrastructures and compression technologies.

The first technology is based on less expensive broadband communication to the home and to companies. For many years, there has been a battle between different technologies trying to provide the infrastructure to make it possible for anyone to access more advanced applications (such as broadband Internet connections, live video and hi-fi sound). Four main approaches are struggling to take the lead in this area:

- *Optical fibre networks.* For many years, the main idea was to build a new broadband network as a basis for services that required high bandwidth. Many people believed that this was the network technology for the 1990s, but the investments are too large to be made without a true customer demand for new services. The discussion of a 'killer application' that would justify the investment has been going on for years, but none has appeared.
- *Community Area Television (CATV) networks.* The cable television network is a network with high bandwidth (in the range of 10–100 megabytes per second). It is based on coaxial cables and sometimes on optical fibre networks. An important aspect is that it is already in place in many countries. The problem is that it is only working in one direction (only broadcasting, with no signals in the other direction). Different alternatives have been tested to get around this problem (for example, using telephony in the other direction or adding equipment to the network to create an upstream channel with less bandwidth). The technology to add services other than television is created by connecting a set-top box to the television through which other services can be added (Internet, interactive television or telephony). This market is driven by television and media companies that want to make the television set into the gateway to all future multimedia services.
- *The telephony (copper) network.* The old telephony network was for a long time seen as an obsolete infrastructure, not at all suitable for the new generation of broadband services, but in the past few years new technology has totally changed this picture. The technology is called ADSL (asynchronous digital subscriber line). This makes it possible to use the existing copper network for speeds up to a few megabytes per

second (the current limit, although this is constantly being enhanced to handle even higher byte rates). Suddenly, the old copper network that has been in use for a hundred years is a primary candidate for the multimedia services of the next century. Several trials have been carried out in which this technology has been used as the basis for various broadband services to the home and to small businesses.

■ *The electricity network.* The existing electricity infrastructure is another network that reaches virtually all homes in developed countries. It is accessible almost everywhere in a home or company. This overwhelming abundance leads to a great interest on the part of electricity companies. Technology that makes it possible to send information over this network has been developed very rapidly. At the moment, a number of tests, for example high-speed Internet connections to the home, are being run. This may become an interesting future alternative to telecommunications networks.

The second type of technology that is making broadband services a viable alternative even for the private market is compression. It is now possible to get near-television quality using connections of only a few hundred kilobytes per second or even less. The development in this area is also very fast and quickly reduces the need for advanced high-speed networks. Many interesting concepts are deployed to compress the bandwidth. The concept of fractals is one of the latest trends, and it has showed tremendous results in laboratories.

The two trends, compression and broadband communication in existing networks, will together form the basis for the new network market that we discuss in this book. One conclusion that can be drawn is that we do not have to wait for very long in order for advanced services to be realised.

Internet technologies

The Internet is not a new phenomenon: it has been around for almost 30 years. What is new is the multitude of tools and techniques that make this network easy to use, both for people and companies that want to make information and applications available on the Internet, and for people who want to get access to all the information that is offered. Because of the focus on information and multimedia (text, pictures, animation, video and voice), the Internet was for a long time seen as a new publishing tool that had major implications for media and publishing companies. However, it did not take long before it was clear that this was much more than a simple information channel for a small number of people who were using the latest IT appliances.

Today, it is often said that the Internet represents a completely new paradigm for distributed computing and services. Internet technologies have also achieved something that has been a long-time goal in the computer industry, namely to be able to use the right applications and access information independently of the technical platform used.

Internet technologies include the Java programming language, web-browser software and search engines that include names such as Alta Vista, Yahoo, Lycos and a number of others. There are also a number of other new industries that have developed as offshoots of the growth of these basic Internet technologies, for example conferencing systems, electronic commerce products, fire walls (to protect from hackers), web publishing tools and Internet access products.

The network is the computer

The WWW started as a new medium to publish information. It is easy to see how it can be used for this purpose, but why should we suppose that the most efficient way to transfer information should be limited to such a marginal role in society? The WWW is equally suitable for other types of communication. In one form, this could mean that we could deliver whole systems of programs that could be downloaded over the network and run on a local computer. With the appearance of the Internet programming language, Java, the whole WWW has become much more powerful as a technological concept. Any piece of software that is needed in the future can be exchanged and run locally on any machine capable of accessing the WWW. Many computer companies have realised that this will be more serious than it may look at a first glance. It will influence how computers and operating systems are constructed and how applications are implemented, managed and distributed. The main interface to a computer may be a web-browser rather than Windows, which is one reason behind the current battle between Microsoft and Netscape.

In fact, this will lead to a totally distributed and network-orientated way of running applications. It is no longer easy, or even possible, to know exactly where a piece of code or some other piece of information came from or where a certain task was executed. An entire network of information and software can be mixed together at run time to meet the user's needs. This is often called a new era in computing. After central- isation, using mainframe computers, it was time to decentralise and run everything on PCs. Now we see a large amount of interest in client/server architectures, which means a mix of programs that are run locally or centrally on different computers. This could seem like a minor change. It may turn out, however, that it is a major change. It will change the entire way in which users get access to electronic tools. Applications can suddenly be made available 'just in time' and delivered to the person and the computer that need it.

Traditionally, users have had to buy a package of software, install it on one PC and use it locally until a new version was available or a better tool was launched in the market. With a whole network of functionality, it will be much easier to find the right tool in a given situation. The user does not even need to plan which tools and software to use; these could be installed automatically together with the service or information being accessed. No time needs to be spent on looking for, installing or upgrading software. The interest can instead be focused on the actual use of tools and information.

Network computers

The success of the Internet depends on how many people have access to it. Today, there are a large number of people who can access it, but many of them can only do so from work. This means that they will not be able to use it as often as they would if they had access from home. Several services today are focused on helping people in their daily lives (finding information, booking tickets or reading the news), and it is therefore vital to access the Internet from more places than simply the office. A new computer, the network computer, or NC, has been launched that is directly targeted at this niche. The goal is to sell a computer dedicated to Internet applications at a price below $500. Many people in the industry argue that this is simply an 'old' PC (a 386 or 486, talking in terms of Intel processor generations) with a new label, but many others believe that this will lead to a broad usage of Internet services and create a basis for a completely new computer architecture.

The development of the NC is an example of the trend to move computing into the network. As a consequence of this, the computer may become less powerful in terms of capacity and have limited storage capacity. The idea is instead based on communication with a network, where most of the computing and storage capacity is located.

Multimedia technology

The development of multimedia communication is one of the corner-stones of our reasoning regarding the changes that are possible in society. Multimedia is the collective name of a number of technological solutions that will make communication much richer than it ever was when communication was limited to telephone and fax. It is also one of the drivers of the real-time trend described earlier.

Multimedia solutions will make it possible to communicate in real-time with sounds, pictures and writing. This means that, in the future, we will be able to see each other's writing on the computer screen as we talk and write, in the same manner as we would have done had we been sitting in the same room and had written on a flip chart. We will find communication over long distances becoming both more personal and more efficient than before. Through this development, we will be able to meet business contacts more frequently. We will be able to contact them when a matter has to be discussed and start discussion immediately, without the delays previously experienced, when travelling to meet and discuss complicated or delicate matters.

This does not mean, however, that the multimedia development stops at the solution of some basic issues of personal communication. No; the term 'multimedia' could be interpreted as having much wider applications than that. It could also mean that the interaction between a person and his PC could one day take new forms. It could mean that a future PC or NC could react to spoken language and that users could actually use their voices to give orders to their computers. It could also mean that a computer could convert spoken language into written text or vice versa. We could, for example, ask the computer by voice to dial a certain telephone number for us and start to speak to the person as he or she answers; then, during the discussion, we could ask the computer to send an e-mail containing some drawings that could be studied together with the person at the other end of the line. This is the type of solution that could take personal communication in all matters, including complex and delicate ones, into the real-time society.

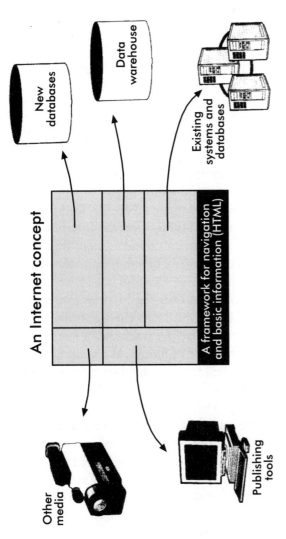

An Internet concept

New databases

Data warehouse

Existing systems and databases

A framework for navigation and basic information (HTML)

Other media

Publishing tools

The first thing that comes to mind when thinking of an Internet concept is a set of static pages with text and pictures published on the WWW. This was true in the early days of the WWW, but today it is just a small part of a typical concept. Information of various kinds can be directly linked to the Internet and made available to everybody. Databases, systems and media from new and existing sources are connected to the Internet without reprogramming or transformations. Users can now take part in dynamic interaction with Internet sites and other users, influencing and changing the information content.

This new scope of an Internet concept is important to have in mind when discussing new opportunities in order not to miss the real potential of this medium.

Figure 4.1 An Internet concept

Sources of information on the Internet

Today, we see how multimedia technologies are making their entry into the Internet. We could, however, expect the Internet to be used for a much wider variety of purposes in the near future than most of us would expect today. It is widespread belief that the Internet and the WWW are equivalent to a set of HTML pages with information, perhaps with some extra services such as making bookings and sending e-mail back to the company that offers the pages. This was true in the early days of the web, but it is not true today. HTML-based information is quickly being reduced to only a small portion of the information that is offered. It only plays the role of a framework, or skeleton, for how to present the information. The information comes from various databases connected to the Internet. This makes the web an integrated part of a company's information systems instead of being a stand-alone system.

Since any digital technology could be connected to the Internet, it will become possible to do a whole range of things over the Internet. We can already see how real estate companies connect their building management systems, which are used to control heating, ventilation and other installations in buildings. In the area of film and music, we could expect to access films and music recordings over the Internet instead of buying or hiring a film or buying a CD. This will also change the concept of a CD by letting the customer put together the tracks he or she wants to buy rather than having to buy a fixed mix of music. As a consequence of this development, the cost of the medium and the distribution of the film or CD would substantially decrease.

One factor that we find interesting in the present technological development is that we are only at the very beginning of a new and challenging era when we will see more and more appliances connected to the Internet. There is already a common policy in many companies that every new computer system must have a web interface. This means that the Internet will be a possible way, and many times *the* way, to access company systems. To think of the Internet or an intranet as a computer system in itself may not be so radical. What could be more interesting is that many company systems are usually seen as isolated islands that cannot be accessed unless people have a terminal for the system in question and experience of using it. We are used to thinking in terms of 'I have to ask the sales department for an update on the sales volume' or 'The status of a customer's order can only be accessed from the production control systems in the factory.' These barriers between different areas within a company have led to inefficiencies in many processes. By connecting these systems to the Internet or to an intranet, a new world is opening up. Suddenly, everybody can access all the information that they need (and are entitled to access) in an easy and straightforward way. They can also feed systems with information and get access to the tools and functionality that they need. The development in this area is very fast, and most IT systems already have, or will soon have, web interfaces of various kinds.

Many companies are aware of this and see the opportunities that it will provide. There are many examples of companies that have taken it seriously and are demanding web interfaces to all new support systems that they buy. Access to information systems over the Internet will not only make it easier for people within a company, but will also help customers to get the information that they need in every situation. Customers could in the future, for example, look into the order system and check whether their products are ready or whether the goods that they need are in stock locally for rapid delivery.

> The Federal Express example that we discussed before is typical of a system that has been given a web interface to extend its use both within and outside the organisation. The parcel tracing system that this firm has developed can be accessed from any part of the company over the Internet and even by the customers themselves (100,000 customers do this every day). This simple extension of the system provides the company with many opportunities to become more customer friendly and to improve the management of parcels.
>
> The computer company Dell (www.dell.com) is also a good example of how information from internal administrative systems can be provided directly to the customer. At their site on the Internet, it is possible to see, for example, the expected delivery times of products (especially useful being to see which parts of an order will delay the delivery) and to see the order status of requested products.

The area of computer systems is not the only one in which web interfaces will be provided. Since the technology is simple and cheap, it is possible to connect almost any type of electronic appliance to the Internet. Today, there are, for example, video cameras connected to the Internet that make it possible to look at the traffic situation in a city centre or to see what the weather is like in another city. The next step could be to connect home appliances such as videos, the alarm system, the electrical heating or the oven. This would make it possible to control the heating at home from any location or to check the alarm at home when travelling.

Let us take a very simple example. A company has a system for security and the registration of entrants with magnetic cards that is used to grant people access to buildings. This system registers all employees when they enter and leave the company's premises. This is usually a local system that can be accessed via dedicated terminals to which only a few people have access. This makes it very difficult to use as an information system to locate where people are. The problem is not the way in which information is collected but how it is provided to the people who need it. With a simple connection of the security system to the Internet, information can be provided to anybody, at any time and in any place. There will, of course, be a need to limit the access to the information to guarantee privacy, but this is possible to handle. This is a typical example of what Internet connections to various systems and appliances can mean.

Push technology: broadcasting over the Internet

Today, the Internet is mainly used as a passive source of information. Through the use of various search engines, bookmarks and links, it is possible to find the information we are looking for when we need it. In many situations, this is not enough. It is often better if the information is actively sent to those who need it. When something occurs that is of interest to a number of people, they should be actively informed. As it is, we currently have to scan a number of sources daily just to check whether something of interest has turned up. At the moment, new technology is being employed that makes it possible actively to send information to a number of users. It is usually called push technology and is similar to a broadcasting system by which certain people can be targeted with specific information.

> Pointcast (www.pointcast.com) is a service provider that has been one of the forerunners in the push technology area. Pointcast is a US company that is providing a piece of software (to be downloaded easily over the Internet) that can be used to filter and customise information delivered over the Internet from various sources. News and information are presented on the computer screen when it is idle or when the user actively wants to look at the information. The information is collected by Pointcast from a number of sources and sent to the user through a number of 'channels'. This term is used to stress that it is possible to select which channels to 'listen to'. This method of sending and presenting information is based on the ideas of push technology.

Channels are used as a concept to send information to people in such a way that it is possible to select the information that is sent. This is becoming more and more widespread as the push technology makes its way into new applications.

Integrated management systems and data warehouses

Transparency is not only a trend that will affect society as a whole: there are tools that are increasing transparency within companies as well. Historically, information systems in companies have been of a stand-alone nature. There has been one system for accounting purposes, one for the administration of production, one for the taking of orders and so on. This has meant that it has been possible to analyse the situation within each department of a company, but IT has not been very helpful in the management of the company as a whole.

Today, all these management systems are tied together into integrated systems solutions in which data that are entered as a customer order are used in many other parts of the company. In the same manner, the quantitative goals that are set by top management could be broken down by each department or each subsidiary so that the intentions of management can permeate the whole company. In this way, management could keep a tighter grip of the whole business than before, and they could always be informed in real-time about everything that went on.

Another technology that is increasing transparency in a company and helps us in the analysis of very complex relationships in companies is data warehousing. Data warehousing means that operative data from one integrated management system, or from a number of unrelated systems, are periodically taken over to a huge database where managers, analysts and other people with access to this information can analyse them at an aggregated level or look for new and previously unknown patterns in the data. The strength lies in the fact that information from various sources is brought together into one single information base to make it possible to use information in the way the user wants rather than the way systems can provide it. This may seem like a minor development, but it leads to a completely new way of analysing different aspects of the business of a company. When information is kept in separate systems, the possibility of finding interesting patterns and new opportunities is limited, but when it is brought together in a data warehouse, the potential uses of the information often increase radically. It takes time, however, to achieve results because people are not aware of the potential that these tools have. The transparency of a company's business that this offers is so powerful that very few can see the real benefits. As an example, we normally think about the financial performance of a company, operational data and customer orders as unrelated items of information, which makes us blind to the information that we may get if we combine these data.

Many companies are already using this type of tool in order to improve the handling of very complex issues of special importance to their business. One example is credit card companies that use these tools to analyse huge amounts of data about customer behaviour in order to find out which variables indicate that a customer will incur bad debts for the company. Some of these companies use the results of such analyses to assess applications from customers, and these companies have managed substantially to decrease the number of bad debts through this procedure.

Other companies use this type of tool for more ordinary purposes, for example to find out how they should use their salesforce better. Such companies may run correlative analyses on data concerning customer behaviour and relate these data to salesforce activities, thus discovering which customers to visit in order to get the best pay-off.

> One of the largest data warehouses in the world is that of the American retailer Wal Mart. Each night, all transactions that are entered as customer purchases in each one of the 2,000 stores of this company are transferred to a 70 terabyte data warehouse. This vast collection of data is then used to analyse the purchasing patterns of the several million American customers who make weekly visits to Wal Mart's stores.
>
> From these analyses, all kinds of conclusion can be drawn. For example, the company has found out that beer sells better on Fridays if it is placed next to babies' nappies. Customers who buy nappies on Fridays obviously tend to buy beer as well if this product is conveniently placed. In stores where beer and nappies were separated, the same co-variation in sales could not be found. This is only one example of how this type of analysis could be used to improve the layout of a store in order to increase sales.

Data warehousing is often based on an intranet solution that provides common storage of information made open to the users of an intranet. By storing information in a data warehouse, reasonable capacity and security can be guaranteed. Because of this, the two concepts of data warehousing and intranet technology are often used to create a service package that makes it possible both to store information and to access it when it is needed.

Data warehousing is only in the very first phase of usage, even if it has been available for a number of years, especially in the United States. The current rapid development is largely a result of the falling prices of storage and processing capacity. A data warehouse with several terabytes of information was too expensive to handle only a few years ago.

Intelligent and mobile agents

'Intelligent agent technology' is a new technology built on the same basic idea as computer viruses. This may seem dangerous, but the technology has proved to be safe enough for a number of applications. These agents have two things in common with viruses: they can replicate themselves and they can be sent out by one computer and reside in other computer systems where they can carry out tasks. Some application areas for this new technology are:

- The collection of information from a number of sources without the need to specify in advance in exactly which computer systems connected to the Internet searches are to be carried out. An agent has the intelligence to replicate itself to send out a whole army of agents that search for sources of vital information and then come back and report the result. In this way, searches can be carried out in different systems in parallel instead of in a series.
- The transfer of information when a certain condition is met in the system where the agent resides. This reduces the need to survey systems continuously to find new information. An agent can stay as a resident of another system and wait for certain information to turn up. When the right information appears, it comes back and reports. This will significantly reduce the need for communication between computers.
- Information management can be described and handled on a higher level of abstraction. Tasks do not have to be specified in detail, outlining exactly what should be done and how. Agents can break a task down into smaller pieces that are easy to carry out and put information together to give a more comprehensive end result.

Intelligent agent technology is an important technology that helps to cope with the increasing complexity and dynamics of the Internet. It is vital for people and companies to find the information they need on the Internet and also to get updates when information changes.

Business intelligence is a typical area in which companies can make use of intelligent agent technology. Companies need to collect information and compile it to maintain a picture of what their customers, partners, competitors and suppliers are doing. On the Internet, there is a tremendous amount of valuable information about all sorts of company that can be used for these purposes. A big problem is to find all this information and put it together to make it useful. Even if companies manage to collect all the information they need at one point in time, it is probably outdated even before it is presented to management as a basis for strategic decisions. To really maintain an up-to-date picture of the market, it is necessary continuously to scan a number of sites on the Internet and collect all the information that has changed since the previous search. This is a typical task for agents. They can replicate themselves to go to all necessary sources and collect information. They can go back regularly to check whether information has changed and even stay in other systems and wait for information to change and report back when that happens. Today, there are products that deal with the continuous collection of information on the Internet, and the next step will be real agent technology that makes it possible to send agents (perhaps Java based) that stay and watch sites of interest on behalf of a company or a private user.

Knowledge-based systems

Knowledge-based systems were viewed in the mid-1980s as having a great future. Many companies put effort into the development of these thrilling systems that had expert qualifications. Programming languages based on logic and rules were the basis of these systems. There are special requirements of the computers that were running these programs, and this hardware became expensive. Methodologies to elicit and formalise knowledge were developed to support the implementation of these systems. Many interesting applications were developed in areas such as medicine (in diagnosis), process control (to manage processes and factories) and sales support (to help less skilled people sell complex products and services). However, the expectations and the cost of the computers were too high to get a reasonable pay-back on investments, and the complexity of many of the applications was underestimated. This went so far that many experts believed the technology was dead, but when computing capacity became less expensive in the early 1990s, the technology underwent a renaissance. Today, there are a number of applications that play a vital role in different parts of society, and with the access to all the information and services on the Internet, it is likely that this technology will play a more and more important role after all. One of the areas in which there are interesting examples is translation between different languages (as we saw in the example above) and between different media, such as text to voice and vice versa.

One example of a type of knowledge-based system comprises the functions for automatic translation that are included in a number of new applications. These functions make it possible, for example, to translate standard letters between a number of different languages.

This development clearly has many implications. First, the market for human translators becomes smaller since an increasing share of all the texts that will have to be translated could be translated by this type of program. Second, the innovation opens up the Internet market so that companies could compete over larger geographical areas without having to invest in translations of their homepages, which would until now have had to be made by human translators.

Secure payment options

Most of the applications and concepts that we discuss in this book are based on the assumption that the Internet is a marketplace for products and services and not just a place where we can find free information and commercials. A true marketplace is not only a place where customers and suppliers meet and discuss potential business, then going somewhere else to conclude the deal. Instead, the idea is that the new electronic marketplace should have all the ingredients of a market. Thus secure payment options are crucial. Ever since the WWW was launched, the discussion of whether or not it is safe enough to use, for example, a credit card number to pay for services on the Internet has been going on. Most people would say that they are not prepared to send their numbers via this medium. However, many would send their credit card number over a fax or tell it to a person over the telephone. They would say that the main difference is the feeling that everybody is 'listening' to the traffic on the Internet, just because everybody is connected to the same network. Behind this feeling lie many misunderstandings and fears with no real background. However, for a company that wants to conduct business on the Internet, it does not matter whether or not a person has made the right decision. What counts is whether or not he or she will buy. As a consequence of the widespread fear of shopping on-line, a number of companies have started to address the security issue in order to come up with a solution that everybody can trust. The result is a new protocol called SET (secure electronic transfer).

SET promises to be the leading protocol that consumers will use to purchase products safely over the Internet. Both Microsoft and Netscape are working along with Visa and Mastercard to develop SET-compatible browsers. There are five fundamental criteria in electronic commerce that SET addresses:

- It must provide confidentiality of payment and ordering information. Consumers want to be sure that the information they are sending is going to be secure yet readily available to the people intended.
- It must ensure the integrity of all the transmitted data. Because of the encryption methods that are used, it is impossible for anyone to change the content of the encrypted 'order.'
- It must provide authentication that the cardholder is the registered cardholder. SET uses a system of digital signatures and cardholder authentication certificates to make sure the cardholder is the right person.
- It must provide authentication that the merchant is authorised to make transactions through a financial institution. Digital signatures and cardholder authentication certificates are again used to make sure that a customer is dealing with an authorised party.
- There must be no preferences for certain hardware or software platforms, that is, there can be no monopoly that holds the rights to the protocol. This will ensure that the system is available for everyone.

The way in which SET provides a service to the consumer is simple. A customer signs up with a financial institution. The financial institution may be a credit card company or digital on-line money service such as DigiCash. Once an account is established, the user has the power to go to a website, select a desired product with a few clicks of the mouse and send the order. Once the order has been transmitted, there are other complex things that happen behind the scenes, which will not be described here.

There are some other fundamental issues of a payment system that also must be addressed to make the real electronic market take off. Importantly, it must be possible to handle even very small transactions. If it is too expensive to process small amounts of money with a system for electronic payment, it will limit the types of service offered on the Internet. It is, for example, important that companies can charge for looking at certain information, such as reading a short report or printing a paper of interest. Say that a news company wants to charge 10 cents for a look at an in-depth story behind a news headline; the customer must be able to pay for this in a convenient way without several time-consuming security checks and passwords.

Another aspect of the security discussion is how to make sure that the company behind a web page is trustworthy. In the physical world, it is possible to get a feeling for this by looking at the kinds of shop or office in which the company resides. However, in the electronic marketplace, everybody has the opportunity to look like a large company. One solution to this problem is to use certificates of different kinds that a company must have to be able to use systems such as SET. These certificates (a kind of electronic key) are only issued by certain bodies that have the permission to do so. Various levels of security are offered to those who apply for a certificate. In the most extreme cases, the Chief Executive Officer of the company must travel in person to the company that issues the certificate and bring proof that the company is legally the 'right one'.

In 1998, the SET system will be launched, and this will probably make the electronic market grow even more quickly. Many of the pioneers of the Internet have already started to plan for these trials. We strongly believe that this is an important milestone in the history of the Internet, which will wipe away one of the last obstacles that have made people reluctant to start to shop on-line.

The decreasing cost of computing and communications capacity

One of the main reasons behind the present very rapid development of new applications for IT is the decreasing cost of computing and communications capacity. A number of famous 'laws' have been formulated to show what is happening:

Moore's Law: Computer performance ÷ price doubles every 18 months.

Gilder's Law: Communications performance ÷ price doubles every 3 months.

In the heyday of mainframes, companies did everything in their power to limit the need for storage capacity. Each megabyte (Mbyte, 1 million bytes) was very expensive, and this was the reason behind this behaviour, which may seem strange less than a decade or so later. Processing performance is another factor that sets a limit to the speed of computers. Today, we are talking about hundreds of MHz (1 million Hz) in most cases, but at the turn of the century 1 GHz (1 billion Hz) processors will probably be used commercially. This will make it possible for even more complex applications to be run on a simple PC.

Today, storage capacity is measured in gigabytes (1,000 megabytes), or even in terabytes (1 million megabytes), and this opens up the opportunities that are needed to make the changes described above possible. Without this decrease in price, it would still have been impossible to run data warehouses requiring gigabytes of information to be handled, or to run Internet servers and search engines that could handle thousands of transactions each second.

The same type of development is taking place for communications capacity. Nowadays, companies can buy 40 gigabytes per second access at the same price as 100 megabytes per second just 7 years ago. This tremendous increase in communication capacity can be turned into completely new opportunities. Companies can establish multimedia conferences between offices, and people who work with advanced graphics and calculations, can transfer enormous amounts of information between different sites, which opens up new ways of working and interacting.

It can be assumed that we are coming close to the capacities that we need for most purposes. It is probable that we will learn how to handle computing capacity more economically in the future, which may mean that we could manage with home computers that have less memory capacity than most new PCs have today. On the other hand, we will probably have to continue to expand our networks for long-distance computer communication in the future.

Part II
Concepts

Based on our observations, we now take our analysis one step further. We describe three new concepts, which we have chosen to call 'network intelligence', 'the valuescape' and 'concept transformation'. In order to be able to take advantage of the developments described in Part I, companies, individuals and governments need to understand these concepts.

Network intelligence means that we will be able to use competence in new ways in the future, which will make society as a whole more efficient.

The valuescape is a way for users of the Internet to configure their view of this information and communications network in the way that is most suitable for them.

Concept transformation means that companies will have to transform their business concepts as they move them from the physical world to the new electronic market.

We argue that the use of the new technologies described in this book will create leaps in terms of efficiency that make it likely that the volume of business done over the Internet will increase and that business in the physical market will decrease accordingly. Any company that currently competes in the physical market has to understand these changes in order to take measures to stay in business in the future.

5 Network Intelligence

In any system of problem solving individuals an increase in the access to structured information from secondary sources or an increase in the quality of communication between individuals will make it possible to maintain the problem solving capacity of the system, even if the average problem solving capacity of the individuals would decrease. ('The Network Intelligence Principle', as formulated by the authors)

Introduction to network intelligence

One of our main arguments in this book is based on the assumption that we, through the 'transparent society', enter into a new paradigm of problem-solving. We see that the complete transparency, which means that everybody who has a PC will have access to all public information that is available, leads to an increase in the form of problem-solving capacity that we may call 'network intelligence'. Network intelligence is not new. As we can see from the quotation introducing this chapter and from the example below, different degrees of network intelligence exists in any system of problem-solving individuals.

Network intelligence is based on two fundamental building blocks, which both refer to the principle above:

1. the assumption that the problem-solving ability of any single human being *will be enhanced* as the access to structured information regarding any problem increases;
2. the thought that the need of problem-solving ability in each person *decreases* as the all-encompassing information networks increase our access to others' competencies and knowledge.

Both these factors point in the same direction, indicating that the need for competence will decrease in the future. This statement contradicts all other contemporary predictions of the need for developments in training and education in the near future: all other analysts say that we will face a continuously increasing need for education and training.

The first point could be supported as follows. We could assume that one main reason for needing competent people is because we, in each profession, face a multitude of decision points at which we have less information than we need in order to make good decisions. We normally assume that increasing amounts of information will require a greater and greater power of analysis. This is only true if the information is unstructured because then we need a high level of education and competence in order to see which bits of information we have to use at each decision point. With an increasing amount of well-structured information, it will become easier to find all the relevant information at each point and make simple rules for how each decision should be handled. (It should be noted that the meaning of the term 'well structured' is not what it may seem to be. The point is not that somebody has to structure the information and provide it to all other people. Instead the idea is that each person can use electronic tools to structure the information to suit his or her current situation and needs.)

Thus less competence should be needed by the person who is supposed to make each decision. This also means that rather simple rules could be used to see when a new situation required a new type of decision. The transparent society will mean not only that all changes will be known at the time when they occur, but also that the consequences of each move can be understood, which will make all aspects of life simpler.

This is not only true for problems that are traditionally seen as well structured. Through network intelligence, we learn to organise spontaneously for the solution of problems that are not structured in advance. The access to information that could be structured through various search engines working with all the information available on the Internet makes it possible easily to find a structured approach to solving problems that have formerly been seen as unstructured.

Information collection, refinement and combination on the Internet is a typical example of how network intelligence can be used in a real case. In our working lives as consultants, we are often faced with the task of writing a report or making a presentation in an area that is not familiar. Before we had access to the Internet, the only way to gather the information and knowledge was to ask colleagues about references, reports and other people to contact. One input led to another, and soon a network of useful links was built that made it possible to compile the result. This was often a tedious task, and it was necessary to have a good existing network from the start or else it would take too much time and effort. Today, it is much easier; we do not need an existing network of contacts and references.

By using both the open Internet and the intranet within our company, we can put together the network of knowledge that we need in a very short time. We can find all sorts of written material and ready-made presentations as well as people whom we need to contact. By doing this, it is possible to pick pieces of information, text and slides to form a new presentation that will meet our needs. It is not even necessary to produce the presentation: most of it could probably be accessed directly over the Internet and be stored in our PC for further customisation before presentation. When we have made the presentation, we could, of course, decide that it might have a company-wide interest and publish it on the company intranet so that other people could use it. This is a typical example of how many people work today. It shows how much easier it is to perform a task that would have taken days a few years ago. As the knowledge base we are sharing on the Internet (externally or internally in a company) grows rapidly, this will become even easier to do.

This development could indicate two different directions. Either it will be easier for anyone with general skills to create a good piece of work on a subject of which the person has little previous expertise, or customers who buy the services of consultants will try to find the person who has the best experience in their current field of interest. The latter alternative would support our assumption that the degree of specialisation will increase in a future system based on network intelligence.

> When the market is very small, no person can have any encouragement to dedicate himself entirely to one employment, for want of the power to exchange all that surplus part of the produce of his own labour, which is over and above his own consumption for such parts of the produce of other men's labour as he has occasion for. (Smith, 1997)

Regarding the second point above, network intelligence means that we will be able to access not only all information and use it ourselves, but also all the competence of other people in the world. This means that we will not need to be able to solve very complex problems ourselves, but we will be able to find people with competencies that complement our own at very short notice. It will thus become more efficient to connect people with more specialised competencies than is the case today, and better to make them solve different parts of one problem than to educate extremely competent people who can solve complex problems themselves. The transparent society will make it possible to find those with the right level of competence and initiate co-operation.

In the example above about the reuse of knowledge and information, it is easy to see that the need for competent people to do such tasks will be reduced. It is possible to work much faster when presentations and reports are produced, and it also requires fewer skills (because one can learn quickly from the input of others).

Network intelligence could be used not only for work-related purposes. It is also, for example, a concept used in new architectures for distributed computing. The question of where to put the intelligence in computer systems has been discussed since computers were born. First, intelligence was implemented in large central computers that had the power to perform complex tasks. Then intelligence was distributed to personal computers or work stations, called clients, close to the users. This way of working has increased dramatically in the 1990s because everybody can use the local power of their own computer instead of sharing the power of a large computer with other users. The latest trend in this area is following the same principle as network intelligence.

The idea is to use the entire network as the computer. It is possible to run one program on a server, another piece of software being downloaded on demand from another server to execute on a PC, and information being collected from several sources together with local information from our hard disk. We may not even realise that different parts of the information have been taken from different sources; it may just as well have been a local program accessing locally stored information.

Network intelligence may be studied in nature, where the human brain and the brains of other mammals are constructed as networks of cells. It can also be studied in a new type of computer called the 'neural network computer' that solves problems in a manner similar to that of the human brain. Such a computer can perform different tasks in parallel and also works much more quickly than a traditional computer. Furthermore, it can 'learn' from input data and get better at solving problems as it 'gains experience'.

The overall structure is simple – independent parts and connections between them

The basic logic behind network intelligence is that a large share of the problem-solving in a network is done not in the minds of individuals but by the network structure itself, by connecting a number of highly specialised individuals with each other and with information sources. In such a network, each person (or computer) carries out a small part of a large and complex task.

Until now, the solving of complex tasks in this manner has required somebody who has consciously organised the problem-solving process. The reason is that it has been impossible to compile all the necessary information instantly when it is needed. Instead, some person in a company or some other type of organisation has been forced to plan the need for competence years in advance and specify whether somebody with a specific competence should be employed full time or part time or hired as a consultant at the point at which his or her competence is needed. In the near future, anybody – a company, an organisation or a person – could access any information and any competence right at the point when the need arose, provided that there was somebody willing to supply the competence at that time and in those circumstances.

This means that network intelligence is created by a large number of people who get involved in spontaneous and unplanned interaction. It also means that people who work in this type of network do not need traditional job descriptions in which a number of related tasks are put together to form a position in an organisation.

The first stumbling steps towards substantially increasing network intelligence in modern organisations have been taken by many large multinational companies. They have seen the need to capture and use knowledge in new areas quickly and without costs being too high. Traditional organisations, especially large ones, are not suited to meeting the dynamics of the new electronic market. Experience has shown that it is not a good idea to build large units when a new business idea has been developed and try to explore it. Instead, a number of people in different positions in the company, and often in different parts of the world, are linked together in informal networks to address the new idea and move it into a new product or service area in the company. These people in the network also have other jobs and come together just because of their unique competence in and enthusiasm for the topic itself. When the area has been developed enough to know what to do with it, the network can dissolve and people can go back to their usual tasks. There are many examples of these types of network in industry today. Most of them are not run directly by management but by the members' own interests. Some of these networks live for more than a year, while others have shorter lives because of the lack of interest from members or a decision from management to cease a network.

An example of how companies can organise spontaneously to achieve a result is the Network Management Forum (NMF) in the telecommunications industry. This is an independent organisation that has telecom companies as members and was formed in order to develop products in crucial areas in the telecom industry. People from different companies (service providers, equipment suppliers and end users) work together to solve problems that the companies involved want to explore. The focus is on how companies should work together in a fragmented market, especially on how they should exchange information.

Companies send skilled people to the work teams with the mission to achieve something useful in a short period of time. By forming a team of experts in an area, results can be produced more rapidly than in any company on its own. The work is carried out in a true network environment, which helps to speed up the process. A basic feature that makes this example different from other organisations is that the work is not planned in advance. Informal interaction between people from different companies is the starting point for the work. When areas and tasks of common interest are spotted, the work can start quickly. The only firm requirement is that there should be a clear business case to prove that there are business opportunities in the project.

We may think that a system in which most people are specialised in narrowly defined areas will be inhuman. However, it will be natural for people with skills in a certain area to develop these further to maintain a good position. It will be difficult for people with general knowledge and skills to compete against highly specialised individuals. Therefore, specialisation will be the natural move in a market like this, and no individual could influence this development on his or her own. It will be up to buyers and suppliers of goods and services to decide whether to choose only the best person for each task or whether to allow people to diversify, which could add some cost to the system as a whole.

We can already see some examples of the trend towards increasing specialisation. In today's society, the consulting services market tends to grow at a steady rate. This indicates that companies now need more and more specialised resources for shorter periods of time. Even if a consultant costs in many cases two or three times as much as a full-time employee, companies choose to employ consultants for many tasks because the additional cost of employing highly specialised people, for whom they have no use when a project is finished, becomes too high.

However, even if companies already buy large volumes of consulting services, they often have a small number of consultants whom they hire over and over again, because they already know them as people and trust them. This means that consultants today incur a large share of the cost for their customers through the process of learning new fields of expertise all the time. If companies could find consultants with the best experience for each project, they could spend less money on consultants than they do today. Sometimes an experienced consultant could even bring semi-finished solutions to the customer and do a project in half or one-third of the time that it would take a newcomer in the field. Through Internet technology, it will be possible in the future to find a better match between projects and the experience of a consultant than there has previously been. At the moment, the consulting market is moving towards more specialisation, and we can see more and more examples of job titles such as 'IT architect' or 'standard packages specialist'.

One aspect of this specialisation is the further assumption that this will lead to a level of efficiency never before experienced in society. This is because of three factors:

1. The decreasing need for managers to organise interaction and problem-solving between people will reduce the costs of the organisation and administration of businesses.
2. Intermediary functions that plan work will disappear in industries and companies where they can be replaced by direct communication.
3. The development described here means that slack will be taken out of the system since people will be able to work only when their contributions are needed. Very few people will have to spend time waiting at their desks for work to turn up.

A practical guide to the use of network intelligence

Traditional organisations have been characterised by hierarchical structures that have been developed over many years. This has been possible because of the stability of the environment and the conditions in the market. As competition is increasing, many markets lose their stability, and it may no longer be optimal to modify old structures to meet new requirements. A new organisational model is needed. In the early 1990s, we saw the birth of a new organisational structure, often called 'process based' or based on the concept of business process re-engineering (BPR). We think, however, that this trend will be of short duration. The process-based organisation may have its merits, but it also has drawbacks. We suggest that the new form of organisation to replace the process-based organisation will be an organisation with an internal network structure. We also suggest that this form of organisation is the most efficient of all possible organisational types provided that there is transparency in the market and within each organisation. This argument goes back to classical economic theory, which says that the invisible hand of the market allocates resources to the most efficient producers. This market-based allocation of resources would work as well internally in companies as it does externally between companies in a market. An organisation that has no formal structure is not easy to monitor and manage, but this is not crucial in a market where transparency and network intelligence provide the basis for the organisation of work.

One example of this is the way in which document archives have been structured in a company in order to make it possible for people to find them. Structured libraries have been created, documents have received an identification number and a number of registers have been used in order to find a document on a certain subject. Most people in organisations are so used to this way of organising information that they believe it is the only way to do it for information to be reused in a company. However, the new search and navigation tools of the Internet have made all these structures and rules obsolete. All documents could be searched through the use of key words. When a person needs to find information, he or she uses a search engine to create a special directory for each particular need. This means that the tool gives full visibility (transparency) of the information. The old solution has been to formalise and categorise the information in a way that suits everybody. Systems of document numbers and classifications are now made obsolete, and large amounts of time and effort are saved.

This example shows how new tools for information-processing increase the accessibility of information in companies. The same level of accessibility could be achieved through intranet solutions spanning whole organisations, regardless of size.

Spontaneous organisations

We would like to divide organisations into two groups. The first would be 'consciously organised organisations'. This group consists of most of the organisations that we would think of as 'organisations', namely ones comprising a number of people who work together for a common purpose. These are organised by a person, whom we think of as sitting 'at the top of the organisational pyramid' or the top of the hierarchy. Process-based organisations also belong to this group since they require a manager who organises each process and general management to decide which processes a company should have at the highest level. The second group consists of 'spontaneously organised organisations'.

It is possible to come up with a number of situations where people organise spontaneously to solve a problem or do something which does not need a formal organisation to accomplish, such as felling a tree on a common or organising a party in the neighbourhood. Even if these are simple examples, there are some interesting parallels with how we could organise more complex matters, such as companies.

> This division of labour, from which so many advantages are derived, is not originally the effect of any human wisdom, which foresees and intends that general opulence to which it gives occasion. It is the necessary, though very slow and gradual consequence of a certain propensity in human nature which has in view no such extensive utility; the propensity to truck, barter, and exchange one thing for another. (Smith, 1997)

The most complex and advanced type of spontaneous organisation we could think of is the market. The market consists of people and companies that exchange goods, labour and services in exchange for money in various unplanned ways. In this 'sea of unplanned activities' we call 'the market', there are 'islands of planned value creation', which we call organisations.[1] With this as a background, we could say that the market is a type of organisation that arises spontaneously and that also changes spontaneously as companies and people choose new suppliers and business partners.

We could assume that each of these two types of organisation is the best in a certain situation. The consciously organised organisation would then be effective in an environment where there is enough time for top management to reorganise departments or processes, because smaller and quicker organisations could be kept out of the market through the use of the large organisation's superior financial power. If, on the other hand, changes start to become so rapid that management becomes unable to reorganise quickly enough, or as often as they need to, it would be more efficient to try to introduce a higher degree of spontaneity in the process of organising interactions between people. As the spontaneously organising market has proved that it can deal with rapid changes and adapt quickly, it is tempting to take a closer look at the market mechanism to see whether it could function as the main organisational principle even within a company.

It is a well-known fact that companies spend a lot of resources on the organisation of work. It is common for these projects to involve many employees and sometimes also consultants, which makes them costly for organisations. Sometimes a new project has to be started when another is finished because the environment changes so rapidly that organisations have problems in following the pace. Many companies have expanded the work in this area to cover both current needs and needs that are expected to arise in the future. They could have as much as two or three versions of processes, which describe the current state, the next generation and the future target. This has gone so far that it is common to have special departments working only with process development and change management, or to spend large sums on external consultants who could lead these activities.

In our work as management consultants we are often involved in such projects, and we have seen their growing need as a result of the ever-increasing pace of change in markets and organisations. One example is that of a large Swedish utilities company that has developed detailed processes for all parts of its business. When it started, it was forced to extend the work to new areas because of the deregulation of the electricity industry (which led to the development of new processes for activities such as acquiring new customers and disconnecting others).

The first versions of these processes were intended to take care of the most urgent needs, but when they were implemented it was already time for a new version, and it is likely that this will continue in the future as changes occur in the environment, internal systems change, the organisation changes and customer requirements change. The cost of these steady alterations could be very high compared with the benefits. It would be less expensive if a system of spontaneous organisation could be applied.

It is not possible to control and describe spontaneous organisations in the same detailed manner as for previous types of organisation. It is still deeply ingrained in most managers that they have to keep a tight grip on their organisation, and many will resist every argument proposing that people should be allowed to organise spontaneously. So, could an organisation with a large degree of spontaneity of organisation be managed? We suggest that we go back to the argument calling for a higher degree of spontaneity in a situation where the environment changes more rapidly than managers can handle through the process of conscious organisation. This argument is key in this discussion. There is a general fear in managers and owners that they would lose control of the business if they did not know exactly how people worked in different parts of the company. This is probably one of the reasons why the number of spontaneous organisations inside companies still is rather small.

Telia (Sweden's largest telecom service provider) has launched a number of information systems that offer operational information, in real-time, on their intranet. These tools are vital for people who deal with service management and customer care. Before the intranet, it was impossible to get this information for someone who did not have a computer where these systems and tools were installed. Therefore, it was a well-planned process to decide who should have which tools and information in the organisation.

With the introduction of intranet-based tools, it is no longer possible to know which tools and which information each person uses. In fact, management has lost the ability to know exactly how a process is carried out. A person in any position in a company can start to use the information and the tools that he or she finds convenient and start to change his or her role in the company. If this is handled properly, it might be a major advantage for an organisation, giving rise to shorter lead times and more flexibility. What is needed is usually to let the organisation develop in the same direction as the IT support. A typical step that can be taken is to introduce performance and quality indicators that focus on the added value of a unit or a person, rather than measuring whether tasks are carried out in line with fixed process descriptions. A change process like this in an organisation cannot easily be reversed, and it is a typical example of how a spontaneous organisation is created.

Let us look at what might happen when an organisation became exposed to transparency internally through an intranet service. The starting point is a traditional organisation. Some people handle customer services, some people produce marketing materials, some people handle travel arrangements. This specialisation of work is planned from the top of the organisation by managers at different levels. Each person is equipped with the tools and support systems that are required to carry out the tasks. For example, those who interact with customers have access to customer databases, and those who develop marketing materials have access to product and service information. This means that it is easy to know who is doing what because nobody has any tools that would enable them to do anything outside the narrowly defined borders of their work descriptions. This often leads to a situation in which customers are sent around the company in order to find the person who can help them with their particular problem. This can be very annoying for someone who wants only some simple answers, but when all companies are working in the same way, customers cannot expect better treatment anywhere else.

Think for a second about what would happen in this organisation if an intranet were to be installed and all present customer support systems connected to it. Through this intranet, it would be possible to find all the vital information that people need and also easy for anybody to search for it. Today, it is also possible to implement a number of applications to help people find the right competencies and manage internal activities and, last but not least, give them access to all kinds of support systems, such as travel bookings. This means that anybody can find the information they need and perform the tasks they need. Slowly, the organisation will learn to use these opportunities and start to work in new ways. For example, when a customer wonders when an order will be delivered, the person who answers the telephones can look it up in 5 seconds without help from others. Those who need a train ticket immediately can book it on their own instead of involving secretaries and travel agencies. A person who needs a customised product presentation to give to a customer can compile it in 2 minutes by using his PC and information provided over the corporate intranet. A person who needs to order a new piece of software makes a market survey in 2 hours instead of involving the purchasing department, who would have started a 2-week project.

All these examples may seem insignificant in themselves, but, let us think further. Would the person who has saved 2 weeks in 2 hours go back to the old way of working? Would the person at the front desk ask an annoyed customer to call again when the salesperson is back from lunch instead of giving the information right away? Hopefully not.

When we analyse what happens in an organisation that starts to use an intranet, it is interesting to note that very few of the changes in tasks and ways of working are consciously planned in advance – they simply happen as people start to use the available information. With more and more advanced features of intranets, the consequences will be more apparent and far reaching. Competition very often starts to arise in the organisation even if that was not the original intention. People start to compare services they can get via the Internet with services they can get through the traditional channels. To book a travel ticket, for example, can suddenly be made much easier using the Internet instead of asking the secretary, and this leads to competition between two different alternatives. One reaction to this is to let these new forces loose in the organisation and encourage them, rather than to hinder the development. By doing this, the first step is taken towards the type of spontaneous organisation, based on the market mechanism, that we describe later in this book.

With this simple example in mind, it will also be easy for the reader to understand that this type of spontaneous organisation will also increase efficiency, decrease cost and change the opportunities for management to plan activities in the organisation. One other effect is that roles in the organisation will be redefined and the organisation will learn how to produce the same amount of products and services through the use of fewer resources, and that is the basic meaning of increased efficiency, is it not?

The market mechanism is making its way into large organisations

For large corporations, network intelligence may seem like a direct threat to their existence, so what could these companies do? Do they have to split the organisation into small units and give them the total freedom to manage their own business? The answer is not that simple and straightforward.

Historically, many industries have been dominated by large organisations because this way of organising work has had many advantages compared with using smaller organisational units. Large formal organisations have:

- decreased transaction costs
- made capital available where it has been needed in the organisation;
- provided a focal point for customers.

Now the situation is changing dramatically. The advantages of being large are likely to decrease in the future society that we are describing. We will start by discussing the market mechanism that will be not just the way in which entire markets are organised, but also how organisations will be able to work internally.

The market mechanism, or 'the invisible hand', has the advantage of allocating resources to the most efficient producer in the market while less efficient producers have to improve efficiency or go out of business. This means that the producers who will be first to clear their stocks will be those with the lowest costs of production. When they have cleared their stocks, producers at the next level of efficiency will be able to sell their goods until producers at the first level have replenished their stocks. Over time, this establishes a price at an equilibrium level where the cost curve of the suppliers intersects the demand curve of the buyers.

The prerequisites for this situation are that all players in the market have access to complete information about what goes on in the market, and that there are goods from different producers that are interchangeable with each other in the eyes of the majority of customers. One other prerequisite is that no producer can use his power in order to influence other suppliers or buyers, or influence the level of supply or demand at any given time. Through Internet trade, the large-scale advantages in administration and marketing will virtually disappear. Instead, we could talk about the advantages of small-scale networks that increase flexibility and innovation.

In most large organisations, we have in recent years seen a development towards smaller and smaller profit units. Members of top management in these organisations have realised something very important: they cannot expect to be able to allocate resources internally more efficiently than the organisation's units can do themselves through market-based interaction. To be able to do this, the units have to have the opportunity to trade their products and services freely between each other. They also have to be able to get resources in proportion to the value that they create internally and for customers. In many countries, this development has been going on both in business and in the public sector. The development that we describe here, however, has the power to have deeper consequences than any planned changes towards market-based interaction that we have seen so far.

In Chapter 3, we mentioned buyers in the Swedish public sector who have formed a large-scale project in the field of electronic trade in order to decrease administration costs. This could be seen as an example of an early attempt to make large-scale use of the new information technology in order to create new opportunities in the market. In the electronic market, large companies will face networks of small competitors who have the advantage of lower overhead costs, less slack in the organisation, more flexibility and a higher potential for innovation.

Managing internal networks in larger organisations

Even networked organisations within a company need to be managed. Without management, the company will lose all of its advantages of scale, and it may as well be split into a number of different pieces. This is likely to happen in many cases over time, but there will also be the means of keeping large corporations as units and helping them to stay efficient even in this new environment. In this section, we will discuss some methods that could be used to manage this type of organisation.

It is crucial for the employees of any company to have a sense of direction, which means that they need overall guidelines describing the direction in which the organisation is supposed to move. Without these guidelines, an organisation using the market mechanism as its main organisational principle could drift into areas that would not be preferred by top management in the long term. Therefore, management needs to set the foundations for the company by formulating and communicating a set of high-level goals and processes.

In order to achieve the goals and contribute to the overall processes, any organisation will need management systems and measurement tools that make people take the right decisions. By this we mean systems that make it possible to measure the value created by each individual so that he or she can be measured against specific economic or other performance goals. Thus tomorrow's organisations will have to discard the practice of measuring people by the time they spend at work. Instead, employees should, as far as possible, be rewarded for their contributions.

In order for an organisation to become more flexible, all employees should be trusted to plan work according to their ideas of how it should best be done, make spontaneous contacts with other employees whose competence or time will be needed in order to achieve the result, agree with them the conditions of co-operation and work towards the goal that has been set up. In such an organisation each individual would sell services to other members of the organisation, either at a preset rate or with the help of market-based pricing mechanisms that could change the price of the time of a particular individual as the demand for his time change.

In this case, each person would have at least one budget, namely a budget for the amount of services that they would have to sell to their peers. People in management positions would be allocated responsibilities for projects or operative processes of different kinds, for which they would have to hire other people in the organisation in order to succeed. With improved computer tools, the administration of such a network will not be as costly as it would have been 10 years ago, and the effects on the identification of slack in the organisation could in many organisations be dramatic.

One example of a company that has organised in the form of a network organisation with a substantial share of spontaneity is WH Gore & Associates. This company was founded in 1959 by Bill Gore, a former employee of Du Pont. Gore invented a new material, called Gore-Tex, which is used in a number of applications in the electronics industry, clothing and medical industries and for other applications.

The company has been described as having no managers and no hierarchical structure, even though communication in this company has not been based on any particular electronic device. We argue, however, that Gore and other companies that use the same organisational principles are the forerunners showing that spontaneous organisations can be both more effective and more efficient than traditional companies.

The organisation at WH Gore is based on personal involvement. People within Gore call their organisation a 'lattice organisation', each individual representing a node that is connected to other nodes by a network of 'lattices'. In the organisation, each individual takes on a responsibility to accomplish a goal, which is set by each person himself in a discussion with his 'sponsor'. One of the reasons behind the very rapid growth of the company since its foundation could be the personal involvement that is created in this process. The culture of the company ensures that nobody wants to set goals that are too low for themselves. Instead, associates are inspired to take initiatives that could increase the turnover and profitability of the company, for example finding new applications for the products or expanding sales and profitability in existing markets or application areas.

The Gore principles lay the foundation of the strong culture. Associates have to live by these principles in order to survive in the company. The principles are only four and they are simple:

1. *Freedom*: Each associate should allow, help and encourage fellow associates to grow in knowledge and responsibility within a field of expertise. Freedom also means that associates should be able to take initiatives under personal responsibility.
2. *Fairness*: All associates should be as honest with each other, and with customers and suppliers, as possible.
3. *Commitments*: Each employee has to accept responsibility for the achievement of goals and manage to live up to these targets. No associate can make decisions or commitments on behalf of another person. All commitments are personal.
4. *Waterline*: All associates have to ask for advice from more experienced colleagues before they make decisions that could damage the company economically or have a negative impact on its image. The metaphor of a ship is used, where very risky decisions could lead to damages under the waterline and the ship could sink (that is, the company could go bankrupt).

These principles, together with the organisation without managers and hierarchy, form one part of the foundation of the success of the company. Each employee has to build a network of contacts within the company, and the bonds that are created in this process are continually re-evaluated and renewed. Some old bonds get weaker as the constellations that have been formed are replaced by others that serve the moment better. Individuals are encouraged to pursue the goals that they have formulated together with their sponsor, and as all associates strive to do their best for themselves and the company, they improve the position of WH Gore in the external market.

The basic organisation principle is the market mechanism. People sell their abilities internally, and those who are unsuccessful at developing relationships with other associates do not last long in the company. Instead, the basis for the success for this type of company is that each individual manages to 'sell' his or her competence and other abilities in the internal market.

Two types of internal market

From the WH Gore example, we can see that an organisation based on the internal marketing of resources could function in at least two different ways. The first is the type of internal market where people actually sell their services for money to other employees in the same way that different departments today already trade their services or products with other departments, as goods and services are traded in the external market.

The second way of functioning is the WH Gore type of market, where only time, enthusiasm and competence are traded against each other. In this type of market, people offer these valuables to each other and form teams that could compete against external competitors.

Although we may see some positive effects of this way of organising work, we have to note a few things:

■ Internal relationships would resemble a market. People who would not be able to add value in the role they are playing might have to leave the organisation or go outside and spend some of their time working for other companies or networks as well.
■ Hourly wages and salaries might have to increase since slack would disappear. This would be for the same reason that consultants have to charge a premium because they always have some slack between projects. Companies that organise in this way are likely to save a lot of money through these measures, but they will also have to make it possible for employees to support themselves within the new rules of the game.

■ Many employees and labour unions will disapprove of this way of organising work. Many will argue that it will increase stress levels and that it will create an inhuman work environment. This is only true if we do not reform other areas of society. Among them are our views on work and unemployment, and the ways in which we choose to treat the latter. The increased efficiency of the organisations that we describe here should be seen as a way of freeing resources that could be used for other purposes. It is important for us to understand that we gain nothing by maintaining inefficient structures simply in order to keep people in work that does not have to be done. Instead, we have to find new ways of improving society by utilising the freed resources in new and creative ways.

The network office

Ever since people started to have specialised tasks in their working life, offices have evolved to meet needs when carrying out different types of task. Each type of work has its specific environment designed to facilitate and automate the work as much as possible. An office has a natural place in the process flow that defines the scope and limits of the task in the chain of activities that characterises an enterprise. Process development, re-engineering and design have been on the management agenda for many years, and this has resulted in streamlined workflows that optimise the production of products and services. The office (as a physical or information-based environment) has followed and been driven by this development to support people who work in these processes. This has made modern offices into efficient environments with tools that meet the complex problems posed for the employees of modern organisations. (We would like to stress that automation is high on the agenda in many office environments. In factories, automation has already gone far and led to great changes in the way of working.)

The network office is built in order to increase the flexibility of the working environment. Stability is a word that is seldom used when the requirements of tomorrow's organisation are described. In this book, we use the expression 'spontaneously organised organisations' to describe the basic characteristics of an organisation designed to increase flexibility. We also say that present organisations, in order to compete with networks of co-operating companies, will also have to take on some of these spontaneous characteristics.

One other aspect of networks as a form of organisation is the argument that we put forward stating that networks will replace processes as the organisational form of the future. One important building block of a networked organisation is the network office, which can be seen as the room and work station (a physical object) of an employee in an organisation, but can also mean the software tools, documents and other information that can be accessed by an individual regardless of the physical position of this individual in the geographical environment. Anyone who has a PC and who is connected to a network of computers, either an intranet or the Internet, could access the same computerised tools and documents from anywhere in the world that he or she could get in touch with a telecommunications network. This way of looking at the network office opens up new visions for what could be achieved in this type of environment.

A networked organisation will consist of any number of such offices that are connected to each other through the same network. Within this network, people should be able to organise their co-operation in such a way that efficiency is optimised by the 'invisible hand' of the market without the need for management to pre-organise processes.

The only thing that has to be known in this type of organisation are the overall goals and overall processes that provide guidelines for the type of work to be done. These guidelines only have to describe high-level tasks and the requirements of the process as a whole. Nothing has to be decided by management about who is doing what and when. This may sound like a very uncertain situation for a person who is working in an organisation, but it is the way a market works.

The idea behind this type of organisation is to provide a set of tools that are not focused directly on solving a specific task. Instead, they are focused on three very important things:

- communications
- access to information
- information management.

By using these tools, the person in each office should bring value to the overall process to which he or she is supposed to contribute. In other words, the overall goals are known and the office is the basis for adding value. Since the market is open to all employees, it does not take any specific entrepreneurial skills to succeed – just the ability to add value to the work of others and co-operate in a market environment. We see co-operation as a natural result of the market-based interaction between customers and suppliers.

A network office has to be created and designed by someone. In an organisation with many people, this can be handled by a central function that looks after all the tools to which the organisation should have access. The exact content of the office is, however, up to the user to decide. He or she can choose between the tools offered and create his office to meet current needs. It could, of course, be a complicated task for every person in an organisation to decide which tools to use, but there are means of simplifying this choice. By introducing measurements of the value that each person is contributing, it will become easier for each person to decide which tools to use and how to use them.

If, for example, the focus is on helping customers who experience problems, the network office needs to have tools like:

- communication facilities to connect the customer support staff to the customer;
- access to various types of information about the products with which the customer has problems;
- access to trouble-shooting tools to solve customer problems.

When the support staff switch over to help the next customer, the communication, information and tools may change to meet new requirements. This may seem like a complex situation that makes it necessary for the user to learn a whole range of tools, but through a common interface to these tools, for example a web-browser, it will be possible to handle this without problems.

Note

1. This expression was often used by the late professor Eric Rhenman, founder of the Scandinavian consulting company SIAR. Professor Rhenman also introduced the concept of the market mechanism as an organisation principle.

6 The Valuescape

The valuescape is an important concept in the new electronic marketplace. It will provide the basis for a new type of market in which customer needs, rather than production and transportation issues, are in focus when the market is structured. We call this new structure the 'valuescape' to stress that the key concept in this new paradigm is value, rather than geography as we are used to in the physical landscape (or market). This means also that closeness in the electronic market should be interpreted in terms of 'closeness of values' or 'closeness to the customer in terms of value creation' instead of in terms of geographical closeness.

An introductory visit to a valuescape

The valuescape is the basis for each user's personal experience of the Internet. Unlike the landscape that we know in the physical world, the valuescape is personal. Each valuescape is created by the person who uses it, and it changes as the person discovers the Internet.

In order to understand the concept of a valuescape, we start by following a person on his first journey on the Internet. Let us imagine a person, Dan, who has never before visited the Internet. He has, however, a knowledge of a number of addresses that he wants to visit to do some errands. First, he wants to do some shopping for groceries. Thus Dan visits an Internet-based grocery store that delivers at home in his area. Just a couple of seconds after he has logged on to the computer, he enters the 'Internetto' store, where he can order everything that he usually buys at his corner shop. It takes 3 minutes to buy bread, milk, cheese, a kilo of beef for the Sunday dinner, sweets, a couple of frozen ready-made dishes and a number of other groceries that are needed. He lists his name and his address, together with his e-mail address and credit card number, and goes directly from the grocery shop to the wine merchant's that arranges delivery in co-operation with the grocery store.

At the wine merchant's, he looks at the list of wines to buy. However, he feels a little uncertain of which wine to choose so he clicks on to a number of medium-priced reds that would go well with the roast beef and comes directly into the homepage of a wine magazine that has published tasting notes on the Internet. Here Dan can read the professional comments on each wine and go even further to check whether there are comments written by Internet users who have tasted the wines. He chooses one of the wines, orders a couple of bottles and adds some extra whites that are particularly recommended by the wine magazine as superior value for money. Then Dan checks the producer records on wine he has been recommended on two other homepages, to obtain their sound judgement just for good measure, and exits the wine shop. Next, he prints the name of a small suburb of Dublin, named Dalkey, which he is going to visit in a couple of months, for a search on the Alta Vista search engine.

Now he finds a number of sites that offer information about Dalkey, among them a complete homepage dedicated to the place (www.dalkey-homepage.ie). Here he finds the homepage of a middle-of-the-range hotel where he could stay. On-line, he books 3 nights and takes a look at the other facilities lined up on the town's homepage. One of them catches his immediate interest because, among the pubs, bars and restaurants that are listed, he finds one that could scarcely be found in the real world: The Virtual Bar (www.thevirtualbar.com). He makes a mental note that the homepage of Dalkey is worth another visit prior to going to Dalkey and enters The Virtual Bar.

The Virtual Bar turns out to be a great place. It offers a steadily growing range of more than 5,000 different mixed cocktails, a number of bar games and information about drink ingredients, and actually adapts to the contents of the user's own stock of spirits and other ingredients. Dan lists some of the ingredients that he can remember are in his own refrigerator and gets a number of suggestions for drinks that can be made with these ingredients. He decides that he has no time to mix drinks at present, downloads The Virtual Bar program on to the hard disk of his own computer and hurries on.

He has decided to buy shares with some of his savings, enters the homepage of a stockbroker and places an order to buy shares for a small amount. The fee charged seems much smaller than he had expected. Now there is only one errand left to do. He needs to buy a book for a friend's birthday present. He enters the homepage www.amazon.com, finds the book, places the order and exits the Internet.

This may seem like an ordinary shopping trip that could just as well be done in a city, despite the fact that it took only 20 minutes instead of two and a half hours and that Dan found both products and information that he would have been unable to find in his own home town, regardless of how long he had looked for some of them.

There is one big difference, however, and that is the valuescape. When we visit the shops on our ordinary shopping tour, we seldom leave any traces. If we do, shops rarely make use of the information that our purchases leave behind. In the valuescape, it is quite the contrary. Each step that Dan took on the Internet was recorded by millions of invisible 'eyes' and 'ears' with the sole purpose of getting a better understanding of Dan's shopping habits and lifestyle. Furthermore, as Dan went along his route, he recorded all his actions as 'bookmarks' on his Internet browser so that he would be able to come back and visit his favourite sites again.

As Dan continues to use the Internet, he will create his own valuescape, an electronic landscape to which he can return time and again. Each of his actions adds new sites to his own list of bookmarks at the same time as the information of Dan's actions is interpreted by millions of electronic agents and other applications that analyse the behaviour of users in order to determine which users should be addressed with a particular advertisement or other type of information.

Now, as we intend to tell the story of the valuescape, the reader can keep Dan's little tale in mind, in order better to understand our arguments.

From a geographical market to...

In the beginning, all markets were local. In a society where it was impossible to transport information further than the sound of a scream could carry, no trade could be carried out over long distances. It was only the goods that were offered in the local market that could be considered for purchase. If people wanted to trade over large distances, they had to bring their goods to another market in order to expose it to customers there.

Today we have various ways of informing potential customers about our offerings even if we are far apart, but we still face the problem of making important deals over long distances. We have also had problems collecting information about all offerings in the market. When we are shopping as individuals, we are still often limited to the choices available in the local stores.

We could say that, in the physical world, we are facing a 'market landscape' that is very similar to the geographical landscape we see on a map. If we want a larger choice of products, we travel to a large city to do our shopping, and if we are in a hurry to get something, we have to make do with our local suppliers. However, even if we go to a larger city, we cannot be sure that we will find something better than we are offered locally.

...Value focus

This market structure, as we know it today, is characterised by trade-offs between convenience for the customer and the rational handling of goods. The problem of dealing with material products, from a presentation point of view, is to make it possible for customers to evaluate different alternatives without spending too much time travelling between shops. One problem with this is that, regardless of how many stores we visit, we cannot be sure that we have found the best alternative. There may always be another shop with an offer that is better than the one we have found so far. Despite this uncertainty, there is also the problem that travelling between shops takes time and costs money. Most times, we investigate a limited number of alternatives and choose the best of these.

In the present market, various middlemen are involved in the value chain to set up stores or showrooms where customers can come and look at products and get more information about services. These points where people and products can meet have become a deeply rooted basis for business in all types of industry. We take them for granted and even use the same concepts when we build new electronic marketplaces. Yet distribution structures will take an entirely new shape in the new market that is being created on the Internet.

In all discussions of future shopping, the social aspect of shopping is considered as there are, of course, other aspects of shopping than the purely economical. Some people think that the social side of it is the most important, stressing that we meet other people in the shopping centre and that many people have shopping as a leisure activity. These aspects are important and will play a role when the new electronic market develops. However, these additional needs connected to shopping can probably be solved by completely new 'services'. Just think of 'cyber cafés' where people can meet friends and surf the Internet. We will come back to some examples of new solutions along these lines when we look at emerging markets at the end of this book. Here we will continue to discuss the market and economical aspects of electronic trade.

For a company that considers different strategies for the future, new concepts and new opportunities have to be well understood in order to take advantage of them. Therefore, companies as well as individuals need to stop, try to see this new market from an objective point of view and start to analyse the structure that is emerging. For a company, this must be a core activity in their development of new strategies for the electronic market. The important question is: How could new opportunities using the Internet make it easier for customers to find, buy and use products and services that cover their needs at the lowest possible cost?

The answer to that question in the physical world would probably be that we would like to create our own city with our own choice of shops. Also, we would like to structure this city so that the shops we visit most often would be in the centre, with less frequently visited shops on the outskirts. We would perhaps also like to arrange small 'trap doors' between shops we often visit in conjunction with each other, so that we could go directly from the baker's shop to the cheese shop without entering the 'street' in between. We could even 'rebuild' the shop to meet our own particular needs and preferences, simply in order to make it easier for us to find products and easily evaluate them. It would also be convenient if, once we found a product to buy, we could compare all other offers of similar products without leaving the store where we found the first alternative.

In the emerging market on the Internet, each market will be structured around customer value and customer needs. There will be no need to consider geographical convenience when it comes to presenting products to the customer. The new communication technologies will make it possible to communicate product and service information to customers in a form that contains more nuances, offers more product knowledge to customers and also brings down the price of the products substantially, as we shall see in a number of examples in the next chapter. In short, customers on the Internet will be able to build their own 'cities' according to their own preferences and ideas of what an ideal shopping experience would be like.

In this chapter, we will describe how each customer on the Internet will be able to create his or her own valuescape and how companies should act so that their offerings can be taken up as part of as many valuescapes of different customers as possible. We will also present some examples of how a valuescape could be structured and what the concept of a 'shop' could mean in this type of market.

Building the valuescape

There are no physical distances on the Internet. Instead, all users have access to all the available information regardless of whether it is located on a server next door or on the other side of the world. This access to enormous amounts of information could lead to an extreme overload of information if users did not have the opportunity to structure it according to their own preferences and values. This customisation of the marketplace is crucial, not just for the success of various services on the Internet, but also for the development of the entire Internet market. If people cannot easily find what they need, they will turn to other solutions that take less time and effort to use.

Dan's story at the beginning of this chapter showed how a user could begin to structure his own valuescape along his own lines. This structure will be accessible again and again as Dan wants to return to the shops that he has already visited. Furthermore, it will become 'thicker and thicker' with information that is of interest to him as suppliers of goods and providers of information on the Internet find out more about his interests and buying habits.

Internet technology allows a pace of change of concepts in the valuescape that we have never before seen and can hardly perceive. Let us imagine that we have spent some time in search of a good CD shop and, after some efforts, have spotted a place that seems to be just right for our needs. We now add it to our list of favourite sites and feel pleased because we have found exactly what we are looking for. Next week, we go back to look for a CD to buy and find that the site has totally changed shape. Nothing is the same; new opportunities and new functionality have appeared. There may also be new and better shops that we do not find unless we actively search for them.

This speed of change may seem negative to people who want stability in their lives. Thus this type of change must be managed by companies so that it is turned into something positive for customers. The valuescape that actively analyses the behaviour of users and 'thickens' it in areas of particular interest makes it possible for users to diminish the risk that they will not be able to get back to a place of their liking. If, for any reason, a particular site has disappeared from the Internet, it will become easier and easier for a user to find other sites that provide similar services and information. If Dan knows of one bookshop from the beginning, he will soon, as he pays a number of visits there, get information about many other bookshops that carry the types of book he prefers.

There are indications that the Internet market will be a structure of two layers. On the top level, there may be search engines where customers can specify wanted products and product features. These search engines will search providers' offers and find the ones that fit the description, sorting them according to any variable chosen by the customer. Such agent-based software is already available.

For suppliers who want to build a presence on the Internet, the issue is how to make users discover their sites. This may happen by coincidence or by active search on the part of the customer, but it is important for companies to make customers want to visit their homepages. This requires the differentiation of offers in terms of the actual products and services, the information content and the information structure (layout) of the site. The site must fit as a natural part of the valuescapes of many Internet users.

The valuescape is the structure that each customer on the Internet will build in order to be able to navigate efficiently in the electronic market. Each person who uses the Internet can create links between different sites and homepages that make it easier for him to come back to 'places' he has been before. The valuescape of each customer will be like a map of the interests and the relationships between the different interests of the person in question. This map will, however, never be static. It will always be in the process of being built and rebuilt as a person's needs change and he or she passes through different stages in life.

Another aspect of the valuescape is that it is not just a solution that makes it possible to surf easily between sites of particular interest. It also has the function of changing the working environment for the increasing number of people who use the Internet for work-related purposes. Sites could be tailored to the needs and interests of different users. Electronic tools and information that is stored could be changed in real-time to fit better and better the intentions of users. Links, information, pictures and tools that are of little or no relevance to one user are hidden in his or her valuescape, and more useful things take their place. This function is very similar to the functioning of our own memory, in which memories that we access often are bright and easy to retrieve, whereas memories of which we have not thought for a long time are pushed further and further back in memory.

For the person who works or surfs on the Internet, it is possible to begin a session with a very faint idea of what to do. We could start to look around in a general environment that shows a broad range of alternatives and then, step by step, focus on subjects that turn up and catch our interest. After some time, when the user knows a little more about his or her needs, the valuescape will start to change shape and begin to select information that is close to the subject of interest to show to the user. The user is smoothly guided towards a solution. This means not only that the information shown must be limited to a narrow scope, but also that complementary services could turn up that are useful in other parts of the user's life. These services could be selected for each user in order to make it as easy as possible to find products, services and information that are, or could be, of interest to them. Very rapidly, these new opportunities to customise the offer to the customer start to become available to us. On the Internet, it is already common that commercials are selected depending on which key words we use in our search engines.

This means that no customer is doomed to wander through the valuescape that is built by producers or other suppliers of information. Users could each build their own valuescape through the addition of bookmarks to their own list and by adding automatic links between different sites on the Internet. This way of creating a personal valuescape is only the beginning. New sites, such as the layouts of information sources owned by suppliers on the Internet, are already available where the user can add a personal touch to a number of things, and it is also possible to customise services to our own needs by using these tools. On these sites, users are asked to provide information about themselves, and the homepage draws conclusions from this information (for example the interests of people with a certain type of job or hobby).

A typical example of customisation in this way is Planet Direct (www.planetdirect.com), where news, information, weather and entertainment, among other things, are provided in a way that is tailored to each user's profile. All the information is adapted to the facts about the user that he or she has provided, and it is possible to customise layout, information and services. This is done through a number of choices between various sources of information and by giving extensive information about interests, job and social situation.

The idea behind this site is that the content of any homepage the user visits is adapted and fitted into the Planet Direct environment rather than just being linked to the site. By doing this extra piece of work, it becomes possible to give all sites that are visited by a user the same characteristics, regardless of who provided the information in the first place.

Another example that has gone one step further on the road to the valuescape is Firefly (www.firefly.com). This is a system that recommends sites to visit; it bases its advice on what other users with similar tastes have said that they like. Each person is asked to rate at least 20 sites and give personal information about themselves. This makes it possible for the system to select new sites to recommend, based on the personal profile and the preferences shown. With this type of filtering, it is possible to create an agent that keeps evolving as the user rates its suggestions. You can take your description of the valuescape with you as you surf the web, and when you visit Firefly-enabled sites, you can get recommendations and advice and bond with people who share your interests. This example contains a number of interesting features and is definitely a step towards customisation of the web. A very important characteristic it has in common with the valuescape as we present it in this book is that the profile can follow the user from site to site and evolve automatically.

The building of a valuescape is one aspect of the transparent society. Each user could see the network from the perspective that they want to. Users, regardless of whether they are a politician looking for information about a certain topic in the field of social development, a purchasing manager looking for the best supplier of newsprint or a person leisurely looking for new experiences and shopping opportunities, could travel through the Internet in their own way, building their own valuescape step by step.

Need chains are the key to the new structure

A basic structuring mechanism of the valuescape is the links between the different needs of a user. The old structure of a marketplace is focused on how information, products and services can be sorted and structured to reduce cost and space. Without these limitations, the structure can be more user-friendly by addressing the total needs that a user is likely to have in a certain situation. These links can vary a lot from person to person, but there are usually patterns that are similar for many people.

One example is a person who has decided to buy a plant for his garden. Which products and services should be presented to him as the next step in his visit to the valuescape? Probably not spare parts for the car or flats to rent in the city centre. Why not present information and support on gardening and other plants that would look nice together with the one that he has just bought? After that, payment options, transportation services (to get a large plant delivered) and gardening services could be alternatives that fit well as the next steps to link one need to another. This concept is central when companies add offers to the Internet and will be an important ingredient in the examples discussed later in this chapter.

Let us look at another example of where the valuescape will be an important foundation for various services and where it is obvious how users' needs will play a major role – the travel and tourism market. Some of the developments that we discuss in this book could certainly pose a threat to the travel industry, in which a large share of business travel is built on the idea that people have to meet in person in order to do business efficiently.

It may, however, be an interesting tool for companies in this market to conquer new market shares. Travel and tourism are so much more than just the trip itself. A travel experience starts with planning, thinking, getting thrilled by exotic stories and pictures from foreign countries and, of course, making all the arrangements and ensuring that we have enough money to turn our dreams into reality. The valuescape is, as we have discussed several times, built around a total picture of the user's needs. When it comes to travel and tourism, the users' needs are many and usually quite complex.

Travel agencies have learned that it is complicated and time-consuming to plan and book a journey. Therefore, they have focused on total solutions and are offering customers complete travel packages. These are fulfilling a broad range of customer needs, but definitely not all. Customers are getting more demanding and want more alternatives and options. This provides travel companies with an interesting opportunity, namely that of customising offers. Using traditional solutions, it is very hard for a tour operator to make individual customisation a reality, down to the level of the single customer. However, the Internet and other electronic markets make it possible for companies to offer a completely new service to travellers. By going back to customer needs when we are planning a journey, it is possible to see how the structure of the valuescape will develop in the field of travel.

Let us start a journey into this thrilling part of the valuescape. The user will first express a general wish to be exposed to travel information. In this early phase, the user is not looking for any information in particular. Instead, he or she wants to surf around and look at a number of alternatives, to 'pop in' here and there to see whether something interesting turns up. In this phase, the valuescape can be general, meeting the needs of many people. After some time, it gets more and more clear to both the user and other actors in the valuescape (who can be represented by electronic agents that analyse each step of the presumptive customer) what the needs of the user are. By doing this, the user is, step by step, limiting the options, and the valuescape responds by showing the entrance of specialised sites with information and offers that are adapted to the needs of the user at that particular time.

By interpreting the moves of each customer and addressing the most relevant information available to him or her the huge amount of information and options can be brought down to a minimum. It is now clear that, for example, the user is not interested in expensive cruises but would rather look at budget trips, for example to go back-packing in the Far East. More specific proposals now turn up from various providers in the travel industry (remember that the Internet is filled with information from all the players in the electronic market rather than a particular company that provides everything on its own). This, however, means that there is an immense amount of information available. The selection mechanisms make sure that information overload is avoided and that most of the presented alternatives make sense. This is achieved by letting suppliers search for potential customers, just as customers are searching for potential products and services.

The user can now use all the opportunities of multimedia technology and travel through space and time to look, hear and 'feel' what a certain trip to a foreign country could be like. The user can 'walk' through hotels, be exposed to thrilling sights and hear the music at the discos or the tropical sounds late at night in the jungle. At this stage, the valuescape has helped the user to get a good overall grip of his or her vacation plans. Now the valuescape follows the next turn in the user's need chain, entering the mode of detailed planning and preparation. At this stage, the true power of this adaptable environment shows. The user can start to plan and book his or her journey based on the intentions expressed so far. Thousands of hotels, airline and railway companies are available to meet the needs of the user, but only the ones the customer has looked at previously are selected as first choices. For each first choice, there may be alternatives presented that are in the same price range, offer the same facilities or are in another town with similar things to see.

The complexity of this task, which has led to the need for travel agencies, is reduced to a simple procedure. The user can easily book trips and plan itineraries because of excellent support from the valuescape. The user's needs are at this stage 'well known' by the system, and the alternatives are therefore few and easy to choose between. The customisation of the marketplace guarantees that the choices shown are within the user's own cost limits and are following the overall intentions for the trip. The user picks and chooses between alternatives, and when everything is ready, the total cost and schedule are presented and the trip is booked via a click on an electronic 'button'.

So far, the valuescape has offered services that are rather similar to those of a travel agency, but the support does not stop here. Even if the travel arrangements are made, much more has to be done to arrange the trip itself. The valuescape tracks this and goes into a mode where the user can select various pieces of information about the places to visit. Maps, guides and practical information are provided in a convenient and attractive way using the opportunities of multimedia. Here, the valuescape offers services from other industries such as publishing and tourist information. When the person finally starts the journey, it is tempting to think that the support has come to an end, but that does not have to be the case. Smaller and smaller terminals with access to the Internet are offered, and information kiosks and other Internet access points will become widespread and easy to use, which makes it possible to go even further and continue to meet the needs of the user even later in the process.

Arrangements, deadline monitoring and additional information can be easily accessed from all over the world. It is, of course, also possible to manage practical things at home while travelling. By offering this type of service, the valuescape can even become a partner that keeps track of all the boring practicalities while the user just relaxes and enjoys the trip. This example is applicable for both the business traveller and the tourist.

Suppliers in all markets have, of course, focused on how to create value for customers in an efficient way. Independent of products and services, it is necessary to structure the business to meet customer needs. However, with new opportunities and new means to communicate with customers and other suppliers, a new market structure is possible. When the dimension of physical distance, which has added a cost to the relationship between the supplier and the customer, vanishes, the target can be turned even more towards customer needs and customer value. The focus is turned away from competition through the increasing efficiency of value chains with many intermediaries. Instead, the focus of the valuescape is on the 'need chain' of the customer, which creates a delivery value chain that can be organised spontaneously as the customer reveals his or her needs.

The change of focus from value chains to need chains means that the concept of customer-orientated business can be taken one step further than has been possible in the physical market. It means that most important initiatives are taken away from companies and given over to customers, who could act as judges of all efforts that companies make to a much greater extent than at present.

This development could also create a distinction between the words 'market economy' and 'capitalism', which have until now been almost synonymous. It has been assumed that a market economy is ruled by the capitalist, who has the power to make investments where they are needed. In the Internet-based market economy, customers reveal their need chains and thereby manage production and supplier networks. These signals from the market in their turn determine where money needs to be invested.

One example of how the present market is structured is that one type of company has been developed in order to sell products and another has been established to handle financial transactions. These two types of company have, in the old market, had different physical locations and have shown different faces to the customer. The two functions of selling and taking care of financial transactions have been kept totally separate in different types of business, namely shops and banks. If customers in the future prefer, all types of errand could be done in one place at the same time.

Shops have been a necessary part in the optimisation of a logistics chain where it has been too expensive to deliver goods all the way to the customer's doorstep and it has been impossible for everybody to go to each producer to make their purchases. In the new valuescape, these obstacles have disappeared, and the time has come to begin to break up the old structures and start from scratch, using all the new opportunities. The starting point should, as we have discussed in this chapter, be customer needs and *not* the value chains of the old markets.

The reason why it is now possible to align the whole production and delivery system to customer needs is the transformation of the marketplace that we describe in this book and that will be further developed in Chapter 7. We see the first signs that all kinds of company can use the opportunities of transparency, real-time communication, information-processing and network intelligence to increase customer focus and create service offerings that can, in many cases, be adapted to the individual needs of each customer. Since each customer can see through the entire production system of any industry, create his own valuescape according to his own preferences and have product and service offerings adapted to his needs, it will be possible to increase service levels and still substantially decrease costs.

The creation of the valuescape may, to many readers, seem to be a small change of focus that will lead to some new ways of offering products and services, but it will lead to much more dramatic changes than that, not only at the overall level described above, but also at the level of each offering. It will lead to the creation of a whole new shopping experience in which the efficiency of the shopping (or purchasing, if we talk about a company) reaches a limit that we have not experienced before, either as individuals or as professionals.

The idea behind the valuescape

Which competence is needed in order to create a valuescape? Will it require high skills in information technology? No, it will not. This technology is much simpler to master than almost any tool we use today. Basically, the technology is so simple that anybody who can read or write can use it a few moments after they have learned the basics. The valuescape in itself is also simple because we can start to search for anything that we need immediately, learn more as we go on, and make a few mistakes and experience a few successes and create the solution we need step by step without the use of any of the shopping skills we have acquired from a long life of navigation through the multitude of offerings in the present market.

It is most important to forget about how shops, mail order catalogues and shopping malls are structured and think about how they should be structured to meet our needs. When these needs are highlighted and the market starts to focus on them, instead of on old, well-known, market structures, new types of solution are possible.

A person may, for example, want to make a certain dish for dinner. In this case, he happens to have forgotten the recipe, but he knows the name of the dish that he wants to make. What would we normally do in a situation like that? We would start to look in cookbooks, at magazine clippings and in our handwritten recipes, which are often in a total mess. We may spend 10–15 minutes, or an hour, looking through all this material and finally find what we are looking for. After that, we still have a long way to go before we have decided what we need to buy in order to complement what we already have at home. Then we go to the shop, where the problem starts again. Products are not exposed in a way that suits our needs, as they are laid out in the recipe. The products in the shop are displayed on the shelves by product category, which means that we will have to pass through the whole shop in order to get what we need. Finally, when we are ready and have found all that we need, we need cash or a credit card in order to pay.

How could the structure of this shop be changed to focus on the needs of the customers instead of on the convenience of the employees of the shop and of the suppliers that deliver the goods? First, we should look at which kinds of business and which different types of service are involved in this example.

When we search for recipes, a number of publishing companies offer their services. Books, magazines and various commercial material give people access to recipes. This information is sorted in different ways, depending on the type of source. A cookbook is often sorted in one way and the recipes in a magazine in another, more random, order. This makes it hard to find what we are looking for when we want something in particular.

We could think about a grocery store that offers the goods we need in order to make the dish. Here, goods are sorted in a way that suits everybody (or nobody…). The focus is more on who supplies the goods, and whether they need special storage conditions because they are frozen or cold, than on the needs of the customers who do the shopping. It is definitely not sorted in a way that is customised to every single customer's needs (and how could it be?).

Payment in the shop is handled separately and managed in the same way, independently of what we buy. On the Internet, the three functions of finding a recipe, ordering the necessary ingredients and finally paying for them could be integrated into one very short sequence. The above example can be transferred into the valuescape by starting from the customer and the needs that are in focus.

These needs can be satisfied in a new and completely different way, building on the new opportunities of the electronic market. First, the complete process of meeting the customer's needs when he or she tries to find something interesting to cook can be kept together in an integrated solution. The customer starts by approaching sites on the Internet where companies have created a 'cooking ideas heaven'. Here, in the future, we may be able to surf around and be tempted by different types of food. We can home in on the type of food we are most interested in, for example diet food, Indian food or food with certain ingredients that we already have at home. Information is easy to use, being a mix of sponsored proposals from companies that want to offer their products and proposals from various publishing companies that offer their recipes. There could also be recipes offered by individuals who want to share their dining experiences with other people, and 'do-it-yourself' support to compose a new recipe.

Through the use of multimedia, it is possible to make this journey into the cooking part of the valuescape a pleasant trip that will stimulate most of our senses (smell and taste are unfortunately not yet possible, but it will be possible to hear the sizzle of a frying sausage). When we have finally found what we are looking for, we do not have to stop and find another place where we can buy the ingredients we need. The valuescape is focused around our complete needs and will not be fragmented, which means that when we have decided what we want to eat, we can just go from the recipes into a 'shop' where the ingredients are offered and order what we do not already have at home just by transforming the recipe into an order slip and crossing out the items we do not need to buy.

It will be possible to scan different alternatives so that we can find the best offers and prices that meet our needs. One supplier may offer instant delivery, but at a higher cost than the one that offers delivery tomorrow, when other items from, for example, a clothes shop will be delivered as well. This means that the shop no longer looks like the shop we are used to. Instead, it takes the shape that is most convenient for us. In this example, it is sorted in the way our recipe is sorted. Next time, it may look different if we want it to. We may have joined Weight Watchers and may then want to see only the low-calorie part of the product line. In this case, we will not be tempted to buy potato crisps, chocolate and other things that are unsuitable for our new lifestyle.

Last, but not least, when we have to pay for the goods, a money-handling agent turns up to arrange that. We do not have to go elsewhere to find it, and we get a bill that can be customised to include the information we want: what the dinner cost or our monthly cost of food, or something else that suits us. We may also want to get a quick look at our account in case we are afraid of running short of money.

A marketplace is always intended to be a place where suppliers can get the best possible exposure of their products and where customers can easily find what they need. Because of physical limitations in markets as we know them today, we have had to make a number of compromises. It has not been possible to have one marketplace for every situation and for every customer. However, the valuescape is not limited to these restrictions. The customer could rebuild it and reshape it at any time. This may sound like a nightmare for any company that offers products and tries to keep the loyalty of their customers, and a dream for any frustrated customer who unsuccessfully tries to find a certain product or service today in the physical market, but it requires some effort from the customer to make use of this freedom.

Companies could, however, also look upon this as an opportunity, but they need to know how to act in the electronic market. There should be an idea behind each step that a company takes. The question is how to come up with these ideas. There are many answers to this. One possibility for companies is to use all possible knowledge about customers, analysing it to find the patterns and hidden knowledge that can be used to conquer the market. We have already discussed some technologies that can help companies to do this. Data warehousing could, for example, reveal many hidden facts that could be used to make changes to the marketplace. Companies could provide certain offers on Friday afternoons, others on rainy days and a third type for customers who just happened to enter the 'shop' from an on-line car magazine where he happened to show an interest in the latest car models.

> However, it is very common for new solutions on the Internet to be constructed in the same way as we are used to in the traditional market. There are examples of shops on the Internet that have the same structure as the shops we can visit in the analogous world. A typical example of this is the grocery store www.internetto.se, which has no physical shop that customers can visit. This shop offers the same structure as any traditional shop. Departments are the same as we are used to, and we even get a shopping basket so that we feel at home. The only extra feature offered is that we can start from a standard shopping basket with the things we need to buy every time.
>
> However, it is obvious that this is only the beginning of a new era. Many examples of Internet food stores are developed rapidly, and the type of service we talk about here is starting to enter the market. A UK example of this type is Tesco's on-line shopping service (www.tesco.co.uk).

There may be several reasons why this shop has not transformed the shopping concept. One may be because we want to feel at home and do not want to change the way we are used to do our shopping. Another reason may be that most companies have not yet realised all the new possibilities that are available on the Internet. This conservative way of building solutions on a totally new medium will not be the way to do business in a few years. Companies that bring our old way of doing

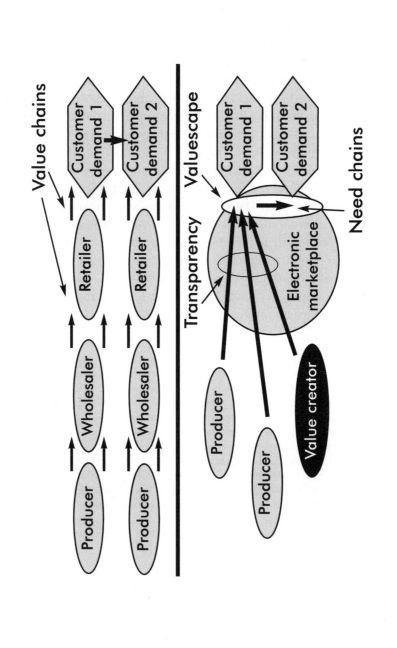

We can see that there may be a fundamental shift in the way in which we think about the market in the future. During the past 15 years, we have used the concept of value chains in order to describe how producers at different stages of a production chain add value to a product. In the market, it is then up to the customer to evaluate different products against each other and to decide which product offers the best value for money. In the present market, it is up to producers to configure the value chain of each product, the focus having been on the specific features of each product that have been the main target of customer evaluation.

In the electronic market, the production chain could be focused on the preferences of each customer, and it could actually become possible for the customer herself to configure the production chain at each point of purchase. This could mean that a customer who wants to buy printed stationery would be able to choose her preferred quality of paper and have it sent to a chosen printer, who would print it using colours of the customer's choice and then deliver it through a transportation network that could be chosen in the same manner. Similar options could be available in many industries, production being done to order, and the number of such industries is undoubtedly likely to increase as proliferation along product (and other) lines increases in the future.

This type of choice would not only be possible from the point of view of different product characteristics. Instead, all aspects of the production and distribution chain could be taken into account, including aspects that are difficult to get information on at present. No customer will have to buy products from a company with basic values that clash with those of the customer, or from a company that shows in some respect inappropriate behaviour.

Figure 6.1   From value chains to need chains

things into the new market will be overtaken by companies that have a better understanding of how the new technologies could be used to satisfy customer needs more efficiently than before. The mind should be set to the new valuescape rather than to the old market with definite boundaries in space and time.

How to build a corporate valuescape

The valuescape is, of course, not useful just for private life; it could be even more challenging to build the valuescape to meet company demands. This is also seen as a major growth area for the next few years. Today, about two-thirds of the world's 240,000 web-servers are dedicated to internal private use, according to Ben Horowitz, Senior Product Manager of server products for Netscape Communications Corp. Horowitz has estimated that there will be 10 times as many intranet as Internet servers by the year 2000. This is an interesting trend. It means that, even if the growth of the Internet is tremendous, the growth of internal networks in companies is even higher. It may seem strange that companies are investing heavily in internal communication when the opportunities are so great in the external market, but one of the main reasons behind this is probably that companies see greater opportunities in sharing knowledge internally than they do in increasing their interaction with other companies in the open market, and want to experiment and get experience of intranet communication first. In a few years' time, when this period has come to an end, we may see an even more impressive growth in external, 'extranet' applications that are improved examples of services that have been available inside companies for a long time.

An example of a typical need in any company is to support activities where people and systems work together to achieve a common goal (to introduce a new product, to put together an offer to customers or to build a house). During the entire life of a project, people have different needs and requirements. These are usually supported by many different services offered over different media using a multitude of technologies. The step from the traditional market into the new electronic marketplace could provide tremendous extra value to people who work in a project, but the current solutions are not achieving this because they are just a mirror of the solutions that are available in the physical world.

A typical example of a project-based valuescape in a company is a project in a large corporation with the goal of introducing a new product. This rather complex task, involving a number of people and a number of internal and external relations, involves the use of many different services in various phases of the project. In the very beginning of this process, the focus is usually turned to the external world. People try to collect ideas about the contents of the offering and identify requirements that a new product can meet. In this phase, there is a clear need for information from many different sources. Today, it is complicated and time-consuming to put this together. Newspapers, magazines, supplier and customer organisations and conference material are typical sources. When this information has been collected by a number of people with various skills, it has to be analysed by experts to find the relevant knowledge in the vast amount of information. When the first ideas of the new product are formed, these ideas have to be evaluated by several people in the company to make sure that they are sound. The next phase is to go from ideas into firm descriptions and concepts that outline the future product or service.

Many people from different parts of the company are involved here, and communication takes place in meetings, via the fax and over the telephone. When the framework is clear, it is time to launch a set of parallel projects that take design one step further towards the realisation of the product. Co-ordination is essential here, and many people have to rely on a common understanding of the products and their future performance in different respects. When the product is almost ready, it is time to spread product information to the marketing and sales organisation and, of course, to customers.

This simplified description of how the process of new product introduction is usually built is presented to give a hint of how complex this type of process can be. It is easy to see that information and support are not offered in one simple form independent of where and who you are. In the early phases, information is, in the present system, spread between different media and may belong to a large number of different owners, experience of how to find it being essential and having to be gathered over a number of years of practice. The next phases are also difficult because people have to rely on old methods of communication with peers within and outside the organisation. In large organisations distributed over wide areas, this can be a very difficult phase with difficulties of co-ordination and inefficiencies as a direct result.

The valuescape concept can be used to build new solutions to support processes like this in corporations and between one company and any number of partner firms. Therefore, the ambition must be to look outside the traditional organisational borders and think along new lines when solutions for communication and information management are built. Just as in the case of the building of the valuescape, the focus must be set on the needs of the people involved. In this case, people are striving to come up with new ideas of products and services and turn them into profitable offers in the market. In order to go through this process efficiently and rapidly, the support offered must be integrated and sustain the entire process from start to finish. This overall support cannot be built top-down with detailed specifications from the start of what is needed and what is not. Instead, a step-by-step implementation will be the case, in which the valuescape for the introduction of new products in a company is made. The goal is freedom for units, groups and people to add value to the overall process.

In the first phase of constructing the project valuescape, different players with various product ideas and solutions will meet and create an embryo of the valuescape in which basic information about product ideas and markets for present products can be found. This basic 'meeting point' will then develop rapidly as more employees see that something interesting is being created. These people will share their information with their colleagues in this electronic forum, and new ideas will be created. In an organisation in which the structure is formed spontaneously, in the manner that we described in Chapter 5, many people will be interested enough to join the 'project', which may be informal, and help in developing the ideas. When more and more people join, the valuescape is developed further by all of them together. This means that everybody can work on their own on the aspects of the project where each person can add the most value.

In the example discussed above, the needs of the people who deal with new products are the focus, and when their needs change, the valuescape is there to change in order to meet those needs. This has nothing to do with firm plans and detailed work descriptions. Instead, it is the most natural way for people to add value together, trying to meet the needs of others and to make a profit from this. Instead of being forced to know exactly where and how to find the right solutions to realise new product ideas, solutions come naturally when a particular part of the valuescape, which is focused on this process, is created and explored.

To enable people in an organisation to add value where it is needed instead of doing unproductive work, it is important that the management systems of a company are designed so that they can measure the added value of each employee and integrate it into the company valuescape. The fact that employees can add value where they want to and refrain from adding value where they do not think that they have the necessary competence will call for types of management system other than the ones that we know today. It will probably also be necessary to redefine which people are allowed to add value during the different phases of a project. In the primary 'search' phase, a large number of people could be asked to add value where they can, whereas at later stages this number of people could be reduced as the project became more well defined. Similarly, a number of people could have access to all the documents of a project, whereas others could have access to the same or a selection of documents only for reading purposes. If one of the latter were to find that they could add value somewhere in the project, they could have permission from the project owner to add documents of their own or make changes in documents prepared by other members of the project team. In this way, any project could be dynamic both in terms of the forms of interaction and in terms of the 'membership' of the project team.

This type of valuescape is not a completely new phenomenon that we have not seen before. There are already advanced examples on the Internet showing how this phenomenon works. A very good example of such a site developed to meet needs in the telecom industry is called Instant Search Telecoms (www.instant-search.com). It is a growing mix of news, information, companies and products that is starting to become a telecom meeting place on the Internet. This site has not yet found its role in the telecom industry, but when its use increases, it will probably find a stable form in which its real use becomes clear. A good guess is that it will help telecom people in the early phases of the new product introduction process, where the need for information about news, products or solutions is especially great.

As we have seen, the valuescape is created by every individual present on the Internet. Structures are built around sites that present information, ideas, services and product offerings. We could call these pieces of information that make up a valuescape 'concepts' of different kinds. In the next chapter, we will describe how companies will have to transform their present business concepts in order to populate the Internet with innovative concepts.

7 Concept Transformation

A bove, we described a completely new type of communication, which has the potential of changing the way we live, the way we work and the way we do business. If we wish to take full advantage of the opportunities offered by the new technologies, we have to rethink many of the concepts and ideas that form the basis of our present ways of organising industries and of how we interact with companies and organisations in our free time. The term 'concept' is a broad one, and we have selected it because in this chapter a wide range of services and products in the market will be discussed. By using the term 'concept' the idea is to broaden the scope of 'tools' that businesses will use to compete on the new electronic marketplace.

In many cases, we can see from early trials on the Internet that companies who want to do business there simply take their current offerings and present them in the same way on the Internet as they do on analogous media or on their shop shelves. This is, of course, one way to do it, but in order to take advantage of the opportunities that are offered by the new media, companies will have to transform their concepts to new forms in which the opportunities of transparency and real-time communication are used. If today's competitors do not do this, there will certainly arrive new companies that have the ideas and the abilities to use these opportunities to their advantage, which will result in increasing service levels to customers, decreasing costs and a faster response to customer needs. One strong force that works in favour of these new companies is that they have no legacy in the form of systems or people to consider, which will help them to think along new lines and better use the power of the new market environment without carrying the costs of withdrawal from present markets.

Companies have to drive the strategic process themselves where they encourage new ideas on how to move into the valuescape. It is, in other words, a core part of any company's strategic planning to address these issues before it becomes too late. It may be that the restructuring of the marketplace means that there will be a need for a smaller number of competitors, and that their connection to a particular industry will be less obvious for the customer (see the case concerning Amazon, below). In this process, it is necessary to plan what to bring, what to leave behind and what to invent to become a successful player in this new environment. As was discussed in the previous chapter, the valuescape represents the basis for a new business environment with completely new rules and new opportunities. However, the valuescape is just the beginning of this process, providing the foundation of a new marketplace. A landscape with no people, houses or towns is not an easy place for us humans to live in. In the same way, the valuescape will not prosper if new business concepts and ideas are not brought into it and developed.

Limited transformation

As human beings, it is natural for us to be rigid in our ideas of how things should work in the world in which we live. Most concepts are so natural to us that we have forgotten that they can be challenged by new inventions and that they may have to be radically changed if our environment undergoes dramatic changes. It is also necessary for us, in order to feel secure, to have a certain amount of stability in our lives. In the same way, society needs to have a certain amount of stability in order to function in the long run. On the other hand, however, it is also important for us to be able to change our basic ideas and concepts when significant things around us change. This is one of the reasons why *Homo sapiens* has been so successful over the millennia of our past development.

It is possible to list a large number of concepts that have been developed over the years and have taken their present shapes, which make them functional in our present environment. To show what concept transformation will require in terms of change, we will discuss some examples.

The telephone book is a simple place to start. This concept is playing a very clear role in our daily lives. The basic need that the telephone call is fulfilling is that of contacting other people. In order to find out how to establish the link to a friend or business contact, we need to know the telephone number. The number is essential, and to find it a telephone book is a common tool. The book we use functions, as everybody knows, as a simple link between a name and a number. So what about moving the concept of a telephone book into the valuescape? To many people this is not a big transformation. It is simply a matter of translating the book into electronic form so that users can find it on the Internet and use it in the same way as we use the present paper-based telephone books we are used to. There are numerous examples of transformations that have been made like this. The *Yellow Pages* is published on the Internet by many telephone companies. In many cases, it gives the user a more convenient way to 'flick' through the pages, but it does not add any new information, and it is very easy for users who are used to the printed *Yellow Pages* to use it and feel at home.

The familiar look has, of course, some advantages because people feel comfortable and can start to use it immediately. However, it does not use the new opportunities offered by the electronic market. Therefore, existing solutions for the electronic *Yellow Pages* that are based on old concepts are not likely to exist long in this form on the Internet. If operators do not develop the concept and adapt it to the opportunities of the valuescape, there will be other companies that do, making use of the information published in the *Yellow Pages* and adding a number of new features that could make the printed or traditional on-line *Yellow Pages* obsolete. The key question is what to do in order to transform the concept of a telephone book into a competitive offer in the valuescape. To do this, it is necessary to remember that the valuescape is entirely focused on the need chains of each user and on how to make it as easy as possible for them to find what they are looking for.

In order to do this, we need to go back to the roots of the concept and consider what its real role is. The idea of a telephone book is not simply to translate a name into a number – it is to help people to make contacts. Historically, the only way to make contacts over long distances was to make a telephone call or perhaps send a letter or a fax. Therefore, it is enough to focus on telephone numbers and postal addresses when a telephone book is created. However, in the valuescape there are more ways to interact than just over a telephone. The telephone wire has been extended to a broad link between people who use different media. Thus the telephone book needs to grow into a tool that the users of all these new opportunities could take advantage of, that is, into a place where they could find information about how to make all kinds of contacts in an efficient way.

A very good example of an enhanced telephone book on the Internet today is the Infospace (www.infospace.com), created in the United

States. Here we can find ways to interact with people in the United States, Canada and, recently, other countries as well. It is already possible to find more than 112 million people here. With a rather limited knowledge of a person's name, one can find not only the telephone number and e-mail address, but also descriptions of where the person lives, shown on maps with different levels of detail. It is also possible to get a guide of how to travel to the person and which shops, companies and hotels can be found in the neighbourhood. This extends the telephone book into a complete guide of how to contact an old friend or a company. However, during the writing of this book, the *Yellow Pages* of some telephone operators have been given similar features, which shows that many companies are already aware of the need to transform existing concepts.

This example shows what will happen in the valuescape. Companies will start to use their imagination and transform the concepts of today into competitive tools suitable for the new market. This will, of course, feel new and perhaps uncomfortable the first time we use the new tools, but when we have learned what the new concepts can add in terms of flexibility and efficiency, we will never want to turn back or long for the old ones again.

Concept transformation by far-reaching customisation

One of the most thrilling opportunities offered by new technologies and the birth of the new market is the possibility of producing products and services for smaller and smaller groups of customers. In fact, there seems to be no limit to how far customisation can be driven. One service package for every customer is no longer a dream. Instead, companies in many industries will set it down among their goals for the future. Telia, for example, already talks about having 5 million customer segments (the same as the number of customers) rather than 10 segments, as they have today. Sceptics would probably say that it sounds extremely expensive and that nobody would pay the costs connected with this extreme type of customisation. However, we have already seen examples of how new solutions, together with a new way of building distribution systems easily, can make customisation both possible and less expensive than existing solutions aimed at mass markets.

In the discussion of what companies should do to bring their old concepts into the valuescape, customisation can be the key to the transformation that is needed in order to become successful. Customisation has the power to add the little extra that is needed to take a unique position in the eyes of the customers. We should remember that the entire valuescape is based on this very crucial objective. We can use an example to show how this could be done.

Most of us are familiar with a newspaper. We all use it to keep up to date with the world around us. A newspaper has a broad scope because it tries to meet the needs and interests of a large number of people. Every day, these papers provide hundreds of pages of information with everything from kittens for sale to the latest news from a war on the other side of the globe. Naturally, nobody is interested in all this information, but everybody can find something in a paper. It would be tempting to bring papers into the valuescape by a simple conversion of text and pictures to a computer screen, to make a paper that is easier to search and easier to distribute (no postman and no newsstand on the street corner). Some rather nice advantages would turn up directly through the use of this method: less expensive newspapers (the cost of printing and distributing a newspaper accounts for approximately two-thirds of the total cost of each paper) and less waste of paper.

Is this transformation enough to create a successful Internet-based newspaper? Most probably not. One aspect has been neglected: the newspaper concept is not really transformed but merely adapted to the new environment. A real transformation must, as we have stressed before, start from the very roots of the concept. So, what are the roots of a newspaper? There is no simple answer to this owing to the fact that a newspaper meets so many different needs. Some obvious examples are:

- the need to have a general knowledge of what is happening in society (locally or globally);
- specific needs of knowing what is happening in specific industries to be able to make the right decisions in business and private life;
- the need to find a certain product or service (a new car, a dog for the children or where to see the latest film);
- to follow current debates;
- to be actively reminded of important events;
- to be entertained and informed at breakfast.

This broad picture of needs and information shows that the newspaper concept is complex and multifaceted. It is not necessary for all aspects of the original concept to be brought into each new concept. Instead, considering the structure and opportunities of the valuescape, it seems more likely that the newspaper concept will be cut into pieces and transformed into several concepts that use different solutions to meet the broad range of needs listed above. In this example, we will focus on the most fundamental newspaper need, namely the distribution of news of what is happening in the world. Today, this distribution is a very blunt tool aimed at a number of readers. The market is often segmented by region or country, so that all the subscribers get the same information.

It is probable that one part of the transformation will be focused on how to meet the needs of a reader when it comes to the distribution of news. Let us think about what those needs might be. We would probably be able to come up with a wish list like this: news from the local community, some news from the closest city, no news from the Middle East, except if something extremely interesting were happening, priority to positive news rather than just wars, conflicts and murders, but natural catastrophes are of interest and so on. This type of list could be made longer and longer until all aspects of news and events were covered. A newspaper can be compiled based on this type of profile for every reader and be downloaded each day to the work station on demand.

Technology can easily do this selection, but is that really what the reader needs? What happens if the situation changes? The interest may suddenly change depending on what the reader is doing. One day, the reader may have to go the Middle East on a business trip. What about the selection he made to exclude all news from that part of the world? He may even have forgotten that he made that decision in his profile a long time ago. No news about that part of the world may have come to his knowledge, and he may suddenly feel unsure about what goes on there and what type of situation he will find. Here we can see why we should not use the opportunities offered by new technology without thinking about possible consequences.

Could there be some other solution that would work better in the valuescape? Yes, when the transformation of the newspaper concept is carried out, it is necessary to consider the opportunities of the new environment. The user's needs are in focus, and services in the valuescape will be built around those needs, following the twists and turns of the user's life. The newspaper should not only go for extreme customisation, giving all users what they want, but also make customisation dynamic by taking over the responsibility for helping the user to find the news needed in any given situation. The newspaper should collect information about what the user would like to read and use that knowledge to complement the user's preferred selection. It should meet the varying needs that a reader has in different situations, such as to offer interesting reading with the morning coffee, vital information at work and evening entertainment. This means that the newspaper is present in different forms in different situations.

News should be filtered depending on what the reader wants, and this information should be collected from various sources depending on what the reader is doing. A reader profile can be designed and changed when the reader is performing other tasks in the valuescape, such as looking for holiday information, buying CDs or searching for information at work. This will make customisation possible without the risk of losing important information because filters are out of date or because the user forgets to change his or her profile.

Dynamic customisation will be a central part of these new transformed newspapers, and its success will to a large extent depend on how they manage to meet customer needs. That, however, is not enough. Newspapers also need to change from a passive search for information to more active provisioning in which the reader gets the information he needs and wants delivered actively. Passive searching should not be necessary. Some such functions are offered by the Pointcast application, described below.

This glimpse of a newspaper fit to enter the new valuescape is intended to give some thoughts and ideas on how a transformed newspaper concept could look. Today, there are examples of these transformed newspapers available over the Internet. A good example is the Pointcast news server that delivers filtered on-line news. Pointcast has started to focus on customisation by offering a number of on-line news channels (such as Reuter's, CNN and Sports news) that the user can customise by defining a profile of which type of information he or she wants. This filter can be changed at any time, but there are no dynamic changes made by the system itself in this solution. News is shown to users as they momentarily stop using their computer. Then the news appears on their screens as a 'screen saver'.

On the Internet, there are also a number of more traditional newspapers that have entered the new marketplace. Examples are many, for example *The Times* (www.the-times.co.uk) and *San Francisco Examiner* (www.examiner.com). These have not yet taken advantage of the new opportunities, which means that they are not yet transformed. They still look the same for all readers and still provide a mix of everything found in the old paper-based newspapers (for example advertisements and news).

Some degree of customisation can already be seen on the Internet in some well-known search engines, such as Alta Vista and Yahoo. They offer customised commercials that use the information we provide as users. The key words we enter to limit the search space are also used to limit the choice of commercials for each user that we see on the screen. In this case, the information used in order to customise the advertising to user interests is already there, which means that it is easy to make algorithms that process this information, look for particular key words and then select the commercial to show. In other cases, this information can be more difficult to get and requires more intelligence and processing to be useful. Examples of this are people who surf around to do errands, at the same time revealing certain habits, wishes and 'secrets' that can be used to customise offers in other areas.

Another example of a transformed concept that focuses on customisation is a number of solutions that are offered in the area of customer support. Most companies have some type of customer support function that deals with everything from customer complaints and customer query-handling to proactive sales activities in which the customer is informed about the latest news and opportunities. Customer support is a vital service for most companies, leading to good relationships between customers and suppliers. However, this in most cases means having a large support organisation, often 24 hours a day, with experts who cost large amounts of money. In the valuescape, customer support will take another shape, following unconventional paths to reach and support customers. Transforming the support concept will require substantial customisation because that is what customer support means. Each customer has his or her particular situation (different products, different applications, different working hours and varying skills and abilities), which makes customer support especially difficult even for trained experts.

The key to excellent support lies in the knowledge of the needs of each customer. Therefore, the transformed support concept will offer a new range of services that have been very hard to offer before without access to a huge support organisation that knows its customers as individuals. Customer support in the valuescape will be centred on exact knowledge of the customers' situation and support history. Every time a customer needs help, it will be built on past services, what the customer is doing at the moment and a knowledge of the customer's skills. Each new problem will start a new case, which is not finalised until the customer is again satisfied.

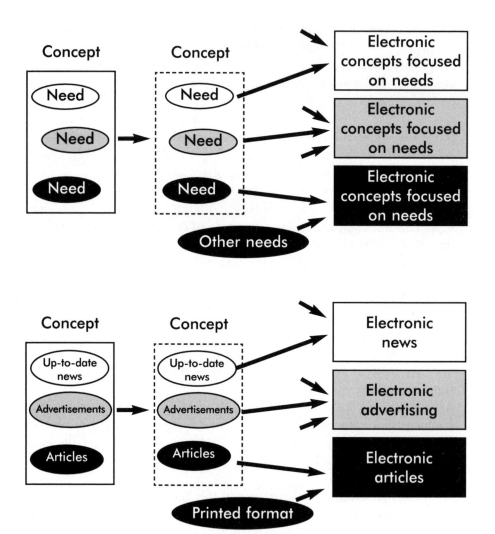

Concept transformation is a three-step process:

1. the identification of needs and preferences for which the old concept caters;
2. the breaking down of the concept package into its component parts;
3. the transfer of each component part into the new electronic marketplace and the completion of the transformation through the addition of other concepts so that the new offers become 'complete'.

Each of the new concepts should focus on the satisfaction of the particular needs and preferences of some customer group. Through the use of offers from a number of electronic concepts, customers could themselves configure complete packages of products and services that cover a whole chain of needs and preferences.

In the list below, we see how the newspaper concept could be transformed into a number of new stand-alone concepts, each covering such a chain of needs in the electronic market. We could see that the present newspaper concept covers a number of needs and preferences, which are likely to be addressed by different concepts in the electronic market:

1. The need for up-to-date news. In a transformed concept, this could be satisfied through the provision of the latest news over the Internet.
2. The need for advertisements and other types of product and market information. On the Internet, any customer could in the future find full information about all market aspects of any product that he or she would like to buy.
3. The need for articles of general interest. On the Internet, articles and whole databases on any subject could be found when they were needed.
4. The preference of having information presented in a paper-based format so that the newspaper could be bought on a train or anywhere else. On the Internet, articles and other information of interest could be printed and bought in the same manner as any ordinary newspaper of today. Preference 4 could thus still be coupled with any of the needs in points 1–3.

This indicates that new preferences could be satisfied through the new concepts, for example the preference of having complete information available.

Figure 7.1   Concept transformation

This means tailored support for every customer and every situation. The support is offered on-line or over the telephone with full knowledge of products and services with which the support is concerned. To make this support as easy to use as possible, it should be tightly integrated with the product or service on which it is focused. Support for computers should be offered as an integrated part of the computer itself, and support in the use of on-line services should, of course, be a part of the service itself. Examples of on-line customer support are common on the Internet today, two being Microsoft's support site (www.microsoft.com) and Sun's similar site (www.sun.com). It is common for the offered support to be a mix of functionality at the customer's site (in systems and products), which means both static and dynamic information and functionality offered directly on-line. Examples like this show the power of on-line, web-based support, but these companies have not entered the real valuescape and turned to true customised support.

A more far-reaching example, which one of us has been involved in developing, is a concept for Web-Enabled Customer Support, developed for a large telecommunications company that wanted better support for the customers of advanced management systems for mobile telecom networks. This concept presented the customer support function as an integrated part of the management system itself, which follows the user closely and actively offers the best solution depending on the customer, the situation and the support history. This tool is intended to build up knowledge about the customer step by step, starting with information about which types of product the customer is using. Every question is then used to get a picture of the customer's problem. That knowledge could subsequently be used actively to propose actions and offer tips. An important ingredient is the use of cases kept together to support the customer better. If the customer encounters a problem, checks a knowledge base for answers, goes over to check a 'frequently asked questions' database and then finally asks for a link into the organisation of human expert support, the system automatically keeps records of what the customer has been doing and the information that has already been given. This is vital information for other systems or for an expert who takes over the case. He or she does not have to ask all the questions again. Another obvious advantage is that the customer can choose to stop the support session and come back later and continue from the point of departure. These types of facility in the transformed support case are vital for a company that tries to make the best of the new environment.

These two examples of transformation focused on customisation are interesting because they show how to make use of the new opportunities rather than just taking for granted that the present solutions will be sufficient in the valuescape.

> One example of far-reaching customisation can be taken from a company in the education and business intelligence sector, Business Intelligence Group (www.big.se). This company delivers customised training programmes for companies that are adapted to the needs of each company. Courses are delivered over the intranet of each customer company, and the people who are to be trained can attend each course when it best suits their schedules. In that way, very little productive time is lost through training compared with the traditional way of delivering such services.
>
> One week before each course, those who are to attend go through a test to assess their level of knowledge on the subject that is to be addressed. They receive the questions and deliver the answers on their PCs, and the results from the tests can be studied either individually or from the perspective of the group as a whole or as different subgroups.
>
> One major client of this company has five different courses that their employees can attend, ranging from management accounting to relations marketing. The power of this type of interactive training can be shown by a simple example. The company name is related to three core values that all employees, and most customers, should be able to associate with the brand name. The category of employee who management thought would be most familiar with these values were the salespersons at the dealers'. When the salespersons all went through the marketing training, it turned out that they were 70 per cent wrong on this particular question. Two weeks after they had gone through the training, they had a follow-up test at which they had improved their overall command of the subject to fewer than 25 per cent wrong answers.

In the near future, traditional textbook information could be developed into personalised training experiences with the help of computer programs that could customise programs to the specific needs of each person and, through the use of films and sound, could deliver a more exciting experience than do most teachers.

Obviously, the best teachers and communicators in each field, blended with interesting examples and fascinating films, could be used in order to make first-class educational programmes that could be delivered to any part of the world. All aspects of the material, from the speed of progress to the contents of the examples and the level of the exercises, could be matched to the specific needs and preferences of every single person.

The Business Intelligence Group, mentioned in the example above, is currently planning for the next generation of training programmes.

They will then utilise the full opportunities of the new information technologies to customise training so that each person who attends gets his or her specific course, which is adapted to personal needs. No two people will follow the same path through training, and both film and sound are used to improve the experience and make those who attend learn more, also making their new knowledge more useful in the business situations they face in their day-to-day activities.

Concept transformation through convergence of services

In Chapter 6, we stressed the fact that the new market environment will have a new basic structure that is not based on geography as the main dimension. We also pointed out that many industries will have to be developed from scratch forming new market structures, in order to be an integrated part of a common marketplace. They will, in other words, seemingly 'disappear' from the scene and converge with offerings from other industries. Some concept transformations focus on this fact. This will lead to distributed functionality that will be integrated into service offerings.

A 'bank' is a very old concept, and the business of banking has developed over a long time. In order to describe how the transformation of at least a part of the banking business into the new environment could be carried out, it is necessary to go back to the very roots of a bank and consider why we have banks and which needs they cater for in our daily lives.

To do this exhaustively would, of course, require considerable space, so we should not try here to reinvent all parts of the banking system with all its different products and offerings. However, we would like to show what concept transformation means in this complex industry. It is especially important to look at those parts of a bank that are tied to the physical world, for example bank offices, bills, money and giro payments.

Most people still go to a bank branch at least occasionally to perform some transactions that could basically be described as electronic transmissions of information between the bank office and another bank or company, and, of course, to get annoyed queuing. This may soon become history because of new telephone and computer services that help us to do exactly the same things as we do in a bank office from our homes. If a major share of customers choose the new ways of doing business, it will be impossible for banks to continue to run the number of branches that they do today. This will, however, be no problem since people without a PC of their own will be able to access services from public terminals such as Automatic Teller Machines (ATMs) or other general information 'kiosks', or will be helped by companies or friends who can do on-line banking for them.

A bank office moved into the electronic market should not look the same as it has always done in the 'real world'. Bank offices have been moved into the new electronic world without too much of a face-lift. Many banks have launched their on-line services with a functionality that is very similar to that of a traditional bank. Transactions can be made between accounts, and statements can be issued that show the balance of an account. The advantages are that queues are avoided (if the bank has enough incoming data connections) and that it is easy to feel at home and start to use the traditional services in a new medium (giro payments even look like the old paper form on the screen).

There are several examples of on-line banks on the Internet today, and the business is growing very rapidly. The services offered are typically the traditional banking services such as checking the balance of an account, making payments and getting information about rates, currencies and loans. A typical example of such a bank is Nationwide Building Society (www.nationwide.co.uk). SE-banken (www.sebank.se) in Sweden is the largest Internet bank in Europe, with about 80,000 customers at present. This is far more than it had expected when it launched the service, and the traffic in the network is sometimes so high that it causes severe congestion in the data communication network between SE-banken's ATM machines.

Some needs that the bank concept meets derive from the need to pay for purchases and the need to manage accounts and loans. These activities are at present kept separate. We buy things in one situation and manage our money at other points in time. The question is: What do we really need? When we think of buying the things we need, we would like to have a good overview of our financial situation to know whether we can afford the purchase. At that very moment, we are expected to know the balance of our accounts or go to the bank to talk about a loan. It is not possible to do that at the point of purchase in a shop. However, in the electronic market, we will be doing things in a different way.

It will be possible to surf around to look for things we want, and we may find a new house or a car that we think is a bargain. The first thing we do will be to check whether we can afford to buy it and what it would mean to our financial status in the long and short terms. In the valuescape, we will not have to stop, search for a bank office on the Internet and start a new session at the bank, try to explain what we would like to do and the price of the item that we would like to buy, and then finally get an answer to whether or not we can proceed with the purchase. The new concept of a bank office will be transformed in a different way. It will be split into several functions and distributed to where the business is, that is, to all places where customers and suppliers meet to do business. The bank must be present in every place where purchases are considered. A bank should be an integrated part of even the smallest shop on the Internet. In this, the smallest of bank branches in terms of turnover, it should be possible to carry out all the necessary activities that a customer may want to do at a bank. We would like to be able to make payments, carry out other types of electronic transaction, arrange loans and make calculations. This new concept will not just be useful for the customer, but will also be better for the bank and the provider of products and services.

The bank will automatically know which customer and which goods are involved in the purchase. The assessment of the risk of a loan for a house, car or whatever the customer may want to buy will become easier when the bank is in the middle of everything. It will be safer for the bank than discussing the loan in an office far from where the business takes place because it will have access to much more information about the customer's historical bank contacts and financial status. Moreover, the shop will be certain that the payments can be arranged. These types of relationship between a bank and a customer or a supplier do not have to be formal ones between the companies, in which an agreement has been made that the bank will have a 'site' on the shop's homepage. Instead, links on the Internet could be established in real-time depending on who the customer is and which type of purchase he or she wants to make. Most important is that they are 'close' in the new non-geographic valuescape, that is, close to the needs of the user.

Seen from a company perspective, this concept transformation means distributing services to all the places where business is taking place in the electronic marketplace. The bank concept is converging with other concepts until it may be impossible to point out what is and what is not a bank.

Concept transformation through the use of transparency

The fact that Internet technology, including Java programming, multimedia solutions for communication and other technological innovations that can be connected to the Internet, gives access to large amounts of information can open doors to a multitude of creative opportunities. We earlier described this as transparency, saying that we, regardless of our geographical location, can have access to all the information about any subject that has been published on the Internet. The crucial factor that will make this information available to us in a structured form will be the existence of search engines, electronic marketplaces or homepages, where a company or an organisation provides us with the information in a structured form and with links to other parts of the market.

In its simplest form, these solutions could be a catalogue of products or services with any number of additional features and functions connected. The customer could, in addition to names and pictures of the product, be provided with test results, information about features and capabilities, opinions from previous customers, the opportunity to order it from the least expensive source (in many cases, this will be directly from the producer) and information about the closest competitors and access to the same type of information about all competitors.

One example of this type of transformation can be taken from the homepage www.amazon.com, where customers can buy all kinds of books in the English language. This is almost a textbook example of what we are talking about here because this firm offers 2.5 million titles. The decreasing costs of communicating with customers and the fact that they rarely have to put unsold books on sale at a loss are probably the reasons why they can offer hardbacks at an across-the-board discount of 30 per cent compared with the cover price, and paperbacks at a 20 per cent discount.

Amazon simply provides customers with information about all the books that are in print at the publishers with whom they co-operate, allowing customers to submit orders directly on the homepage, transfers orders to the publisher in question and asks them to send the books to the customer. Amazon then asks customers to pay with their credit cards, and customers also receive information about how soon each publisher normally ships the books in case they are not shipped from one of their own warehouses.

In order for customers to be able to choose from this immense number of books, a number of features are added to this site. Information about books is provided in the form of reviews and general information from the publisher and other sources. In addition, readers can send in comments on books that can be read by other customers, and for each book Amazon also provides a list of three other books that have been ordered by other customers who also bought the first one. This means that the buyer of books who chooses to buy from Amazon will, in some respects, have much better opportunities to choose books that really interest him than does the buyer who enters a bookshop. The only thing that the customer in the bookshop can, but the Internet-based customer cannot do, is flip through the pages of the book and read a little here or there. There is no reason to assume that this opportunity should not be available from Amazon in the future.

One additional advantage that will decrease the prices of books in the long run is that, in the Internet world, the main share of the stock of each book will be with the publisher. There will, therefore, be no reason for publishers to print many copies of books simply to be able to distribute them copy by copy to a large number of bookshops that are uncertain whether they will sell only one or one hundred copies. This will diminish the costs of inventory in the whole system and make it possible for publishers to print smaller runs in order to hold down both stock and risk. In its turn, this will probably increase the demand for small-scale printing equipment that still can produce books at an economic cost, and it may open up the opportunity for authors themselves to publish books, present them on a homepage of the Amazon type and sell them in an inexpensive binder before it becomes clear that there is a larger demand for the book so that a 'real' publisher can publish it.

All in all, it could be assumed that the discount of 30 per cent offered by Amazon will be increased in the future as these forces are set to work and competition increases in the market. This increased competition will bring down prices of books in the market as a whole. Amazon has managed to get over 1 million unique customers (as of autumn 1997), which makes them the first Internet-based company to reach that level.

It is, of course, possible to elaborate further on the whole idea, just from a theoretical point of view. Suppose that customers in Europe find it too expensive to pay for the transportation of a book from the United States and also find it hard to wait for a week to get it delivered (remember the real-time society.). It may take a month if we choose surface delivery. Then the publisher could make an agreement with any number of printers with small-scale printing equipment all over the world for them to print and bind each copy or a number of copies for the local market. In the future, readers could get their books in a few days without the cost of postage from the other side of the globe.

Another opportunity could be to have the choice of buying a ready-bound book or just downloading the whole text on to the home computer's disk, with the opportunity to print it out or just read it on the screen.

One example of the effects of transparency can be taken from the time when we were writing this book. In order to take correct quotations from *The Wealth of Nations* (Smith, 1997), we decided to order the book from www.bokus.se. When we looked up the author and title, we found 14 different editions in English. The prices of these editions ranged from SEK 89 (£7) to SEK 3390 (£271). There were definitely differences between these editions that justified price differences, but it was also possible to find editions that seemed to be equivalent in many senses but still differed substantially in price.

We can assume that this same type of concept transformation is possible in all industries and all product groups. Any product, regardless of size or complexity, could be traded on the Internet. When it comes to complex products, it would be logical to assume that the basic information, in great detail, would be published by the producer.

It could also be assumed that producers would like to supply the expertise which would be offered to customers at the point of sale. (An example of how this could be done could be found in the section below on transformation through the use of network intelligence, where the computer company Power Computing is presented.) We could easily assume that a marketplace for cars or any other type of goods could arise on the Internet, where customers could find presentations of cars of all makes published by the producers and where other players in the market could supply additional information such as test data, users' opinions and price comparisons.

The Microsoft Carpoint service (www.carpoint.msn.com) is an example of how the buyers and sellers of cars can meet on the Internet and do business. This service has been tremendously successful, and in October 1997 20 per cent of all new cars in New York city found their buyers through this site.

One example of the effects of transparency can be found in the business intelligence sector. Many companies try to monitor the development in their own industries and often also in neighbouring industries, so that they know as much as possible about the actions of their competitors and the development of market volumes and other related issues. Only a few years ago, the collection of this type of information was very time-consuming, and companies often had to hire consultants in order to both update their knowledge of market development and to get outside help to analyse and interpret it.

Today, there are companies that provide computerised tools to search automatically for this type of information on the Internet. One example of this type of company is the Business Intelligence Group (www.big.se), which offers a product that always delivers the latest articles on any subject a company wants to follow. Through searches on the Internet and other sources of information connected to the Internet, this article database is continuously updated. A person with access to this type of tool could, within an hour, collect relevant and updated information about competing companies, their products or current activities among customers, competitors or governments. The contents of the database depend on which key words have been used to define what the system should search for on the Internet in the first place, but, regardless of what has been predefined, it is also possible for managers to add new key words on an *ad hoc* basis.

Concept transformation based on transparency often leads to major changes in roles in the industry value chains. The main effect is that producers and consumers come closer to each other. Consumers get more information and more insight into production, while producers learn more about consumer needs and behaviour. This means that both parties gain from the development and that middlemen such as wholesalers and retailers will get squeezed, their roles being threatened if they fail to add new types of value to the chain. This development is, in a way, to go back to the old structures in society where customers and suppliers interacted directly with each other. Farmers, for example, sold their goods directly to the people nearby, which led to openness in production conditions.

Since concept transformation is based on the idea that companies should bring old concepts into a new business environment, it is not always wise to start from the perspective of a particular company when we try to find new and transformed concepts. The risk is that there are fixed boundaries, which allow little room for drastic transformation.

Instead, a whole industry or value chain would be the preferred focus. In electronics industries, this approach is definitely to be recommended, but it is likely to work well in other types of industry too. A situation in which this type of thinking can give an extra dimension to a concept transformation is when new strategic directions are set for companies in middleman positions. These companies may otherwise try to preserve their position in the market just because they are tied to old relationships and agreements with customers and suppliers in the value chain. These old relationships can very easily be changed if a producer suddenly decides to redefine its position in an old market and try to squeeze the middleman out. The best solutions for the new electronic market are often to be found when traditional roles and relationships are forgotten.

Concept transformations of entire value chains are based on more or less the same ideas as the transformations we have presented so far. They start from the basic needs, find other or new needs to meet and arrive at a new electronic concept that supports the whole need chain. One difference, however, is that new concepts have to start from the needs and objectives of companies in several roles in the value chain. It is vital that everybody who is supposed to take part in the concept both contributes to the value creation *and* sees an added value in being a part of the concept. If this is not the case, the concept will not be successful but will soon change or die. Transformations across company borders can be based on any of the types of transformation that we have discussed in this chapter (that is, transparency, network intelligence or real-time.).

Let us take the food industry as a practical example of a concept transformation based on transparency. Long ago, this industry was to a large extent transparent. Food was sold directly at the farm or in a local market, and people had the opportunity to see where and how it was produced. Industrialisation changed this situation. Food is now delivered into a large production system, with no links from the consumer back to the producer or back through the chain of distribution. The food that we find in shops is instead related to a brand name rather than to its origin and the way in which it has been processed and delivered. Yet current developments in society have made food into a product that many people would like to be able to trace to a farm, a field and the craftsmen who produced the refined products. The brand name is the only thing that we, as consumers, can relate to the quality, healthiness, taste and value for money of the piece of food we are buying.

Until recently, most consumers were content with this level of insight into the production and origin of food, but recent events in the market, such as 'mad cow disease', the use of antibiotics, 'inhumane' transport conditions for animals and the breeding of 'monster cows', have totally changed this picture. Consumers have started to be suspicious of the entire production system of some types of food and are grabbing for facts that they can trust.

In the physical market, there are few opportunities to get the information that is needed. Either alternatives are expensive, such as ecological or functional food, or we cannot be certain of their superior quality, for example when buying food that is produced in countries that are generally thought of as better at keeping high-quality standards in their food production, such as Sweden or Ireland. Authorities try to address the problem of re-establishing the confidence in producers through rules, regulations and databases containing information about animals and farming conditions. These actions are based on old ways of regulating market conditions, and they provide customers with an illusory safety that depends on their trust in marketing campaigns and authorities. In the new electronic marketplace, the steps to be taken will be completely different and will create safety through new means. The concept of mass-produced, anonymous food will be replaced by 'transparent food'[1] that is produced to meet the demands of each individual consumer. Food with a traceable origin and profile could in the future be chosen by customers who want this type of service, and this will be possible only if the entire value chain of food production and distribution is transformed. Farms must provide information about their conditions at the same time as needing insight into what the market requires and values. Producers of different kinds need to make food traceable through the whole chain from farm to customer. They must also take on board the wants of the customer to adapt the product range to customer needs.

Retailers are also a part of the value chain. They must help customers to choose the best products based on information about origin and production. With new tools, retailers will be able to select a profile that suits their local market and gives customers confidence in what they buy. These shops can, of course, be both the old supermarket and the new electronic shops on the Internet, which can be customised and adapted to the needs of their customers. These new electronic food shops will be perfectly suited to the increasing transparency of the food industry. Food that is adapted to customers' preferences (their valuescapes) is likely to be in great demand in the near future.

An interesting example of the creation of a transformed concept that follows the lines of the thinking presented above is Swedish Farm Assured. Here different players in the Swedish food industry have created a new standard based on the ability to trace food, through the whole value chain, back to farms. The goal is to re-establish the confidence in this industry and to diminish the risk of more alarms about unhealthy food. Consumers are able to trace the food back through production and end up at the farm from which it came. The Swedish Farm Assured concept also gives retailers the opportunity to get more information about the products they sell, and also the ability to influence and customise the offer of meat and milk products. This is seen as a natural next step of food tracing: the growing wish of the market to influence production through demanding a certain type of product (for example, one produced in a certain way or originating from a certain area). By using the Internet as the platform for these services, the people behind Swedish Farm Assured foresee a number of other opportunities. It is, for example, possible to bring market information back to producers and farms in order to support decision-making. It is also possible to extend the concept to make administration and logistics easier and less expensive.

Concept transformation by real-time communication

In many industries, it would not be sufficient to have only complete transparency in order to be able to get the best service or to get products at the lowest possible price. There is simply a need to be able to collect many different services, produced by different companies, in real-time into a package in order to have the complete service delivered.

We could think of the buyer of transport from a small village in Bavaria to another small village in France. In order to get the best offering in this case, a consumer would have to compare prices and service levels from a number of different sources in order to know which alternative would best fit his or her needs. For example, oysters and frozen mushrooms would require refridgerated transport, whereas nails or beer would not. The price of the service would depend not only on the type of product, but also on the weight, the type of packaging used and how fast it had to be delivered.

There would definitely be any number of alternatives, ranging from a taxi directly driving the 800 km with a small package in the boot to any number of short transports with different carriers reloading at several terminals along the way. It would also be possible that the most cost-efficient alternative for a parcel would be with one transportation company to Rome, reloading there, and then with another transportation company to France from Rome, if these companies happened to have free space on their trucks that they were willing to offer at a discount.

The solution to this could be a form of simple booking system for journeys, like the one described at the beginning of Chapter 2. In this type of self-organising system, suppliers and buyers of transportation enter the city or village from which they would like to send a package, and the places they would like to send it to. Each of them could also enter the price that they would like to pay or receive if there were a field for that purpose. This would create a marketplace for transportation in which there would be complete transparency from both supplier and buyer perspectives.

Customers could then register their needs each time they wanted to send goods somewhere, and they would instantly find out about the best alternative at any given moment. It would then also be possible for transportation companies to reduce the prices of surplus space for buyers who wanted to make late bookings in order to get the best prices, and it might even be possible to handle confidential information, such as the discounts that large customers might have with one or more transportation companies, since the actual calculations of prices would go on only inside the computer of the offering company, where the asking company would be recognised and where the price would be calculated in relation to all the data available about each specific customer.

In this example, the real-time aspect of the electronic marketplace plays an important role, but it can easily be seen that it is this aspect, in combination with the other aspects presented here, that makes up the total opportunity package.

The result of this type of marketplace would be a substantial saving for customers as capacity utilisation would increase and a large amount of excess capacity would go out of business. This is because each transportation company today only has information about its own routes and the routes of some partners, and each customer works with only one or two transportation companies at a time. However, if the total picture could be presented to the customers who were paying for these services, they could drive the development in the direction that would be most interesting for them, which means in the right direction to get the best quality at the lowest possible price.

Another factor that would bring prices down would be the decreasing need for management of the Internet-based system. Any transportation company in the present society will have a large overhead cost in the form of managers, salespersons and other types of supporting personnel, which adds a cost to the services. The Internet-based solution could function without the major part of these costs, and this would be to the advantage of customers, who would pay lower prices.

Concept transformation by network intelligence

In Chapter 5, we described how connecting people with different competencies decreases the need for competence in society in the long run because the competence of each person can then be utilised more efficiently. This is also said to increase the level of specialisation, because each person will need to be competent in only a rather narrow field, if it becomes possible to connect competencies with each other at the point at which a certain combination of competencies is needed.

> First, we could look at an example of a computer company that offers on-line sales support to customers, so that they can configure their own computers according to their needs without the pressure of a salesperson who wants to sell as much as possible in as short a time as he or she can. The name of the company is Power Computing (www.powercomputing.com). Each customer who enters the company's Internet site is led through a questionnaire that ends up with the offer of a custom-configured personal computer. After all the questions have been answered, the customer receives an immediate price quote and can place an order. Despite the fact that the customer gets exactly the computer he needs, the company eliminates a large share of the sales costs, eliminates dealer mark-up, reduces inventory in the whole supply chain and shortens sales lead times.

In this example, the company connects the expertise of an unknown number of different people, but the competencies need not be available to customers in real-time; instead, the competence is collected in a computer system and offered in real-time in this form. It might be possible, however, for a company that sells complex products to choose to have a number of experts in different fields available all the time. The rule could be that there should always be one expert in each field available in some service centre over the globe at any time, so that any question could always be answered by the right type of person, regardless of the time at which a person was calling, if the electronic customer service function was not enough.

In the future, this could mean that a company could offer the same type of self-service kit as described above, with the opportunity for a customer at any time either to print an additional question on the screen, which would be routed to the person who should answer it, or to be visually connected to an expert to whom questions could be asked in person.

The advantage in this case could be that, instead of having 500 different agents selling complex products all over the world, the producing company could control the quality of information that was offered to customers, both before and after each sale. This would also give the producing company direct access to unfiltered feedback from customers, which they could use if they so wanted to in order to improve products and service offerings.

This would also mean that sales costs could be brought down, because a 24-hour service could be provided but only a limited number of customer calls would have to be taken care of by salespersons. Furthermore, products could be produced to order to a higher degree than today and, to a greater extent than today, could be tailored to customer needs, which would diminish capital costs and other costs connected to the storage of products.

This type of concept can be applied in many cases when customers buy complex products and services. In a customer service system of this kind, even very infrequent needs could be addressed by questions, and customers who, because of their unusual demands, have difficulty in getting good service today could get better treatment. In the same vein, customers who really need personal service could also have better treatment than today because their needs could be addressed by people who really would have the time to treat each customer in a personal way.

We have now discussed how network intelligence could be used in order to transform concepts that to a large extent consist of a product offering. In some cases, we deal with companies that produce pure knowledge. The product of a consulting firm may be only a package of knowledge that is presented to the customer in the form of information, such as computer code or a consulting report, or that is directly transferred to the customer company in the form of knowledge about how to perform new routines. Network intelligence could also be used when a certain company produces knowledge about itself, about how to improve routines or in the development of new products. In this case, work is often done in projects, and network intelligence could be used in order to make the best possible use of the knowledge of each individual. The following is an example of how projects could be managed in the future using network intelligence.

Many companies use the concept of 'projects' to deal with a wide range of tasks in the organisation. A project is usually formed when something has to be carried out that has not been done before, that is, a task for which no exact processes are defined. People from various parts of the organisation come together to offer their skills and experiences to achieve a common goal. After the task has been carried out (which may take several years or just a couple of days), the project is dissolved and people go back to their normal tasks or join another project. The fact that a project cannot be defined in detail before it starts and that people could come from different parts of the organisation and different parts of the world also makes it complicated. Projects are built on knowledge, and knowledge is handled very differently in the traditional organisation compared with an organisation that uses the power of the new valuescape. This makes the concept of a project interesting in terms of transformation into the new electronic market.

People in a project need to share knowledge in various ways in order to achieve their common goal. In the physical world, there are a number of tools that could be used to support a project, for example libraries, conference rooms, mail distribution, project secretaries or common calendars. These types of tool are crucial to make people work together and share their knowledge. They are, in other words, the basis of a networked organisation that is trying to optimise the use of knowledge and experience. These tools are often seen as so natural and central to a project that they look exactly the same even in the world of computerised support systems. Libraries are turned into computer-based libraries, a conference room still looks the same, mail is transported electronically but looks very much the same as it always has, secretaries are still human and calendars keep their characteristics, even if they are stored in a computer. This means that, even in the world of computer support, there is no real support for new ways of working and the more efficient sharing of knowledge.

Where are the new concepts that could take project work into the valuescape? There are only some very simple embryos of project support that have been transformed. However, there are some very clear needs to focus on, and if we use our imagination and keep some existing examples from the Internet in mind, it is possible to get a feeling of how these transformed tools will enable network intelligence. The basic needs of project tools are rather easy to summarise:

- communication between members of the project;
- the ability to share knowledge in any form;
- efficient planning and administration (for example, the sharing of calendars);
- easy access to information from the outside (knowledge, information or customer contacts);
- the easy distribution of results (to customers of various kinds).

People who work in projects have more specific needs than those for computerised mail and libraries. They need a new platform that enables them to work together in a distributed environment. They need tools to be able to add their particular value to the process without having to maintain a complete and detailed view of how the whole process is organised. They also need to be as independent as possible from the rest of the project. People should not have to wait for results from someone else before their own next step can be taken. All these things point in a very precise direction: they need an overall process to guide the work but a large amount of freedom in how they carry out tasks. This was discussed in Chapter 5. In this area, we will see a tremendous development in terms of tools and techniques to be able to work in this way. The project support concept will be transformed into tools such as virtual offices where people can work together as if they were in the same office and have tools that could stimulate interaction and creative work. Everybody will have their particular view of the office, get information presented in a useful way and get tools that enable them to do their tasks. Communication will be much more selective, with information customised to avoid overload. We will soon see personal electronic assistants that administer information and communication in order to help users to make use of a number of new opportunities within the electronic market.

Some interesting examples of these workplaces have been created in the European ACTS (Advanced Communication Technologies and Services) projects, on which people from several countries and organisations collaborate. The distributed nature of the projects and the fact that they are all in the IT and telecommunications business have led to project sites on the Internet where members can share information (documents, presentations, pictures and sound), administer e-mail conferences, publish deliverables, chair meetings and sign on new members. All could be done in a way that makes tools easy and attractive to use. These project sites also meet the demands of the distribution of information about the projects to other people within or outside member organisations.

Concept transformation by changing the scope of an offering

Using the opportunities of the Internet often has to do with breaking down artificial barriers. These barriers are there mainly because the information-handling capabilities available in the physical world have been restricted by our limited ability as human beings. This is true when we act both as customers and users of information, and as sellers and providers of information. What we need to be able to do is to cope with far larger amounts of information in a constructive way.

We only need take a walk in the city in order to understand this argument. Why is it that we have to enter a bookshop in order to get good advise about which books to buy, an electronics shop in order to have an expert salesman to sell a video recorder and a paint shop in order to buy paint and wallpaper from a person with the right competence? Why is it that if I were to buy these products from a supermarket, I would not get the expert help that I may need in some situations?

One of the reasons behind this is that it is very difficult for a person to become an expert in all these fields at the same time. Once someone has started to work in a bookshop, he or she gets loaded with information about books, publishers and different subjects. It is natural for a person who works in a specialist shop to develop more knowledge about the products than a person who works at a supermarket would do during the same time.

Therefore, producers who want their products to be presented by professionals who have an expertise in a certain field choose to sell them in specialist shops, while producers who do not want their products to have this support could sell through supermarkets. In many cases, however, products are available through both these channels.

From the point of view of the customer, on the other hand, we tend to associate a specialist shop with good quality and good service because we think that those who run that type of shop know more about their products and have the ability to select the best products to sell to their customers. Supermarkets, however, could be assumed to sell products of any quality, just because they do not have the competence to distinguish between good and bad quality. This view may, of course, be wrong, but many people still see it this way.

This logic will not be there on the Internet. Information about a product can always be published by the party that has the best information about each aspect of it. The producer could supply general information about the product and about how to use it. An environmental organisation could, whether the producer likes it or not, publish information about the environmental aspects of the product's manufacture and use. Owners of summer houses could publish information about the advantages and disadvantages of using this particular product in a summer house during the vacation. There will be no need to assume that all the best information about a product can be found in any particular geographical spot, such as a shop. Instead, those who search for information can see the whole picture of all aspects of a subject. The richness of the information depends on how many people have something important to contribute to the matter. These contributions from different people will not even stay within companies. It already happens that people add value to an area on the Internet simply because they have a personal interest and are keen on sharing their knowledge and experiences.

In Chapter 6, we saw how the concept of a shop could be transformed. However, it was not the shop as we know it today. The concept of a shop blurs as publishers of information and customers use the new advantages of the electronic marketplace. Here, a shop is not something that we enter to buy a certain type of product and then leave, just to go to another shop to complete the shopping. Instead, it is a complete solution to meet the particular needs of a particular person in a particular situation. From a certain Internet site, customers could surf over to another page with the flick of a finger, and the whole valuescape could be seen in total as one new shop that is much more than just a place where customers meet producers: it is a tailored way to meet a complete need with a complete range of solutions.

From another perspective, we could see each homepage as one separate shop, where a limited number of needs could be satisfied. However, the analogy with shops blurs once more when we note that we would rarely leave a shop on the Internet with the goods that we have bought. The shopping experience will be divided in terms of different functions, such as the presentation and selling of a product up until the point of making the order and paying for the product electronically. After that distribution comes in, but the customer will not need to know whether the company that happens to stock and deliver the product is located next door or in another part of the world. Nor will the customer need to know whether the product is taken from the shelf or produced at the point of order. He will just know that the product he ordered will be delivered in the time that was promised at the point of making the order, unless he has a special interest in diminishing transportation distances. In that case, the above-mentioned type of information would become of interest.

Federal Express is using the new electronic media to move up the value chain and start providing added value to their customers. Federal Express offers a service that helps companies to sell products on the Internet. The service means that a company can let Federal Express set up a database with all products for sale. It presents this database on the Internet together with facilities to order products. The only thing that Federal Express demands is that it handles delivery of the products. For small companies, this is a valuable service as they do not have to set up databases, servers and Internet connections, or deal with maintenance and support.

Actually, the most frequently bought goods may be stocked in a local or regional storage house, where milk, bread and butter are located next to white shirts, inexpensive watches and lawn mowers. In order to make distribution as efficient as possible, it is a good idea to distribute goods with similar distribution patterns or similar buying patterns through the same channels, but this could still mean that shops could be structured in a manner very different from that of today. In this case, an order for groceries could be sent to the same distributor as an order for a new pair of trousers, or an order for bread, milk and butter could be divided between two different distributors if that were the way in which these goods were stored and delivered in a particular region.

In this case, concept transformation means that concepts will be broken down, expanded and narrowed, depending on the logic of the physical flows and the information flows that are connected to the purchase and service of each type of product. The information will be structured in the valuescape, where different offerings can be linked to each other in order for customers to find the products that they want, and for suppliers to be able to communicate with those customers whom they assume will have an interest in their products. However, this presentation will then be cut off from the physical distribution of products, so that the process of delivery can be made as efficient as possible. After that, the servicing of products that need to be dealt with by professionals will be disconnected from the two previous processes.

Nothing new under the sun

The process of moving old concepts into a new environment was a key issue for companies long before the birth of the electronic market. It is a general business problem, and people have made the same types of mistake in the past when a new technology has been born and a number of new concepts have had to be transformed to make use of the new opportunities. When a technology evolves, it is common for the concepts to be adapted to the new circumstances rather than transformed. The new challenge that is created by the valuescape is that it now becomes possible for many new competitors to enter established markets and that it becomes crucial for established firms to transform their concepts in order to stay in business.

As an example of a case in which it would have been possible to transform a concept but companies failed to make use of new opportunities, we could take the invention of telephony at the end of the nineteenth century. It was suddenly possible to talk to people all over the globe independently of location. A telephone network was built to connect people. Naturally, it was not possible to have a complete network where every person was directly connected to all others. Instead, switching centres were built to establish physical links between people when they wanted to talk to each other. This was done manually through the use of a switchboard with cables that were plugged into holes. This cumbersome procedure was the only way to do the switching before electromagnetic, and later computer, switches were invented to make this procedure automatic.

The invention of the automatic switch was a tremendous step forward, and a whole profession became superfluous. However, the concept of a person who did the switching still lives on, and electronic switching still works in almost the same manner as did manual switching. The concept has hardly been transformed. The technical solution used today is to a large extent the old way of switching dressed up in new technology. The development has, of course, led to a tremendous improvement in efficiency. Telephone calls are routed automatically in microseconds, but the question still lingers: Is the present way of switching really using the opportunities of the new technology? Probably not. New networks are being built that use a completely different way of connecting people with each other.

Datacom networks of various types are based on other concepts of how to establish a link between people and computers. The Internet itself, to mention one example, is not a switched network. It uses the concept of hierarchical addresses that are read and interpreted by nodes in a hierarchy where each node does its particular part of the routing task. These nodes perform the task as far as possible and then hand it over to the next node in the network. The rapid expansion of the Internet and the technology that is used there poses a threat to traditional switching solutions offered by the large telecom companies of the world. People in the telecom industry are starting to think about new ways of switching calls that will make it possible for calls to bypass substantial parts of the network, and thus saving network capacity and increasing speed. This is usually referred to as IP-based telephony.

The most essential thing behind concept transformation is that it is built on innovation and creativity in order to become competitive and successful in the new marketplace. Old ideas and 'truths' are left behind and replaced by new solutions. Concept transformation should become a natural part of strategy development in most companies in the near future. When new products and services are developed, companies should always start by looking at how they fit into the new marketplace and the new environment in which they will evolve in the future. It is only when current companies transform their concepts into a form that could work well in the valuescape that they can hope to be successful in the next millennium.

Note

1. The expression 'transparent food' was mentioned to us by Peter Wennström and was developed in parallel with our own concepts of a 'transparent market' or a 'transparent society' which are presented in this book.

Part III
Challenges

The development described so far will pose several challenges to all players in our economy. Companies, individuals and governments who think that the future will be similar to the present in terms of opportunities and requirements may find that they will have no position in the future market.

In Part III, we describe the structural changes that will follow and the challenges that companies, individuals and governments will have to face, and we will also describe how a number of industries might be influenced if consumers and companies started to use the new opportunities.

8 Structural Changes

Throughout the book so far, we have described developments that will affect the whole structure of society. We have, however, not made all these effects explicit, which means that it may be difficult for readers to see which types of change lie ahead of us. These effects may be even more dramatic than most of us would expect even after having read the book this far.

Many people argue that the development of an electronic market and of opportunities to organise markets and work in new ways is a technical issue rather than an array of factors that will influence society as a whole. In this chapter, we will discuss the development from different perspectives to show some of its potential consequences. However, predictions of the future are always just predictions, visions and thoughts. We argue that only consumers have the opportunity to choose whether or not the development we describe here will become a reality, because if consumers use the available opportunities in the electronic market, the change process will gather momentum.

Transforming the economy

Changes in international trade

The discovery of the abundant mines of America reduced, in the sixteenth century the value of gold and silver in Europe to about a third of what it had been before. (Smith, 1997)

We are used to thinking of international trade as if it has purely positive effects on the economy of each country involved. With increasing opportunities to communicate, this may change. As it becomes easier to communicate over large distances, it will no longer be the case that any country with high labour costs will be able to hold its own in competition against countries with lower labour costs. In future, the importance of being geographically close to the customer will decrease, which means that low-cost countries that can compete with production in high-cost countries will have an advantage. Customers from high-cost countries will soon discover that they can get the same quality of products and services for a much lower price if they buy on the global market rather than from the local company.

As everybody is aware, this development has already started. The difference now is that the pace of change may become much faster. Once we have tested the possibility of global shopping, most of us will never turn back to the local market. This development is very hard to stop even if many of us would want to do so in order to protect jobs locally. The reason is that it is very hard to convince people that they should pay a premium of, for example, 100 per cent just to save the local shop.

It must be noted here that it will not only be tasks related to the pure production of information that will be exported. Instead, the increasing opportunities to communicate efficiently over large distances will make it possible to move all kinds of activity to low-cost countries.

If we take the production of clothes as an example, it has been possible for companies with a substantial market to organise low-cost production in Asia, Portugal or the Baltic states. With the opportunity to 'visit' a company far away through electronic means, it will be easy even for small companies or individuals to move production to the country where it is most advantageous. Examples of how to interact electronically with production units far away are making 'electronic visits' to production facilities through video cameras that could be mounted all over a plant, making frequent such 'visits' to companies that may cause problems and even studying sewing patterns or other details together with the employees or managers of the foreign companies, and electronically moving computerised management systems to handle production in other locations.

Until now, it has been possible for customers of some size and in some industries to move production abroad, but in future it will be possible even for children to have their school magazine printed abroad if it brings down the cost. In the case of printing a school magazine, the children could find an inexpensive printer abroad by looking on the Internet. By double-clicking on a button on the homepage of this printer, a video line could be opened so that the children and their suppliers could see each other. The producer could present a price and a delivery time, and also offer to take the children on a visual tour of his printing shop. They could even decide on a date and time when their magazines would be printed, so that the children could watch the process from start to finish. After the children had placed the order, they would simply take the documents containing written text and digital photos and send them over the Internet to the printer, who would receive it a few minutes after despatch.

Even if we do not know how many of our companies in high-cost countries will face this type of competition, we can assume that they are legion. Even in industries that have until now been thought of as secure for high-cost countries, because they require employees with high competence, competition from low-cost countries may become severe.

One example of Western companies moving service functions to low-cost countries are advanced IT and communications solutions in the field of customer support in telecommunications operator organisations. This task has been handled by a number of highly skilled people specialising in narrow fields (subscriber line maintenance, fault handling, customer contacts). When the old technology was used, they had to be highly skilled specialists since the tools they were using did not provide enough support and guidance. In many operator organisations, this is changing rapidly.

> Of two countries having precisely the same population, and the same quantity of land of equal fertility in cultivation, with the same knowledge too of agriculture, the prices of raw produce will be highest in that where the greater skill and the better machinery is used in the manufacture of exportable commodities. (Ricardo, 1996)

A similar development will be seen between countries that have different tax rates, for example for VAT. It is already a fact that people in Sweden are able to buy groceries from Germany at almost half the Swedish price over the Internet (occ.warendienst.se). If the volumes traded in this way increased, it would mean that Swedes could get their groceries at a lower price but that the Swedish state would lose tax income, which would create a problem as volumes increased.

The substantial price differences are the result of not only differences in VAT, but also differences in factor costs, other taxes and different levels of efficiency between countries, which makes it even more difficult for governments to counteract this trend by changing the Swedish VAT rates. If Swedish tax incomes decreased, we would either have to create new tax incomes from other types of transactions or decrease the level of public spending.

If we take the effects on employment in Western countries that we have described into account, we find not only that the labour market in the developed countries will decrease, but also that competition for the remaining work will increase. As this competition will come to an increasing degree from countries where wages and salaries are lower than in developed countries, we may find that the export to low-cost countries of work currently performed in our own countries creates problems here.

Increasing market stability in the long run

One aspect of today's society is that it can be described as fairly unstable. We see this instability in different situations. We see it in our economic system, where the peaks and troughs of the economic cycles create problems for states and households, and opportunities for investors who want to take risks. We also see it in business, where companies compete and where fortune for one company may mean bankruptcy for another.

These instabilities are likely to diminish as the transparency of society increases. This is because instability is another effect of the lack of information that we experience today. In this situation, a person who is better at predicting the future, or has more luck than others, can gain a substantial advantage over competitors. We see this in the financial markets, where people can earn large sums on their willingness to take risks, where those who happen to be right about the future are the winners and those who make the wrong guesses are the losers. Instability is created by the tendency for investors to follow each other so that large amounts of money are moved on a daily basis between different investment alternatives. That many companies represent a very high stock market value and that large holdings are traded each day account for the large fluctuations. If the economy consisted of smaller units of self-employed individuals tied together in networks, the system would become more stable simply because there would be fewer large transactions each day.

Transformation of industry structures

Large overheads mean disadvantage

In the case of the transportation industry that was presented in Chapter 7, we see how a worldwide network of transport could be established by independent companies in the transportation business who offered their services in the same electronic marketplace. This network would become more efficient than any transportation network that could be established by a large company and managed by its managers, since it would do away with the large overheads that the big companies have. The costs of management at head office and the salespersons and managers in the regional offices will be ones that the large companies have but that will be unnecessary in this new type of structure. A transportation network structured with the market mechanism as the main organisation principle will not become more efficient if one or more managers are employed in order to manage the network.

This also means that there will be disadvantages for the owners of large companies. The most efficient transportation network will be created by a multitude of small companies with no ties between each other than the mutual interest of producing the transportation services that their customers need.

One example of the kind of information system that can be used to form an unmanaged network is the transport management system that Federal Express has managed to create. In this system, it has exact information on the route that packages take in its own network of trucks, aeroplanes and vans. By using this information, it always has full visibility of transportation needs and transportation resources. A system like this could become the foundation of a more market-based network in which all customers could express their needs for services and match these to offers.

This type of application could be complemented through a system in which producers could meet consumers. Owners of trucks could list their routes in one database, where all points of reloading could also be listed. In this system, customers could do their bookings with the help of automatic functions that calculated the price based on individual tariffs and discount systems.

There are many examples of industries in which the same type of opportunities exist. We can think of the printing industry, where the company www.iprint.com offers customers the opportunity to pay 30–40 per cent lower prices for the printing of stationery than in other print shops. This company does not do any printing itself; it only acts as a powerful middleman between the customer and a number of print shops that it uses as subcontractors. Iprint uses the buying power created through the volumes it handles for its customers in order to achieve much better prices than customers could get on their own.

This company, however, is in a rather fragile position in the market since transparency in itself could provide customers themselves with the buying power that they needed in order to get better prices from printers. It would only require printers to offer their services over the Internet for each customer himself to choose the supplier with the best price. This would take away the middleman function that Iprint currently performs, and unnecessary overcapacity would be taken out of the industry at the same time as putting prices under pressure to move towards the equilibrium level.

Small-scale production

In future, it will be at the discretion of users of the Internet to build their own valuescapes, and the configuration of each valuescape will to a large extent determine which type of information will be addressed to a certain user. Furthermore, it will be possible for users to focus more on unprejudiced sources, such as test results, rather than reading advertisements from producers who have the sole aim of selling as much as possible to consumers. The very foundation of consumer behaviour can change when we can use a broader range of market information more easily. A faint memory of a commercial slogan will be replaced by firm market information, provided by companies themselves and by a number of independent sources, for example people who have had problems with, or good experiences of, a product or service. This type of information has existed for a long time, but it has only been provided on media that are not accessible at the point of purchase. This type of information will be very easily accessible when we transfer the market to an electronic medium. A filter set up by a customer of an electronic foodstore could filter all products from a certain company or foods that have certain ingredients.

This, together with the trend towards customised products and the large-scale disadvantages mentioned earlier, will increase the share of small-scale production. It will simply not be possible for large-scale producers in many industries to find the large markets that they need in order to continue their domination. The access to more comprehensive information, together with more aware customers, will lead to a number of new product niches that small companies can dominate. The main competitive advantage that the mass-producing companies have at present is that of large-scale marketing and production. When this is gone, it will be possible for small and local producers to compete on fairly equal terms against much larger companies. If we take the production of low-technology goods such as most food products, clothes and other goods of the same type, the large-scale advantages of production will not be substantial enough in the future to offset the advantages of small and local producers of speciality products. We already see this development in the brewing industry, where new local and regional breweries are rapidly being established in many countries.

One example mentioned above is the availability of 14 different editions of *The Wealth of Nations* (1997) by Adam Smith that were available in English through one Internet-based bookshop. We could think of someone who may have a printing press in his garage; this person would be able to print a fifteenth edition of this book. With limited overheads, it may well be that it could be advertised and sold through the same bookshop at a price lower than that of any of the existing editions.

In the physical market, this would not create an advantage because of the capital that would be needed in order to market it to bookshops all over the world on a bookshop-by-bookshop basis. In the Internet market, it would be possible during an afternoon to call fewer than 10 major Internet-based bookshops that sell books in English and, in a few hours, have the new edition displayed to all Internet shoppers alongside the present 14 editions. It may even be possible for publishers or printers to add books on their own to the homepages of these bookshops.

In our work as management consultants, we have also noted that the minimum volumes required to run efficient and profitable production are decreasing in many industries as production equipment is equipped with more computer software to replace mechanical functions. The example from the brewing industry can be mentioned in this respect as well, but we could also think of the development of photocopiers, which makes it possible to have such machines even for companies that copy only small numbers of documents.

One of the historical reasons behind the development of large corporations is that they have been owned by people with large capital resources. These owners have, through their position in society, personified the security and stability that have been a requirement for capital investments in the old system. This has created owners with large capital resources that have been backed by banks and other financial institutes. Their existing capital base and their financial strength, which they can use to acquire new capital when needed, have made it possible to build large empires of businesses and other holdings. The development towards decreasing advantages of scale in distribution and in the building of brands means that the advantage of being a large player financially decreases.

This trend is also visible in the field of marketing of IT solutions. In the case of Netscape, this company acquired 7 million new customers in 1 year when this market was still rather small, which meant a major share of the world market for Internet browsers. In this type of industry, it does not take the same degree of capital resource in order to develop and sell advanced new products all over the world as was needed in traditional markets.

At present, Microsoft is taking over a large share of Netscape's customers, but this should be seen largely as an effect of the inefficiencies that still remain from the physical market, where Microsoft can use its dominance in the field of office software to take over the market for web-browsers. There is no reason to believe that this would have been possible in an electronic market because of the opportunity for customers to choose the best supplier for each particular product.

Even if the offer of a company consists of a physical product, the cost of informing the world market of its existence is much smaller than it has been in the past, which in itself reduces the need for capital.

Fewer players

We have argued that the structures of the present will be changed in the future, but we have not yet paid any attention to the industry structures that are being built on the Internet. It can be assumed that the retail structure of, for example, the clothing industry will not look the same in the future as it does today, when all clothes from any major producer are sold through one store in each city. Would it make sense for a clothing producer to sell through several thousands of Internet-based outlets? Probably not.

Instead, we are facing a future when the value added by industries that could be replaced by Internet-based businesses diminishes. This means that the margins a clothes retailer makes today in the physical world will decrease substantially when business is taken over by an Internet-based company. This also means that in many industries there will be room for fewer companies than there are today.

Typical of this development is the rise of companies such as www.amazon.com and www.bokus.com, which sell books in a worldwide or national market. They have started the race by cutting prices and cutting costs. The question still unanswered is how many of these there are room for in a worldwide book market. We will probably see more of them enter the market with new ideas that can cut costs still further. Services will also be developed that are more attractive and convenient for customers, but in many industries there will only be a number of producers, who sell their products directly to customers.

One area in which the number of big players on the Internet has started to stabilise is the market for search engines. There are just a handful of these that have succeeded in positioning themselves at the top. It will probably not make sense to have dozens or hundreds of these search engines offering more or less the same services. The only weapons that newcomers in this market have are new and more advanced search facilities that help people to find what they are looking for and to get as many 'hits' as possible for the sponsors who pay for the advertising. The problem is that new search facilities can be copied or improved by established competitors at short notice, and customers know that they can be sure that their favourite search site will follow the leader and very soon offer the same new services.

Transforming the labour market

Increased efficiency may lead to a surplus of labour

> If five millions of men could produce as much food and clothing as was necessary for ten millions, food and clothing for five millions would be the net revenue. Would it be of any advantage to the country, that, to produce this same net revenue, seven millions of the men should be required, that is to say, that seven millions should be employed to produce food and clothing sufficient for twelve millions? The food and clothing of five millions would be still the net revenue. The employing a greater number of men would enable us neither to add a man to our army and navy, nor to contribute one guinea more in taxes. (Ricardo, 1996)

Our message is one of optimism. We can, with the help of new technologies, create a more efficient and more humane society. We need, however, to change our ideas on a number of issues in order to avoid problems that may arise in the wake of the changes that may come.

One of our main arguments is that it will be possible in the future to produce the same amount of goods and services as today by using far fewer resources. The main savings in the process of change will be savings on human labour. For this reason, the visions that are put forward here will seem horrifying to many people who are deeply in love with work. The view that we are putting forward is that we must expand our vision of work and realise that the negative connotations we find in words such as 'unemployment' are probably based more on the historical view that all of us need to work at least 8 hours a day in order to create the resources for society that all of us need in order to survive.

If the future means that we will not need to work so much to that end, nobody will need to look down on people who do not work 8 hours a day, and nobody should feel bad if they do not work that many hours. Instead, we have to see this as an opportunity that we should grab and make the most of. The opportunity comes in many shapes:

- We can work where we like and spend less time travelling to and from work. This means that we can spend more time with our family and friends.
- We can use our shorter working hours to improve the quality of our lives. We can take on new hobbies, join a sports club, take part in local politics or spend time with friends.
- We can use shorter working hours to do more of the things we think are not done enough in society. Thus we could care more for the elderly or people who are ill, without the cost of this care being seen as a burden on society, as it often is today.

Today's labour market is suited to working well in a society where the goal is full employment (full employment meaning that everybody should work 8 hours every day) and where many people expect to spend their lifetimes with the same company or at least in the same profession.

The result of the development described above could, however, be that salaries in different professions become more equal than they are today. With a surplus of labour in many professions, including those which require a high level of education, it would be difficult to maintain higher wage levels in some professions than others, as long as there are enough people who are capable of taking on any piece of work that is offered in a particular vocation.

Transforming democracy

Over the past 200 years, we have seen how political, as well as economic, power has been spread to a larger and larger number of people in the democratic societies. A few hundred years ago the king, or an equivalent person, ruled the country. Power was based around a small number of aristocrats who could support the king with money and soldiers when he needed. The majority of people were to a large extent powerless.

This has gradually changed, and both wealth and power have become more evenly spread in society. There are still a number of people who earn much more than the average man in the street, and there are also people who have more power than others, but society has become much more democratic over the years in both these respects.

As people spend less and less time on their jobs away from home and more and more time at home, people will be able to take on more responsibility for the development of their communities. If we wish, we will not need professional politicians to the same extent as we do today. Instead, we will all be able to take part in decision-making in various types of local committee, either through personal participation or through electronic debate and voting.

Even if we see it as unlikely that all would like to participate in this manner, we can assume that there would be more people than today who would be willing to get involved. The main forces driving this development would be more spare time, increased cost-efficiency of the political system, with fewer politicians to be paid for their work, and better opportunities to keep informed about political issues.

Transparency will also find its way into politics and democracy, and we will see a number of consequences in these areas. Access to all kinds of information and the ability to combine and analyse it will lead to a better opportunity to see what is going on in society. Political decisions will be easier to see through, and citizens will be able to decide more objectively what the best solution would be for them as individuals, for example in terms of where to live, which public services to use and how to use the system in an optimal way to get maximum benefits at minimum cost. This may pave the way for whole new systems of society in which the participation of each citizen could increase to a previously unprecedented level.

In Sweden, there is an example of how the Internet can be used to increase the power of the people and make it possible for us to influence politicians directly. In the south of Sweden on a small island called Ven, children are linked directly to politicians in Stockholm (600 km away) via the Internet in order to give the politicians their views about current issues.

9 Challenges for Companies

Many companies need to enter the electronic market as quickly as possible

The fact that suppliers can serve all the customers with whom they can communicate makes the potential market for each supplier enormous. This means that a producer who has substantial competitive advantages in production can initially grab a larger share of the market than he or she has at present. This, together with the fact that customers on the Internet will be able to compare offerings from different suppliers much more accurately than they can today, could lead to a situation in which many companies that have seemingly secure local markets today could lose a large share of these to Internet-based players. Therefore, companies are advised to enter the Internet as soon as possible, for several reasons.

First, they will need to learn about Internet competition in order to be able to compete there. Old truths and rules are no longer valid (as we have tried to show throughout the book); experience will not come automatically. Companies need to make some mistakes before they find their way to success in the new electronic form of business.

Second, the development of the Internet as a marketplace may well be very quick, which could mean that the players who arrive there first will be able to slice the initial pie between them and keep others out by quickly developing the right competitive advantages for this game. Over time, a different situation could arise, in which there will be room for many competitors on the Internet, even with a local nature, but the transition phase between a physical market and an electronic market could make many weak companies bankrupt, and it could take time for new companies to be established.

Third, even for companies in industries in which there will be no globalisation of their markets, local competition may move over to the Internet. With improved opportunities to communicate with customers, with suppliers and within the company itself, Internet-based companies may become more efficient than their competitors, and because of that position themselves in the forefront. It is very important not to forget that requirements for new services and increased efficiency will come from customers rather than internal forces.

All in all, the potential advantages that could be achieved by a company moving on to the Internet make a good case to support this decision. Historically, we see that customers tend to prefer to do business with companies offering a high level of service at a comparatively low price. Since cost advantages in the physical market have often been in single digit percentages, we can assume that companies that could gain advantages of 30–40 per cent by entering the Internet, and at the same time improve service in certain respects, would attract a large number of customers.

> One example of a company that really is taking the Internet challenge into account is the Swedish national mail company Posten. It has launched a number of new business concepts based on its firm belief in the future increase of this new market.
>
> At present, it offers its Internet market site Torget as a platform for Swedish companies that want to do consumer business on the Internet. It has set up storage and distribution facilities for Internet-based companies that want to sell in the Swedish market but still prefer to avoid the physical handling of goods. Additionally, it offers these companies the service of financing their dues from the customers and also handles the payments through its giro system. The latest addition to this portfolio of services that are based on an assumed increase in Internet trade is the offer of the home delivery of parcels in the evenings for the benefit of people who have ordered goods over the Internet.

We cannot be sure that the Internet market will grow in the way we predict, but if many people and companies believe that this will be true, it is likely that it will come true simply because the believers will start the move in the direction described here. If large players such as Posten take on this challenge and try to develop concepts for the Internet market, the growth of this market will become even more rapid than it would be if only smaller players drove this change.

Another factor supporting this assumption is that many Internet-based companies could be competitive against companies in the physical market even with only a small percentage of business on the Internet. This is because the geographical market of these companies will be very large, whereas companies in the physical market will face problems as their business shrinks, with difficulties in covering fixed costs as a consequence. When this happens, the competitive position of Internet marketers will gradually improve as traditional shops have to increase prices in order to cover fixed costs with decreasing sales. In many industries, this could soon put a strain on traditional businesses. It is interesting to think that, when business declines locally, it is possible that parts of it have moved far away, maybe to the other side of the globe. People may in the near future still visit a shop, but without the intention of buying – just going to look and try. After the visit, they may go home and buy the same product at 50 or 70 per cent of the price over the Internet. This trend may not be easy for single shops to discover because local decreases in turnover will initially be small. It will be much more difficult to see than if a similar shop started up business next door. The trend may not be spotted until trade statistics reveal that the purchasing patterns of customers have changed from purchases in shops to Internet shopping. Even when these figures are available, many companies might argue that it is due to a temporary decline in business rather than to an irreversible trend.

> The company www.amazon.com is reported to have a turnover of more than $150m per year at the end of 1997. This turnover and the turnover of other Internet-based bookshops is taken from the present large number of physical bookshops. This means that the percentage of sales lost by each of these physical shops is small, but as Internet trade grows, the market share of Internet-based bookshops will increase. The problem for many physical bookshops may be that they are almost out of business before they realise that they have a problem, because once they start to notice that they are losing trade volume, it will be difficult for them to maintain prices at the present levels. In order to cover fixed costs, they may have to increase prices. At the same time, the cost advantage for Internet-based bookshops will increase, and they are likely to be able to decrease prices as the volumes traded over the Internet increase.

Companies will have to learn to make use of new technologies in order to save money and increase creativity

When companies have entered the Internet, this will not mean that they have entered a safe haven where they can live in peace and comfort. Competition on the Internet will be fiercer than in the physical market at present. This is because the most efficient competitors will reach a much larger share of the total market than before, and because new competitors with different concepts and new ideas will try their luck all the time.

Many experts say that companies will be more niche orientated than before so that even very small segments of customers, down perhaps to a few people, will be addressed with specific offerings. This means that companies will have to be both very cost-efficient and very targeted in their approaches on the Internet in order to be able to keep their foothold. In order to achieve this, companies will have to use the latest technology to a maximum in order to become more efficient, both in production and distribution.

A big problem for large corporations with complex and inflexible support systems is that they cannot introduce new services with the frequency that they would like to (and definitely need to). This is the result of too much old technology and too many old processes in the area of new product introduction. The increasing requirement for new services is not only driven by the need to introduce new products more often, but is also a consequence of the need to develop and launch services for smaller customer segments (possibly one service for each customer in some industries). There is a battle against time in many companies to change this situation and become faster and more flexible. The use of new technologies such as Internet, object-orientated technologies or middleware will help in this battle.

Also, big companies will have to apply new small-scale production technologies in order to cater to smaller and smaller market segments and niches. This will, to a large extent, take away the competitive advantage of the size of these companies, but still this seems to be the only way forward for them.

Companies will have to work at maximum speed and discard long-term strategic thinking

The speed of development in the Internet market will be very fast. If companies use all the opportunities that are offered by the latest IT, the development of the most advanced competitors will be very quick and new competitors will arrive all the time, using new approaches to Internet marketing. We can assume that companies will be tempted to try using the new technologies to the maximum simply because they will be afraid that competitors will do it and they will be left behind if they are not fast enough. The fear of losing the race will increase the speed even more.

In this type of race, strategic thinking will take on a new dimension. How much strategy do athletes apply during a 100m race? In the market we describe here, the speed will be comparable to such a race. If one of the contestants slows down for a second in order to think about their situation and develop a strategy for the finish, they may discover that they have been left behind by the others. It is probable simply that competitors who do not stop and think but take decisions as they go, more or less at random, will prove either much better or much worse than those who try to develop a strategy. The hard reality will strike those who take one or two wrong steps, but those who have the luck to make the right decisions will be successful.

In our work as consultants, we have seen many examples of companies that still expend much effort trying to make long-term plans. They feel comfortable if they can write directives of how business activities should be co-ordinated and make detailed plans for each part of the business. In the transparent marketplace, with the speed and challenges that follow in its footsteps, this will not be enough. Companies have to make it an ongoing process to try to find new ways of using technology in the short term. As we discussed in Chapter 3, technologies develop faster than the ideas of how to use them, which means that when ideas are being defined, it is very likely that it is possible to implement them. Why should companies write their ideas into a strategy? Mainly in order to communicate the decision, but it is important also to develop new products and service concepts before somebody else does. No company has ever increased its turnover or profits by asserting that it was the first to develop an idea and that it actually wrote it into its strategy a year before. This will become even more true in the rapidly changing Internet market.

Companies will have to develop multiple concepts

One way of avoiding wrong decisions becoming fatal is to run several races. With segments as small as the ones that will be possible in the Internet market, each company will have to focus on and cater to needs in several segments in order to survive.

This means that each company could try many alternatives all the time, which could diminish its risk of going bankrupt, even if some of its concepts proved to be wrong. Thus one way to avoid the most fierce competition would be to try to develop new markets by launching new concepts aimed at customer segments with specific needs that have not yet been catered for. Over time, however, these new segments will become more and more difficult to find, and it might take many unsuccessful tries before a good concept can be found.

This is another aspect of competition without a strategy. It might pay better to try a number of different concepts during a short period of time than to sit back and develop a strategy, simply because the new concepts may not be possible to find through analysis. Instead, a large amount of trial and error may be the only way to arrive at the best solutions.

Multiple concepts can lead to a number of conflicts in organisations. Many companies are focused on reaching unidirection in the organisation to avoid costly duplication of work and, perhaps more importantly, to have one single face towards markets and customers. However, speed will be even more important in the future, and in the long run investments in multiple concepts are likely to pay.

Companies will have to rethink structures and support systems so that they support new ways of working

Companies that think they soon will have to change their way of working in order to be able to compete on the Internet, according to the rules that have been described in this book, may still be at a loss as to how to make the necessary changes in their organisations.

One way to start the process of change is to accelerate the development towards more market-orientated structures and internal management systems, which many companies embarked on a long time ago. We see it as crucial for any company to address the need of changing present hierarchical structures into more and more flexible ones that make organisations more dynamic and spontaneous organisation possible.

Such a change of structures should encompass both internal interaction and the systems for measurement of performance that are used within a company. In order for each individual to trade his or her competence or time internally, it must become possible to support this way of working with inexpensive administrative systems keeping track of individual performance and making it possible for people to prioritise between tasks. This often requires investments in new IT systems, but the main investment will probably be that in the process needed in order to change the corporate culture to the new way of working.

Companies have to remember that customers can change suppliers easily and frequently

A relatively high customer loyalty has been a natural ingredient in many industries because customers are not able continuously to evaluate alternatives to find the best offer, and it has often been very hard to switch to another supplier. The reasons behind this are, of course, that information about alternatives is difficult and costly to find (for example, driving around and visiting different shops) and the amount of work to change suppliers is often great as a result of inefficient administration (for example, switching to another bank). Many of these reasons have started to vanish in the new electronic market. Some examples are:

■ It is easy to access information about all alternatives. This is due to increasing transparency.
■ The distance to different alternatives becomes equal. It is just as easy to buy a piece of software from the other side of the globe as it is to get it from a supplier next door.
■ The efforts to switch from one supplier to another will disappear. A company can no longer claim that it will take days to register a new customer or transfer information from one place to another.

In the market for mobile telecommunications, it is now possible in many countries to switch between two different network operators between calls. Many operators sell cards that can be inserted into the telephone. These cards are 'loaded' with a certain amount of calling time. By changing cards, it is possible to change to another supplier within minutes and, by selecting codes on the telephone, a certain service provider can be selected to connect the call.

The same situation is being realised in the electricity industry. In most countries, it has, until now, been completely impossible to change suppliers, but deregulation of the market is making it possible in many countries to change suppliers in the same manner as in the telecom industry.

In the banking sector, lead times for the transfer of money from an account with one bank to an account with another could be brought close to zero. This would take away the 'float', which is still an important source of income for banks and still makes banks want to keep these lead times. As new entrants in the market appear, established banks will be forced to take away such obstacles that mean unnecessary costs for customers.

In many industries that deal with physical products, it will be as easy and inexpensive as in the above-mentioned examples to change suppliers. The present trend towards a closer and closer relationship between supplier and customer is based on the fact that there still are inefficiencies in communication and information-handling, which incur transaction costs each time a company wants to change suppliers. These transaction costs will diminish as information becomes more readily available and companies learn to play by the new rules. Furthermore, companies that are quick at adopting a new way of working in this respect will be able to gain an advantage in the race for survival in their industries.

The reduction of 'churn rates' (the annual turnover of the customer base) is at the top of the agenda for many companies, owing to the high costs of recruiting new customers. In the long run, companies cannot rely on obstacles in the form of inefficiencies to keep customers. They must find new ways of building customer loyalty, true customer loyalty that is not based on the fact that it takes too much effort to move to another supplier.

The forerunners in this area are companies that use the network market to offer their products and attract customers. These companies show their offerings directly on the network and let customers see all the details, test different alternatives and sometimes even try products. For the customers, this is a positive development that gives them the opportunity to make the best possible decisions before buying. However, for the companies it is a dangerous activity. They may have to disclose information that has been a company secret in the past. Competitors, just as easily as the customers, can look at what is offered at what prices, and then change their own offers. Some forerunners have already experienced this threat, and some have even decided to withdraw services from the network to avoid showing too much to their competitors.

A smallish Swedish insurance company published its complete insurance offering, including tools to calculate prices, on the Internet. After it had done this, it realised that its competitors could easily get full information about the competitive position of the company and compare its own pricing of different services for each offering. When the company realised this, it quickly withdrew this new way of serving customers from its Internet site, even though it understood that the new way of communicating would attract new customers.

So, what does this mean? Was this company travelling down the wrong road when it entered the Internet? Would the best thing be to go back and reintroduce the obstacles to get information in order to hide secrets from competitors? Probably not. What is usually forgotten is that this is a new market rather than just the old market on a new medium. Customer loyalty will be built differently, and it will no longer matter whether competitors know all the details because a company that just watches what others are doing cannot become a winner. In this medium, a market or a market niche is *created* by successful companies; it is not something that can be copied.

In many markets, the reduction in customer loyalty has become a major issue. One example is the market for mobile telecommunications in Great Britain, where the churn rate has reached 32 per cent for some companies. The biggest threat is that churn rates have increased quickly, while the cost of getting new customers has risen instead of gone down. This is because many companies are still convinced that customer loyalty is necessary. Thus they try to force customers into long-term contracts. In many industries, this costs substantial sums because customers are starting to know their value and want something in return for their loyalty.

In many industries, most companies offer customers different types of loyalty programme or bonus system to make them stay. Operators of networks for mobile telephony use telephones as give-aways when new contracts are signed. Gasoline companies in many countries offer gifts to loyal customers, and airlines offer free trips in return for secure business.

Even if the basic characteristics of the market is that customers are continuously scanning various opportunities to find the best possible alternative, there are still benefits in the building of long-term relationships with customers.

■ It is possible to get to know the customers' needs better by having a long relationship rather than just a single purchasing occasion. However, as electronic agents can monitor customer behaviour, the same data may be available to all competitors who want to look for it.

■ It is possible to know exactly when the customer is starting to look for a product again (for example, replacing the car, finding a new flat or searching for a complementary product or service). This advantage may soon disappear for the same reason as above.

Today, it is extremely costly to acquire a new customer. Competition has led to the need to put a lot of money into advertising and into various campaigns to tie up customers in long-term contracts. This makes it very expensive and takes a lot of effort. A common figure for companies that deal with customer contracts is that it costs 5–6 times more to get a new customer than to keep an existing one. Therefore, many companies have started to invest more money in customer support and customer care.

The response from customers to this development is, of course, to use every opportunity to increase competition between suppliers. One way of doing this is to switch suppliers as often as possible. In order for this to be done in an efficient manner, customers, especially professional customers, need to identify all possible suppliers for a certain product or service.

The technology of 'intelligent agents', presented in Chapter 4, can be used for this purpose. A purchaser can send out such agents all over the Internet, these being programmed to scan the network for new suppliers of a product. When such a supplier enters the Internet with new product information, the agent returns to the sender and 'reports' the finding on the sender's computer screen. An agent replicates itself automatically, so all parts of the Internet can be scanned.

In many industries, the best way to build up a longer-term relationship with the customer is to have some kind of after-sales support that creates additional value to the customer. This support can be built in various ways:

■ providing help, tips and information about services or products that have already been sold;
■ actively helping customers to get the most out of the purchase (to make sure maintenance is carried out regularly, to administer the product to keep life-cycle costs down or to add facilities that help in the management of the product or service);
■ to make sure that the customer always has the latest versions and knows which other complementary products are offered (automatic updates).

Despite all efforts to increase customer loyalty, it may in the long run be very difficult to stop customers frequently changing suppliers as long as different alternatives vary to a large extent in terms of quality, service level or price. It is, however, possible to forecast a future situation in which customer loyalty would be much more secure than today, without loyalty programmes. In the section below on the increasing stability of the Internet market, it will be shown that it is possible that many companies, in a later phase of Internet competition, will offer similar services at the same price levels. In such a market, there may not be room for any costly bonuses or loyalty programmes, but customers may nevertheless be loyal because the advantages of changing between two suppliers with similar offers in terms of quality and price will be limited.

Companies will want to move backwards in the value chain

Even if we say that the concept of the value chain will be replaced by the concept of need chains, there will be companies that will want to cling to the value chain concept for as long as they can. This should, among other things, be true for large companies that are dominating their industries. They maintain their competitive positions largely on the basis of creating value through administering the value chain from which they make a profit.

In order to explain what we mean, we could think of a major car-maker. In the beginning of the mass-marketing of cars, the producers manufactured both the car and a large share of the parts themselves. Over time, the major car-makers have increasingly begun to concentrate on four roles in the value chain of car manufacture:

- assembly
- design
- marketing
- administration of the value chain.

While the first three roles are rather simple to understand, the fourth may need some explanation. It is up to the leader in any value chain to manage the value chain by setting the requirements on the other companies, and often also to provide the tools that the different companies in the chain need in order to maintain the standards of profitability, development and quality, and to improve these standards all the time. In the value chain of car manufacturing, this role has included the implementation of such tools as just-in-time delivery, ISO9000 quality control and other similar tools, and has also provided tools that improve the financial follow-up of all the companies in the value chain. During the early 1990s, some car manufacturers, such as Volkswagen, even started to exit the assembly role, Volkswagen having outsourced some of its assembly plants to subcontractors.

Throughout the book, we argue that the increase of electronic trade will mean that we will need less administration of relationships both between companies and within companies, and that the large-scale advantages in marketing and the building of brands will also decrease. This means that it will become more and more difficult for companies to make a profit from the roles of the marketers and administrators of a value chain. This also means that companies wanting to return a profit to their owners will have to become more competitive in their remaining roles, namely assembly and design, and may want to take back some of the tasks of parts production that they have given away to suppliers. This may be one of the challenges that these companies will face in the coming few years. The ones that do not manage the transition may go out of business.

Companies will have to rethink investment strategies

Most industries will be affected by the developments described in this book. In some cases, this will mean that whole industries that today have worldwide turnovers of billions of pounds will disappear. Thus many assets in the form of shares in industries that have historically shown stable developments may prove to become valueless in just a few years' time.

Companies that have finance and investment as an important part of their business will therefore have to re-evaluate their whole investment or business portfolios. The problem for companies heavily invested in industries that will suffer under this development is that potential buyers will do the same type of analysis, and it will become difficult to sell off such assets at a reasonable price.

Examples of companies that need to evaluate their portfolios are:

- investment companies needing to evaluate their share portfolios;
- banks needing to reconsider their loan structure and their investments in real estate;
- insurance companies needing to analyse their total investment portfolios;
- real estate companies needing to evaluate the future of different locations and different cities (see Chapter 12);
- corporations and conglomerates needing to think through their structures of production units, sales companies and overheads.

...but over time, the Internet market will be more stable than the present market

We have focused on describing the transition phase from the present type of market to the Internet market. From a historical point of view, we can see that such transitions have caused upheaval and instability. One example can be found in the transition from the agrarian society to the industrial society, many people having to move from the countryside into the cities because that was where new jobs were created. Farmers were facing increasing difficulties and had to invest in motorised equipment, which meant that they needed less human labour in their production at the same time as more people were needed in the industries. We might expect a similar situation to arise during the transition described here, except that this development will be much more rapid than the previous transition from farm to factory. The increased speed here will mean that society will come under much greater strain than ever before.

We will, however, see a new situation when we have been through the transition period. When the major part of the cost savings and the opportunities to make large profits by improving customer service have been realised, it will be much more difficult than it is today to earn money through innovation. Over time, we will reach a situation in which many industries produce a large amount of all goods and services at a cost that is close to zero, as was discussed at the end of Chapter 3. As more and more functions are taken over by IT and as these solutions mature, it will be very difficult for people to find innovations that will be interesting either from a cost perspective or from the perspective of customer service.

Existing solution providers will instead be able to run their solutions for users who connect to the Internet or sell their solutions to users or companies, but there will be little room for new entrants to receive a pay-back on the cost of developing new solutions. This could also mean that a number of natural monopolies or oligopolies will arise that cannot be challenged from the point of view of efficiency. Instead, companies may be able to increase their charging in their market as the opportunity for new competitors to enter virtually disappears.

A typical example of a new market that has arrived on the Internet, become the focus of early conquerors and then very quickly become stable is the web-browser market. Mosaic and Netscape were established very quickly, and Microsoft rapidly managed to settle as one of the leaders after them. At the moment, there seems to be no room for other competitors, and the market has become rather stable (although it is, of course, still a very competitive one for the players).

In most industries, we could expect another situation in which a number of companies could offer their services at a price level established by 'the invisible hand' of the market. In many cases, this stable situation could mean that markets are local or regional to a much greater extent than they are today, because when companies have used up all the opportunities of increasing competitiveness by becoming more efficient in production, physical closeness to the market will become a competitive advantage of increasing importance. During the transition phase, companies could thus use their overall efficiency in order to establish a global market, but when this first phase was over, the remaining competitors would be able to become more competitive locally if they focused on taking advantage of differences in transportation costs. In a situation where a large number of players use similar concepts in terms of cost and quality, it may be very difficult for many companies to compete outside their local market.

What may shake the stability is the opportunity for companies to adapt to trends in society and start to focus on providing products and services that are geared towards preferences such as environmental friendliness or care of animals. We may end up in a very stable market situation, in which only new types of customer preference or radical innovations could take us outside the competitive dimensions of price, service level, customer orientation and low distribution costs. This, however, is not a topic for this book.

10 Challenges for Governments

The changes we have discussed so far may seem only to affect companies, but the consequences will not stop there. We will see a number of rapid changes that have to be considered by states and governments if they want to avoid ending up with two types of society, one physical in which the government has a substantial influence, and one virtual, in which other rules apply, that is, the Internet and its players.

In this new scenario, the strains on the state and the limits of what any state can accomplish will be higher than ever before. It is even possible that the whole concept of a state will be challenged and that states will have to give up several of the functions they have fulfilled historically; and it may be difficult to find new legal entities that could fill this gap in the near future.

We have been used to a situation in which the borders of a state were clearly defined and any state aspired to control all transactions that crossed these borders. If goods, services and even information crossed a border, a state could decide whether or not to levy a tax or customs tariff on that type of transaction. It is already obvious that this is no longer possible to the same degree. States have also, to a large extent purposefully, given up their right to control cross-border transactions and have deregulated trade on the assumption that the wealth of any state increases as trade with foreign countries increases. Even the flow of capital, which has historically been regulated, has, over the past 10–15 years, been deregulated in many countries. We can also say that information can already flow freely between countries, even before the deregulation of the financial flows, but there has been great difficulty in retrieving all the relevant information on almost any subject. This free flow of information has never been very important owing to the high cost of collecting information. For several reasons, it has always been more difficult to find information in other countries.

In the future, the transparent society will become a reality on a global scale. This will mean that all the information that is available in one country will be so in all other countries. Thus there will be no geographical borders to the production or retrieval of information. It also follows that it will be possible to locate any services pertaining to the production or retrieval of information anywhere on the globe. The same will be true for all productions of goods in which communication between producer and customer can be carried out using the new information and communications technologies described above. Since the benefits for any company that manages to handle communication over large distances, with partners in countries where costs are low, will be immense, efforts to move the production of both services and goods could gain a momentum that few of us expect today. It could be expected that new capacity in low-cost countries could be created very rapidly and that equipment in many industries would be moved or sold to developing countries. This could mean that large numbers of people in developed countries would be unemployed and that, because of the rapidity of the change, it would be very difficult for companies and governments to create new meaningful jobs for these people at the rate at which jobs were being lost.

Governments have to renew legislation

Laws and rules in society are developed over a long period of time to regulate all the possible situations that may arise. Everything is regulated to make markets work as people in a country would like them to, to avoid information that is not accepted by people in common being spread and to determine what is a crime and what is not. Laws have always been national. The ongoing globalisation with an increasingly borderless society has, as a result, already changed this situation to some extent, but the real challenges to the basic system of legislation are yet to be seen.

The step into the transparent society will change this picture considerably. Information can already flow freely between people and companies in different parts of the world, with no, or very small, influences from laws, regulations and tax policies. The reactions from politicians today are often that the laws are all right but that the possibilities for the police to search for suspects and get insight into what is happening on the Internet is, and will be, difficult; that, however, is not correct.

What we have presented in this book points in another direction, namely that it will be much easier in the future to scan the market to find out what is happening. The police can continuously search for transactions that are illegal, just as ordinary people and companies can research anything they want.

One technology that will be of interest to the police is intelligent agent technology, which could decrease the cost of investigating Internet criminality. However, it would in many cases be difficult to prosecute, because of insufficient legislation. This problem is much bigger than it may seem. It is extremely difficult to envision all possible alternatives and situations that may arise. Even if it were possible, the whole process of changing the legislation would take too long compared with the speed of development in this market.

The Internet is a global market with no borders, at least not in the geographical dimension, and this is the root of the problem. Countries are defined by geography, and laws are valid only inside the borders of a country. The only thing on the Internet that is related to geography is the place where a server with a certain piece of information is located, so that has been the target for legislators. Internet services that offer illegal information, pictures or services are banned if they are produced within one specific country. If they are offered from another country, it is more or less impossible to stop them. Thus if a service is found that offers, for example, betting services, it can be illegal in one country and stopped but can move to another country overnight and become legal. Customers all over the world will not even notice the move.

The company www.bet4abetterworld.com offers three different betting alternatives for Internet users. This company, which has its office in Gibraltar, has some 65,000 members worldwide, most of them in the United States.

The founder of the company first applied for a licence to run the company from Sweden, but the Swedish authorities are hesitant to allow Internet gambling. Now the company offers members the chance to win $1m every 30 minutes in one of its games, and there is no possibility of Swedish authorities stopping Swedes using the services.

Many governments try to fight this type of activity by discussing how international laws can force all countries to introduce laws that are adapted to this new environment. Even if they succeed in this in the coming years, the development will make them obsolete. The kind of market that we have discussed in this book will not be easy to control through traditional laws. The introduction of network intelligence has a basic feature that will make legislation extremely difficult: services will be built by several pieces of information, different pieces potentially being held by a number of different computers in all parts of the world. If the end result – the service offered to the end customer – is illegal, it may still be built by pieces that, individually, are legal.

If we go back to the betting example once more, we can envisage a situation in which a number of football matches are listed on one server, the odds for each match being held by another server in another country, and the terms of betting and other types of information by yet another server. The person who would like to place bets on a couple of matches sees a perfectly normal view on his screen and will have no idea that the information comprising it is distributed between a number of countries. In this case, the gambler may be a criminal if he or she is in a country where betting is illegal, but the company offering the service may be immune from prosecution in any country.

Now we start to see one of the reasons why legislators need to address the problem of the electronic market more seriously and think along new lines to become as advanced as the players in this new market. In other words, even legislation must go through a concept transformation to be valid in the new valuescape.

One other issue that governments will have to handle is the problem of different types of 'Internet warfare'. The opportunities to communicate have developed at a speed much higher than that of improvements in the security of computer systems and of single transactions. This has opened the field for individuals and organisations that want to commit crimes with the help of the Internet or that simply want to create problems for nations, governments, companies or individuals.

One example of such efforts is the problem of computer viruses, but these are only the tip of the iceberg. There have also been occasions when 'hackers' have entered homepages of various organisations.

Even the CIA has encountered this kind of problem: hackers changed the title of its homepage from 'Central Intelligence Agency' to 'Central Stupidity Agency'!

This type of activity creates challenges for companies as well as for governments since they will have to guard against actions like these, which may in the future be more destructive than the one mentioned above, but governments will also have to learn more about this development in order to legislate against it. This is a vast topic in itself and cannot be covered in this book.

Governments have to find new ways of keeping trade in balance

Overall, governments in high-cost countries will face an enormous challenge in terms of how to maintain the living standards in their countries as it becomes obvious that even their high-value production is threatened by decreasing demand for competence and an international surplus of competent personnel.

The problem facing governments is that they at present lack the means of coping with such a problem. Through gradual deregulation and internationalisation of trade, they have, over the past half a century, dismantled barriers to trade, and it will be very difficult to invent new types of barrier that will work well in a labour market based on electronic communication.

If the labour market, even for services that require high competence, moves towards a situation of permanent surplus of supply, and if the traditional means for artificially regulating wages and salaries becomes ineffective, the pressure on all wages and salaries may lead to a situation in which the market sets the wages. This means that the wages for all types of job, regardless of the competence required, could move towards subsistence level as they would be defined by people in countries where costs are low. This means that, if this prediction comes true, wages will be much less differentiated in the future, both within and between countries and professions.

> Labor, like all other things which are purchased and sold, and which may be increased or diminished in quantity, has its natural and its market price. The natural price of labor is that price which is necessary to enable the laborers, one with another, to subsist and to perpetuate their race, without either increase or diminution. (Ricardo, 1996)

Governments may have to find new ways of making productive use of human resources

We must remember that the development described here is not a sign of diminishing wealth in the system as a whole, but only leads to wealth being redistributed between and within countries. Even if high-cost countries manage to keep a sufficient share of the world's production of goods and services, their governments will face an internal surplus of labour. If this is the case, it is possible for work to be divided equally between the people within a country, by the invisible hand of the market. All those who want to offer their time in the labour market will be able to do so at the wage rate set by market forces. If our vision of the future comes true, there may be work for each person for fewer than 4 hours a day, and this could allow for a larger amount of goods and services to be produced than at present.

Unemployment has historically been a problem because it has usually meant that the production of society as a whole has decreased as people have been forced out of work. In a situation in which the same amount of goods and services can be produced with the use of fewer resources, the freed resources will represent an asset.

This may call for a whole new view of the concept of work. Will there be those who still want to work full days even though they will have to offer their final hours at very low wages simply to reach that amount of work? Will there be people who would rather give up their 3–4 hours of work to these people, assuming that it is better for society as a whole if those who really want to work are allowed to do so, and people who do not have the same urge to work in the traditional sense are allowed to do other things? Will it be uneconomical to educate people for some types of task simply to let them work for a few hours each day? Will it not be more efficient to require more work from people who are given an education than from those that remain less educated? Will work that has to be performed away from home be seen as less attractive than work that can be performed at (or near) home?

There could be any number of questions of this type, and most of them do not have to be answered now. We can already see, however, that the number of unemployed is increasing in the Western world. Politicians in many countries still think that it is a realistic goal to reach full employment and that work can be looked at through the same paradigm as before. We should, however, take the following arguments into account:

- If we want to keep 35–40 hours of work per week as the norm, new meaningful jobs have to be created at a higher rate than at which present jobs are wiped away.
- Reduction of the hours of work by law is effective only as long as the main part of the workforce is not self-employed. As more and more people start to work as independent specialists, charging by the hour or by the amount of services delivered, the labour market starts to work more as a 'real' market, in which prices are set relative to the

relationship between supply and demand. In this market, suppliers of labour can supply as much of their time as they like.

In the situation described above, it becomes much more difficult to regulate labour markets than it has been historically, and it may be necessary to change the concept of work to a new one very different from the one that we have today. Even if the market only requires people to work for a few hours each day, it may be in the best interests of society to make use of more time for common purposes. Ideally, this would be regulated by the initiatives of people themselves, who see the value of contributing more to society for the common good.

In this respect, we could go on to the next chapter where we discuss challenges for individuals. There are already signs that individuals with an interest in doing various types of work in the field of information production in their spare time publish it on the Internet.

Governments will have to take measures to increase the stability of financial markets

As mentioned earlier, many industries may disappear altogether as an effect of the developments described in this book. This means that the financial markets may suffer great damage as companies go out of business. Since many of the pillars of our economic system, such as banks, insurance companies, investment companies and corporations and conglomerates, have made it their main business to finance all types of business, using the assumption that the basic rules of our economic game will remain the same in the foreseeable future, many of our most important economic institutions will take severe blows if it becomes obvious that these changes are under way.

Examples of institutions that are threatened are stock markets, financial markets and institutions tightly linked to these markets. One important aspect of this that governments have to keep in mind is that national finances are intimately linked to the well-being of these markets. Such national systems as various parts of the tax system, the system of national bonds and many national pension schemes are dependent on them. If financial markets break down, without the likelihood of a fast recovery, and if, at the same time, unemployment substantially increases and other problematic developments make the situation worse, it is very difficult to foresee what will happen.

11

Challenges for Individuals

I ndividuals will face a threefold challenge. First, we will have to learn how to work in new ways; second, we will have to learn new ways to live our lives; and third, these changes will force us to develop new ways of thinking about many ordinary situations in our daily lives.

Individuals will learn to work in new ways

In the near future, unemployment may be created at a rate higher than before. Large numbers of people may become unemployed for no other reason than bad luck, that they happened to work in the wrong industry or in the wrong position within their company. Overwhelming unemployment figures will make it clear that most of the unemployed will never find a full-time position again, assuming that a full-time position means 35–40 hours of work per week.

For many people, it will come down to learning how to compete in a new type of labour market, where self-employed people in all walks of life will find work in the same way as consultants do today by working part of their time for each of a number of employers. In this new market, if it is allowed to develop without regulations, it is likely that we will face a higher degree of specialisation or specialisation in new dimensions, as seen in the earlier discussion about network intelligence (Chapter 5).

It is difficult to envision at this stage of development exactly how the present workforce should act in order to be employable in the new market. We could, however, give a few hints:

■ We can already see that everybody will need an understanding of IT, since computers or other types of advanced electronics are used in almost every job. We also find, however, that applications and hardware become more user-friendly all the time. Both these trends will continue as the use of the Internet becomes more widespread. All kinds of transaction and communication, many of which were carried out over the telephone a few years ago, will be carried out over a computer network, but it will become so easy to do many of the tasks that everybody with some experience of computers will be able to carry them out. Thus it is advisable for everybody to try to acquire a basic knowledge and experience of the Internet and of basic programs for word processing and calculus.

- Everybody will need to be able to describe their field of experience so that they can market their services on the Internet and other electronic media. Many of the tasks of a secretary will have to be performed in the future, and it is possible that the division of labour caused by the growth of network intelligence will increase the demand for some of these services over again. Yet there may be few 'secretaries' as we know them today.

- One way to develop new areas of competence and make new contacts may be to jump on the bandwagon and use some free time to collect, structure and publish information on some subject on the Internet. There is a growing tendency for people to write about their favourite subjects on a homepage and thus compete with established commercial information sources. This could have two different effects. The first is that they may find other people with related interests, or even customers to whom they could sell their services. They could use these new contacts in order to earn money as consultants, self-employed specialists or freelance writers. The other result is that this alternative information 'business' grows, and it becomes more and more difficult to earn money producing the same type of material for magazines and newspapers, or even producing it as a consultant for a company. This would, in itself, be likely to improve the situation of the unemployed, since the more quickly it becomes obvious that unemployment figures are increasing, the more rapidly governments will have to take action in order to find new ways of organising society, in the widest possible sense. This could be a way for those who are unemployed, or are about to become unemployed, to take work away from the traditional labour market and force action to be taken.

Hunting and fishing, the most important employments of mankind in the rude state of society, became in its advanced state their most agreeable amusements, and they pursue for pleasure what they once followed from necessity. In the advanced state of society, therefore, they are all very poor people who follow a trade that other people pursue as a pastime. (Adam Smith, 1997)

■ Start a small business in a field where work will have to be done in the future as well as today. Alternatively, start one in an area in which companies are likely to become extinct, with the ambition of moving into a more stable industry before this actually happens.

■ Prepare a functioning work environment at home and save some money to be able to make necessary investments in technology when that is needed. It may, however, be advisable not to spend unnecessarily large amounts of money on technology before it is needed, since development is extremely rapid and it may be both much less expensive and safer in a few years' time, because technology that is bought today may not be needed in the near future. One example of this is whether or not we will need PCs of our own with substantial memory capacity. In the future, both programs and documents may be located on a computer network, into which we will plug a work station with limited memory capacity. In this case, it may become possible to get the same amount of computing capacity at a substantially lower cost than today.

Think of a taxi network in a city. At any one time, there are a limited number of people who want to be driven somewhere. Over time, all taxis get almost the same amount of income per hour, provided that they use the same method of getting customers. It is possible for a driver to earn more money by working more hours, but only up to a point. If all those who owned a car could use it as a taxi in their free time, it would soon be impossible to make a living from driving a taxi since there would be so many taxis but only the same limited number of customers. This type of surplus may soon be the situation in most markets where goods or services are provided.

The conclusion of this is that selling our labour in a labour market functioning according to the rules of a market economy will not only change our working conditions, but also have an impact on how we live. In a functioning labour market, we will have to work in such a way that we can make a contribution to a product or a service when our contribution is needed. It is not clear to us how this exactly will work in practice, but work and free time are likely to become more intertwined than they are today. This may mean that we can spend whole days without doing any work at all, then getting a call on the mobile telephone telling us that there is a message on the Internet. If we then still use only the number of working hours to determine the size of our income, we may have to rush from the golf course in order to be able to offer our services as quickly as possible. If, on the other hand, we have developed a more flexible way of distributing society's wealth, we might only check whether the same message had been sent to other people with similar qualifications at the same time and leave it for someone else to handle, allowing us to finish our round of golf.

We tend to think that the future, with all the electronic enablers that will make it possible for us to work anywhere we like, will increase our freedom, but if we have to work in a traditional labour market, the truth may be that we will have to 'sit waiting in our taxi' all the time in order to be there when a piece of work comes our way. We may, on the other hand, look upon this as a challenge making it possible for development to go in the direction that we want so that we will become free to use all kinds of electronic devices to allow us to live where we like and work when we like.

Individuals will have to accept more freedom and more responsibility

Today, we are to a large extent forced to live under the conditions that are dictated to us by local, regional and national cultural norms. Even if we have come a long way along the path of internationalisation, we still have to function in our local environment.

In the future, each person will be able to choose whether he wants to belong mainly to the local society where he happens to be located geographically, or to a 'virtual society' of people who share the same values, as described by the term 'valuescape'. In the same way as the valuescape helps us to tailor the marketplace to meet our needs and make shopping easier, it can also have the same meaning in social life. By defining closeness in terms of interest and values, it will become possible to create a virtual neighbourhood where 'friends' are near and people with different interests are far away. The Internet will be a place where we can chat and exchange the ideas and information we value.

This means that, regardless of where we live, our main interaction with other people could be either locally, by meeting people in person as we do now, or electronically, meaning that we interact with people over the Internet. Via this medium, it will be possible to select the people to interact with, based on any criteria. If we want, we can choose people with the same or complementary interests, or of a certain age, sex or political or religious background.

The opportunity to choose our friends from all over the globe and to be able to choose to have a very narrow span of views and interests among our friends could have a number of implications for society's development. We could look upon it as a challenge for ourselves as individuals to take advantage of these opportunities and to arrive at a sound mix of personal and electronic friendships. From the perspective of society, it may be one of the great challenges to ensure a development of a pluralist society in which different groups still talk to each other and solve problems in consensus instead of having different groups with different opinions that fight each other. The fear that the development described in this book could lead to a more hostile climate in society may seem a little far fetched. Let us hope that most individuals will use their increasing free time to develop their understanding of other people and their views instead of narrowing their range of interests so that personal communication between people becomes more difficult.

All in all, the new society will mean not only more freedom, but also greater responsibility for all individuals. Since we will be able to use the transparent society to see what we want to see in society, we will have access to information about any aspect of life. This information will make it possible for us to act more responsibly than we could ever hope to do today. On the other hand, we may find it so difficult to make up our minds on what is right and what is wrong in everything we do that many people will simply stop bothering to look for the relevant information on many complicated subjects. Regardless of how well structured our information may be, information overload may still make many of us passive and without knowledge and opinions on many issues.

The Industry Perspective – Examples of Primary Effects

12

Changes will affect companies in different trades in different ways and in different time perspectives. In some industries, we will find that the effects of new technologies are of a 'primary' nature, meaning that new technologies will have a major impact on how work is organised within these industries. In other industries, the effects will mainly emanate from technological development in other industries and from society as a whole. These effects we call 'secondary'.

> So, when someone within your organization starts messing with their paradigm and says, 'Don't worry, it's got nothing to do with you,' start worrying. It is never just one paradigm that is changed. (Barker, 1993)

Telecommunications companies

The case of modest technological diffusion

If the trend towards transparency is proceeding more slowly than we expect, the telecom market will still be relatively local. Only international corporations will use the opportunities of the global market to buy products and services where they get the most suitable service at the most competitive price. Telecom service providers have already entered other markets with their services, but they still act locally in the markets they enter. They build local organisations and adapt to local rules and business conditions. Customers are not able fully to use the benefits of always choosing the best and least expensive service independent of the geographical location of the company.

Service providers will move up the value chain in the industry and try to add as much value as possible. Telecom companies will enter other markets and start to become providers of information, entertainment and computing services. Competition in these niches may be weak if the lack of transparency of the market makes it impossible to buy services and capacity in an international market. In this case of modest technological diffusion, telecom companies are still doing business as usual. They may only to some extent offer services with a broader scope through the use of new solutions.

Effects of the transparent market

Telecommunications operators, or service providers as they are now called, are in the midst of a dramatic change as a result of increasing competition. Deregulation started several years ago in many markets, and many operators have gone through change programmes in which the goals have been to reduce staff, develop new services and take better care of customers. Telecommunications is an industry in which the new electronic marketplace is very real. The whole industry is focused on providing technologies that facilitate communication between people and provide the basis for electronic business.

The fact that they are, and always have been, very close to this development has led to an interest in taking a more active part in this rather than just providing the 'basic transportation of bits and bytes'. One way of describing their role is that they provide the 'roads' in the networked marketplace. Many players in this market have a long tradition of providing this basic service and have great difficulty in moving up the value chain and starting to add more value. A highly relevant question in these old organisations is, of course, whether they should move at all or whether they should stay as competitive providers of network services. It is, however, likely that this niche will be squeezed from different angles and that there will be very thin margins in this market in the future.

Considering what will happen when transparency increases, it is also highly likely that profits will decrease and that operators who stay as pure transport providers will experience problems. Today, most of these companies, both old established ones and newcomers with alternative networks (cellular networks, networks formerly owned by large companies and organisations, or infrastructure owners from other utility industries such as electricity who want to use their networks for tele-communications) realise that they cannot keep prices up in those parts of the market where competition has been low but is increasing (for example, international and long-distance services). The reasons behind this are:

- New players in the market try to target high-margin niches.
- Increasing transparency makes it easier for customers to get a total picture of the market and find the lowest price on each purchasing occasion.

The last reason is rather new in telecommunications but will very soon become a major threat. Today, it is very difficult to swap operators and choose the least expensive alternative in each situation. Most operators have tried to tie up customers for long periods of time (one to several years is common in the area of mobile services), which means that customers have to make a general assumption on which types of tariff and service best meet expected usage patterns. In the future, this will no longer be possible. Customers will see the opportunities open up in the transparent marketplace. They will start to buy capacity and services when they need them and always go for the best price. There are already indications in this direction. For example, there are whole-salers who buy capacity at a low price and sell it to customers on demand. There are also brokers who act as middlemen to find the best service to use at a given moment.

However, this is just a beginning. Real transparency will mean that customers themselves will be able to evaluate the entire market at any point in time. A customer can find the lowest price for a service without having to call several companies or read complicated price plans. When prices and services start to become available on the Internet, it will be easy to build services or applications that quickly scan the market at the time when a call is to be made or when data are to be transferred. When this becomes possible, price differences will be very hard to maintain if operators cannot deliver superior services, better quality or something else that can make customers pay a little extra.

The fact that Internet communication costs only the price of a local telephone call, regardless of whether we communicate internationally, is posing a threat to telecom service providers. Since we are able to communicate by voice over the Internet, it is already possible to use that alternative instead of making regular telephone calls. This will force down the prices of telephone calls to the level of Internet communication.

This could mean a serious shake-up in several national markets in which various types of monopolists have made it possible to charge a premium. Large operators with too many overheads might have to become even more efficient, and new lean organisations would have to stay efficient in order not to lose the battle for basic transportation services. These organisations have to look at new ways of doing business, such as using the benefits of network intelligence.

Effects of the use of network intelligence

Network intelligence will make many overhead costs and other hidden costs surface in large telecom organisations. This will start a new wave of head count reduction in this industry. The process is driven, as usual, by the new, small companies that target a particular niche and work together with partners to create a complete service offering. One way for telecommunications operators to survive increasing price pressure is to divide organisations into smaller units in order to be able to adapt more quickly to these changing market conditions. Smaller units imply more flexibility and faster decisions and adaptations, but this also means that organisations will become more difficult to manage and optimise from a traditional management perspective. Here the use of network intelligence will make it possible for companies to communicate dynamically in order to find the best solution in any given situation. This means that we will see more loosely connected groups of people within operator organisations that try to optimise their activities to meet overall goals. We can see the first signs of this development in most operators, but the real effects of network intelligence will come when these organisations forget strict organisational principles connected to the use of processes and start to let spontaneous organisations develop. Then we will see a split between market-orientated companies, service-orientated companies and network-orientated companies. Today's typical operator can be the mother of dozens, perhaps hundreds, of small units, each focusing on the particular goals it has selected. Communication will be handled spontaneously, but some simple rules and agreements will have to be developed in order to work together. This will lead to a number of very important changes within these organisations:

■ Far-reaching customisation will be possible because of smaller units with a narrower customer focus.
■ More efficiency is possible in the production of services (both end user service and network services) because of a narrower focus on a particular task or a particular domain.
■ There will be better customer service as a result of better information flow within organisations and a faster response in the network of loosely linked units that all strive to become better and more focused on their particular niches.
■ Increasing flexibility arises when new services and functions can be added without having to plan the restructuring of an organisation made up of large units with a built-in resistance to change.

These fragmented and specialised organisations will also become more open to external services and products. More intense internal communications form the foundation for more frequent external interactions. The border between external and internal personnel, information and other resources will also become blurred as a consequence of an increasing level of network intelligence.

Effects of the emerging valuescape

When we step into the new market environment we call the valuescape, a set of new challenges emerges in the telecom industry. In Chapter 6, we discussed how the market grew on the basis of customer needs and values. Closeness was defined in terms other than geography. For a telecom operator, this will mean substantial changes. Telecommunications will not be separated from other services, as has been the situation in the past. Instead, it will be an integrated part of other service offers, just as we showed when needs were linked to other needs in chains. When, for example, we want to get access to a piece of information from somewhere in the world, telecom will be there as a natural basis for communication. This does not mean that we see this as a separate aspect; it will simply become integrated with other services and products with which we come into contact.

For telecom operators, it is vital to start to address the issue of what the shift to the valuescape will mean and what the right strategy should be. These discussions are going on for most large operators already. The question is whether to stay in the low end of the value chain and continue to provide transportation services, or whether to move into the market for value-added services. Many companies have started this transformation by moving into the media business (for example, by providing marketing services) or by becoming Internet service providers. Some operators, for example the Swedish firm Telia, are even trying the Internet search engine business by operating the Swedish mirror site for Alta Vista (www.altavista.telia.com), and the marketplace provider business by providing Passagen (www.passagen.se), in which a number of companies offer their products and services.

The trend of combining telecom services with other types of service has been visible for a couple of years in the telecom industry. It is usually referred to as 'convergence', which points to the fact that media, telecom and computer services will become closely linked to each other, maybe going so far that we can no longer distinguish one industry from the other. Many articles have been written about this trend as something special for the industries involved, but seeing it from the perspective of the emerging valuescape, it is not a trend that is unique in these industries. Instead, it is something that will influence a large number of industries.

Examples of concept transformation

With the new market structure, the valuescape, in mind, it will be important for telecom operators to find out how they are going to move their current business concepts into the new environment. One example of concept transformation that can be seen already on the Internet is the possibility of calling an old friend after having found him or her on Infospace (www.infospace.com), the search site described earlier for people in the United States and Canada. Here, there is a button to push to make an automatic telephone call (if the equipment is right). By doing this, telecommunications are linked directly to another service from which a need for communication arises. At this site, it is already possible to see how communications can be linked directly to the location where the need arises, and that communications services can be linked in such a way that links become almost invisible to the user. The user can easily choose between making a telephone call or sending an Internet e-mail (these may be distributed through different infrastructures by different companies), and the system will manage all the manual tasks of finding the telephone number or e-mail address, dialling or addressing the message, and making the connection.

Consulting companies

The case of modest technological diffusion

At present, we look upon people with high education as 'the winners' in the labour market of the future. We assume that Western countries will lose many jobs that create low value to countries with lower costs of labour, and we also think that many of our low-value jobs will have to, to a large extent, be taken over by machines if we still are going to keep production in the developed countries.

Work that requires high competence will be more difficult to replace. Among the more advanced services that are produced in the West are many kinds of consulting service. The fact that these services require high competence means that companies in developed countries will be safe from competition from low-cost countries. The fact that consultants today always need to make regular visits to customers means that the market for consulting services will largely remain local. The most competent companies will be able to keep the prices of their services at a high level, and volumes will continue to increase in the foreseeable future.

This may be true, but it can be questioned. If it were true, the new means of communication and the opportunities to find all kinds of information about companies and their products over the Internet would mean only modest improvements in the efficiency of the consulting market. We might not expect the customers of consulting companies to have an interest in using all the possible opportunities to their own advantage, or we might think that it will be impossible to improve the buying position of customers for consulting services through the use of new technologies.

Effects of the transparent market

If we assume that the situation of even the most advanced consulting companies will change radically over the next few years, we have to focus on three arguments to support this position:

1. Customers will want to use the Internet to get an overview of the total supply of consulting capacity and the pricing of it in their field of interest at all given moments.
2. The increasing access to information about the whole supply of consulting services will decrease the total volume of business for consultants and increase the competition on price.
3. The present main customer base of consulting companies, namely large companies and corporations, will decrease in size.

If we look upon the present situation in many industries, it is difficult for most buyers to get a complete overview of the suppliers in a market. It is also difficult and costly to get information about the prices of all suppliers, since someone has to call each supplier and ask questions about capacity, quality, prices and a host of other matters in order to form a first opinion about them. After that, someone may also have to call other customers for references, look in industry catalogues or telephone a number of consultants in order to get enough information to decide whether or not to start negotiating.

This is the situation in many industries, but it is more obvious in the consulting sector, since it is probably more difficult in this industry than others to evaluate the quality of a service offering in advance as this is intimately related to the competence and experience of each consultant. There is also a further complicating factor in that it is very difficult to get hold of a consultant who has done a similar job before. Instead, most consulting projects are carried out almost from scratch each time, requiring the consultant to learn about each industry and the type of problem for the first time in each project.

This is, of course, not totally true, since all consultants build on their past experiences when they take on new projects, but it is very difficult for a customer each time a new project is about to start to find a consultant who has done almost the same before and to understand the competence of this consultant. Instead, the customer hires someone they know to be reliable and accepts the fact that this person may never have done anything similar.

In the future, all kinds of service may be marketed over the Internet. This may also be true for consulting services. If consulting companies choose to advertise their competence with lists of projects and detailed descriptions of them, it will be very easy for customers to find a number of consultants who have done a similar project before. It may also be possible rapidly to get information about the quality of the results since some companies may want to publish references from customers in order to boast about the quality of their work.

We think that the drawbacks of publishing competence, capacity and prices will be so obvious so that companies will refrain from doing it, since it will put customers in a much better position to choose the right supplier and negotiate a good contract with them. In order to avoid this, however, all companies would have to be able to withstand the pressure to do so. Once one company or a few companies published this information, others would have to follow suit in order to compete. This is because the advantages for customers of buying over the Internet will be so large that they will want to do it simply to force more suppliers to publish more and more detailed information about themselves on the Internet. This development may sound strange for people in large, established organisations, but think of it from the perspective of a small (one- or two-person company) that wants to break into the market. It certainly has nothing to lose from publishing details of its offers. A consultant, for example, may present a competence profile, current availability and prices per hour, which a large consulting company would never dream of doing today. However, from the customer's point of view, this will seem like a good idea: if enough people presented this information, customers could scan the market quickly and compare the price/competence of many consultants in a short period of time. This would threaten the established companies; some would then perhaps decide to reveal a little information, and the ball would start rolling.

The fact that many consultants might publish their prices per day or hour on the Internet will also mean that customers can estimate which consultant will be least expensive to hire. It may sometimes be less expensive to hire someone with more competence in an area at a somewhat higher price, since the time it will take for the experienced consultant with a high price per hour will be less than that for the less experienced one with a lower price per hour. It will also be in the customer's interest always to make sure that there is more than one consultant who can do a particular type of job in each market, since this will increase competition and keep prices down.

Another consequence of this development is that the consulting market will be larger from a geographical point of view. An American company may hire a European consultant to do a special project in an area where he or she has particular competence. At present, this would mean a lot of travel expenses, but in the near future, it may mean that interviews and other types of data collection will be done over the

Internet and that the consultant may only have to travel to the United States once, if at all, in order to present the final result.

This lack of geographical restriction will mean that competence from low-cost countries will also slowly take a share of developed markets. Starting at the lower-value end, people in these countries with good education will slowly develop more experience and become more and more competitive.

All in all, consulting companies in developed countries may experience the following development:

- price pressure from increased competition in the home market;
- decreasing volumes of consulting work as the reuse of results becomes more common;
- further price pressure as geographical limits diminish, the total market comprising all developed countries;
- even further price pressure as low-cost countries start to compete at the low end of the market;
- further decreasing volumes as the reuse of results becomes possible over the whole globe. Consultants in India can reuse their experiences when they work for a Norwegian company with the same type of problem.

Effects of the use of network intelligence

As we mentioned above, many of today's consulting projects are carried out more or less from scratch. This was probably truer 10 years ago than it is today, but compared with how the situation may look in the future, we may still find the expression 'from scratch' to be appropriate. In the near future, it may be possible to find whole documents for sale on the Internet with titles such as 'A Purchasing Strategy for a Midsize Grocery Wholesaler' or 'The Development of an Order System for a Concrete Producer'. Consultants who have done a project in a given area will be willing to sell the main results (with the names of client companies made anonymous) more than once in order to prove their competence and get new projects. If a consulting company thinks that it can sell such a document at a profit or entice new customers by publishing some results from earlier projects, without infringement of the rights of the customer, it may do so. Just as references are used today in order to sell new projects, so they will probably also be in the future.

If most projects today involve an 80–90 per cent production of new material, this share of new production may decline to 50 per cent or less if customers can always find the most experienced consultant in each field. When a consultant has achieved a couple of projects in one area, he may publish the main experiences from these projects in a document that can be sold to customers at a fixed price. This may be used in order to get more advanced projects in the future.

Network intelligence will lead to increasing specialisation in the consulting business. The general results will be much more difficult to use and sell, whereas it will be much eaier to do this with specialised material with a sound focus. A market based on network intelligence will build the necessary results on items from different sources and different people. To be able to do this efficiently, results in the market must be described in a way that facilitates mapping of the requirements to the contents and focus of consulting services or ready-made consulting material (presentations, reports or software).

> Within the international consulting company Cap Gemini, there is a large knowledge base that includes these types of material for people to reuse in various situations. This system is self-organised. People can offer their reports or presentations by downloading them to a web-server somewhere in the company. If the right key words are used in a certain document, a number of people will find the material and use it, and the author will be contacted often.
>
> Applications like this show how links can be formed in the organisation. All these links taken together create a network of intelligence within a company or in society as a whole. The real power of this way of working will be revealed when more and more people become good at picking up pieces here and there to form something that can be useful in a project or a particular presentation.

The types of skill that will make people successful in such a network of intelligence will be different from the factors that create success in our current organisations. People who can make use of large amounts of information in a short time, and make use of it in a given situation, will be successful. People who struggle with this and want to have time to learn and adapt to new situations will face problems.

This development also means challenges for consulting companies. The whole award system in most companies must be changed in order to make people want to provide material that they produce on the open network. There may be no way of tracing how and where results that have been put on the network have been used, but it is important for companies to create systems in which producers of information that is often reused are rewarded for this in proportion to the value that they create for the organisation as a whole.

This means that people must have the opportunity to create a good position in the company, both by producing new material and by using material that other people have produced. Many companies have noticed how difficult it is to get enough information on the internal networks. They do not reach a 'critical mass' because people have no interest in feeding them, since information is, and always has been, a basis of power in organisations.

The fact is that such problems are just as visible in the Internet market as a whole, when companies co-operate and compete in a common market where information is sold and bought. This is also likely to be remedied when systems are created that make it possible for information providers to charge users directly for use of the information that is supplied.

One other aspect of the development described here is that the growth of network intelligence is likely to decrease the average size of companies. In some industries, this development may be rapid, as spontaneously organised networks of smaller companies take market shares from present industry leaders. This means that the customer base of consulting companies, which to a large extent consists of large companies, will decrease in size. This decrease represents the third threat on the list above to the existing type of consulting companies.

Retail and wholesale

The case of modest technological diffusion

People will always want to do the major part of their shopping in shops. Shops will continue to be located together in city centres or outside city centres in malls, or so we tend to think will be the case in the future as well. This may be true. It is hard to predict how people will be able to change their buying habits, so we may assume that the increase in electronic shopping will only complement the traditional way of buying goods. Admittedly, we find that there are many advantages to buying things in shops compared with buying them from the type of mail order companies that we encounter today.

Most people would probably say that it is an advantage to be able to look at items before they make a decision to buy them. This goes for any purchase of goods that we seldom buy or on which we spend a lot of money.

How could we even envisage a world without shops? Where could we then go shopping? What would happen to city centres if neither the offices nor the shops needed to be located there? Surely, most people will also want to do their shopping in shops in the future.

Effects of the transparent market

Electronic channels between companies and their customers have been expanded to make it possible to shop in a new way, which will mean better service and lower prices for customers. The bandwidth is now broad enough to present products and services in the same attractive way as we can do in a shop or product catalogue. Through the use of new multimedia and communications technology, it is even possible to get better quality from electronic information than from direct contacts with products. These new technologies do not just provide information on offerings and show pictures and videos of products. They can go one step further and offer customers the opportunity to design their own products, try products and services before they decide what to buy and configure products to meet their specific needs.

The advantage of buying over the Internet is that every customer can have full information about all available alternatives and their prices. In order to get this full information today, we would have to travel over the whole world, visiting hundreds or thousands of shops, and collect all the mail order catalogues in the world that offered the type of product we needed. In the future, this information, sorted by any variable that we chose, would be available at the press of the Enter key.

Many companies today have taken a first and very simple step and moved the catalogue as it is on to the Internet. A proof that this is rather common is the catalogue site (www.catalogsite.com), where hundreds of catalogues can be found. Some of them offer simple on-line ordering facilities, whereas others just offer the possibility of ordering the printed catalogue. This puts too much focus on the catalogue itself and does not use any of the new opportunities offered on the Internet.

Furthermore, when we stand in the shop of our choice, we are in the hands of a shop assistant who is intent on selling us something. The shop assistant wants us to choose a product from his or her shop. Thus we can never really rely 100 per cent on the information we are given.

When we shop on the Internet, we will have access not only to all available information about all the possible choices, but also to all the tests that have been made by professionals throughout the world of the different products between which we may want to choose. In the choice of a stereo, for example, we could have access to test data from all the leading audio magazines in the world and also access to commentaries from various audiophiles who want to publish their opinions over the Internet.

> This situation is already becoming a reality. Anyone who visits the site www.carterhouse.com will find the homepage of a wine shop, where visitors can go from the price list to the tasting records of *The Wine Spectator* and then to maps and information about the American wineries represented in the assortment of wines in the shop. Over time, access in this way to information about the products will probably increase as competing firms find new ways of presenting more and more information. We may expect, in a few years, that such a shop would simply offer a direct link to the homepage of each winery and to the homepages of the magazines that had tasted each wine. This, however, would mean that customers might as well buy directly from the homepage of the winery instead, at a lower price. If customers choose the Internet as a preferred market for shopping, it will most probably mean the demise of the types of shop we know in the affected areas of business.

The future Internet customer will have access to an immensely large amount of information and will also be able to buy products at substantially lower prices, but what about the marketing aspect that we were discussing above?

The argument is as simple as this. In the extreme case, when most customers choose the Internet for their shopping, they will have access to all types of information that they need about product capabilities. It will simply be much more difficult to try to persuade customers to buy something for reasons other than rational ones. Marketing has its natural place in a society where information is scarce and where customers will never be able to get information about all the available alternatives. Companies with the money to run extensive advertising campaigns are able to persuade customers that their products are superior to competing offers regardless of any objective evidence to the contrary that may only be known by experts in each field. Shops will want to carry the brands that are most heavily advertised because more customers will ask for these.

On the Internet, all customers will be able to find the supplier with the products that have received the best ratings for quality, price or value in most of the tests, even if this product comes from the smallest of producers. Will this mean that buyers will refrain from reading advertisements and only take rational information into account? Time will tell. We may, however, assume that a large proportion of customers will have access to much better information than almost any customer has today.

Effects of the use of network intelligence

In all industries, the existence of shops as intermediaries between a producer and a final customer means an extra cost. The size of this cost depends on which type of product we are talking about. In the case of groceries, it may mean mark-ups of 20–25 per cent, and in the case of clothes ones of more than 100 per cent. This is because the turnover of stock in a clothing shop is much slower than that in a grocer's shop. In addition, a clothing shop will have to sell a part of each season's clothes on a sale at the end of the season, which means that they tie up a lot of capital in clothes on which they will never make a profit. The fact that customers want to do their shopping in shops actually means that the whole distribution system from producer to customer is filled with goods all the year through, which tie up capital.

If intermediaries in the form of shops could be bypassed in the future, it would mean large savings on price for the customers. However, it might not be only the mark-up of the shops and wholesalers that would be saved. Today, producers also pay large amounts of money for marketing in magazines, on television and in shops. If we assume that extreme changes will take place in the marketplace and that we should try to predict the most spectacular developments, we can propose that marketing campaigns in many product areas would have much less effect than they do today. This would lead to a substantial saving even in the price that shops today pay to producers.

In the case of the extreme diffusion of Internet technology, the structure that would emerge would be one in which producers marketed and took orders for their products. They might also take over informing customers about the products through their websites. The products would then be delivered by distribution companies carrying a wide range of goods from all kinds of producer. The role of these distribution companies would simply be to get the goods to the customer's doorsteps at the lowest possible cost.

In the case of frequently bought goods, such as groceries or standard clothes like underwear or everyday shirts, we could assume that there would be networks of national, regional and local distribution centres through which the goods would flow almost in the same way as today. The difference would be that future customers might not have to do the shopping themselves. Each distribution centre could have automatic systems for collecting the products for each order, and for packaging them for delivery. It may then be inexpensive to deliver the products once a day or on a couple of days every week since most people would be able to use this service, which would make the volumes delivered fairly large. It would also be possible to deliver goods to a local storage facility from where customers could collect them themselves.

Media companies

The case of modest technological diffusion

Many people are likely to think that, in spite of the development of new technology, we will always have our traditional newspapers and it will always be possible to finance television through commercials. Even if the Internet develops into a marketplace and an information source that we use more and more frequently, we will still want to pay for the service of having news and other readable items presented to us in the paper-based format.

Effects of the transparent market

The main purpose of the newspaper or a magazine, if we start with the written medium, is to work as an intermediary between the writer/ journalist and reader. In a newspaper, articles from a number of different sources are collected each day and printed and distributed to readers or subscribers. The content of each issue is the same for all readers, regardless of their educational level, profile of interests and age. The same is true for publications in other sectors of the media.

Music publishing companies, film distribution companies and television stations work only as intermediaries between the person who has produced the material and the listener or viewer.

The main arguments of a person wanting to suggest that the case of modest diffusion is too conservative would be that:

- The value that a newspaper or a magazine could add to a number of articles written by different writers may actually be seen as negative, with the Internet as the main alternative for distribution.

In order to support this argument, this person would have to be able to show that it is possible for any person with modest competence in the use of computers to get a better product each day by searching directly on the Internet than from a traditional newspaper.

The very nature of transparency in the marketplace makes information more easily accessible. This means that even news, articles of general interest and video clippings that have not been structured, edited and included in a certain newspaper, magazine or similar publication can be useful to people, just because it will be possible in future to search for and structure large volumes of information without having a large organisation such as a newspaper publishing company doing it for the reader.

Cost is a major driver in using the benefits of transparency. One very obvious reason is shown by a study that was made by one of us a couple of years ago. Only about one-third of the cost of a newspaper is incurred by the actual research and the writing of articles. The rest goes on administration, printing and distribution. All of these costs bring little or no value to the reader. If good search engines that could search for articles on the Internet were to be offered, many people would be tempted to choose these instead, simply for cost reasons. Today, readers only pay a fraction of the total cost of each issue (maybe one-third), the rest being paid by advertisers. However, if costs could be brought down to one-third, Internet service providers such as www.hotmail.com, from which users can access news, would be able to sell advertising to companies and offer their services free of charge for the user.

Second, we can already see that many topics are covered on the Internet by numbers of ordinary citizens, who publish their accounts of all kinds of subject on their homepages or in discussion groups on the Internet, without charging readers anything. If this tendency became more widespread, it is questionable whether professional journalists could add more value to this flow of information and charge for it when thousands of articles could be found and read at no cost. This would make the scope of the commercial newspaper more narrow than today.

> In the radio broadcasting market, transparency is already starting to become real and tangible. Most radio stations today, for example Real Audio, offer the opportunity to listen to programmes such as news, sports and the weather over the Internet through the use of plug-in software. For the local listener who can tune the radio into the same channels as found on the Internet, this may be a small change, but when we can start to listen to other radio stations from all over the world, it becomes more interesting. Why not select the radio station located where an event is happening rather than listening to a local station, where the correspondents may be thousands of miles from the real events? It would also be possible to hear more than one side of a story, directly from the people at the scene.

The transparent market may also have a major impact on our ability to finance newspapers and television through advertising. As we have already mentioned, the transparent market will make it possible for consumers to choose products using whichever criteria they find most suitable for them. If it turns out that consumers want to make their choices on the basis of criteria other than information from producers in the form of advertising, it will be very easy to set up Internet functions that make selections by the preferred criteria. This could mean that advertising will not have the same impact in the future as it has today. If that were the case, the advertising income for television stations would be radically diminished.

The difference between advertising on the television or radio and advertising on the Internet is that television advertising requires consumers to keep advertised brands in their minds until they enter a shop where they can buy the product that is advertised. Advertising on the Internet is connected to opportunities of immediate purchase, which makes Internet advertising more advantageous to suppliers than the present type of advertising.

It is probable that this will represent a serious disadvantage for television advertising, which may force television broadcasting into the Internet in order to make it possible to offer advertisers the same functionality as Internet-based advertising opportunities. This development can be seen in the trials around digital television, which will add interactivity to the television medium.

Effects of the use of network intelligence

Network intelligence will open up the field for a new type of actor in the media industry. It will lead to the creation of spontaneous networks of people and companies that come together to produce media products of various kinds. This will become an alternative to the established media companies with a planned creation of media. Individuals can also produce media products by combining sources on the Internet. The idea is to join forces and merge materials to produce something that is of interest to many people.

We could take an example to show what will happen. Assume that people with a common interest would like to make an electronic magazine with a certain focus, for example pop music from the 1970s. Various people and companies will meet in the valuescape, where distances between people with common interests are small. These people will each be able to contribute a small part, for example information about artists, music videos or reviews of interesting tracks. Each of these people will be able to build their particular part of this magazine depending on their background and interests. Companies will be able to offer material depending on their objectives. Some companies want to sell products such as music recordings and therefore want to sponsor and add commercial material to the electronic magazine, but the multimedia future will make it possible to include music recordings and films in the electronic format.

This type of input is similar to the input that we have today in an ordinary magazine. The difference lies in the way in which this will be organised. Nobody will have to plan and manage the work. Instead, it will evolve and change dynamically depending on the people who are involved and which competencies they have. This process can be compared with a workshop where people come together with the common goal of achieving a certain result. In the media industry, this type of phenomenon is known as an 'information workshop', in which media products are produced in a spontaneous way. In this type of situation, the border between the producer and the user of the material blurs, because a certain person may at one moment enjoy reading an article and in the next provide a new song for the same media product. The result develops as different people act as users and providers of information, and there may never be a 'final' product. The product may simply 'disappear' if nobody uses it or adds anything to it for a long period of time.

The same types of challenge will be true for the radio stations broadcasting news, as discussed above. When we can tune into the local station where something is taking place, why listen to another station thousands of miles away? And why should all the large news companies have local correspondents everywhere when it is possible to use network intelligence to put together a radio news programme with the assistance of people from other companies (and independent people) all over the world? One reason is, of course, language, but with better means of translation, this will be less of a problem in the future.

Effects of the emerging valuescape

By the 'personality aspect' of media marketing, we mean that each reader of a newspaper or magazine will have preferences different from those of most other readers. Today's newspapers have to choose a mean position in order to cater to the tastes of their whole readership. Nevertheless, we have to assume that each reader will want articles on some subjects but not others, and that someone will want detailed information on one topic but could do with the headings and first few lines of articles on others. This proliferation of tastes within the readership of each publication may be a problem for newspapers in the future if it turns out that one company will be able to offer a search engine for the Internet with which each person can specify the criteria around which they want their specific newspaper to be composed.

> In 1995, a colleague of one of the authors of this book had already managed to create a search engine that each day produced and printed a personal newspaper with a content similar to that of any commercial newspaper, albeit a little smaller, but filled with articles chosen with the help of criteria specified by this person himself. He did this in order to show that it was already possible. Commercial search engines for this type of application may soon be available. With more and more people having access to the Internet, it is possible that this type of Internet newspaper will become more and more common in the near future. If this is the case, how many people will then be willing to pay for another less personalised newspaper?

By the 'time aspect' of media marketing we mean that traditional newspapers publish a specific article on a particular issue, which appears on a particular day or in a particular week. This means that, however interesting the material may be, the reader may have thrown the paper away before it is actually needed. Many newspapers already publish their news on the Internet as well, and it may well be that back-issues are still available for many months. However, one can still wonder whether there will not soon be a company that could sell only the articles that one really would like to read and could also make them available when one actually needed them instead of when the news-paper wanted to publish them.

This argument could be relevant for all types of article of lasting value. One may primarily think of tests of different types of product, for example cars, but almost any article might be of interest to someone even years after it was first published.

The Industry Perspective – Examples of Secondary Effects

13

Infrastructure companies

The case of modest technological diffusion

Most analysts who look at the future development of travel predict a steady increase in the frequency of travel over at least the coming decade. Since vehicles are steadily improving in terms of speed and comfort, we can see how plans for new infrastructure investments are developed further year by year. New high-speed train connections are planned, the most advanced of which require completely new tracks for the trains to run smoothly and safely at high speed. In the same manner, new airline routes turn up all the time as regional airlines with smaller planes find that the frequency of travel between two regional centres is high enough for a route to become economically viable. In the car industry, we see how companies develop new types of car with lower emission rates that need less fuel.

All of these companies predict that travel will increase in the future and that this increase will come both from business travel and from tourism. These forecasts may not necessarily be wrong, but some of us already doubt that they represent the best guess on the future development of travel.

At the same time as we expand our infrastructure for the transportation of people, we can see how new opportunities arise that may start fierce competition between traditional business travel and new electronic means of meeting people, which may make a large part of our travel obsolete. In Chapter 4, we can see that it is already possible to have video meetings over the Internet. This means that it is possible to talk to people over the Internet in almost the same way as if they were sitting in the same room as ourselves. With the help of a small and inexpensive camera that can be placed on top of a PC, it is possible to meet electronically for small chats or longer meetings. It is also possible to have larger video meeting rooms for meetings in which more people are involved. This equipment is more expensive, but it is likely that it will become less so as more and more companies acquire it as a means of communication over long distances.

We can assume that the use of these means of communication will increase in the future. We can also look at other technical innovations that have made life easier for business people who want to increase their ability to communicate with customers and peers. The fax and the mobile telephone are the innovations in history that have been the quickest to be spread to a large part of the business community in the developed world. We may therefore assume that this will apply also to the new means of video communication. Since the use of the Internet for communication purposes is currently spreading to all parts of the world, the adoption of this new technology is even more rapid than in the two cases mentioned above.

In the case of modest diffusion, we may assume that this technology will be used as a complement to business travel. People will probably still want to meet in person for most talks, and it is likely that the new technology will be used instead of the telephone. Those who take the opportunity to meet over a video link will feel more comfortable when they talk about important matters. In the case of modest technological diffusion they will, however, still travel at almost the same frequency as today. The urge to meet people personally is so strong that traditional travel will persist despite all economic and environmental reasons to the contrary.

The case of extreme technological diffusion

A relatively, but not extremely, frequent business traveller may spend £1,000 per week, 40 weeks a year, on travel. He or she will also spend 10–20 hours a week travelling and 2 or 3 nights a week in hotels away from family and friends. This means that the direct travel cost for this person will be £40,000 per year. For the employer, this means that some of their most valuable employees spend 20–30 per cent of their working hours travelling. The equipment needed in order to be able to meet over the Internet costs less than one or two ordinary business trips; the hardware to furnish a video conference room will be paid back after a few months of usage. It is easy to see that these investments make sense from a cost perspective.

There seem to be substantial gains for both the company and the employees, who may want to travel less. First, the company will save the direct travel expenses. Second, they may need fewer of the most expensive employees who do most of the travelling. Third, they will increase their competitive position from each trip that they can dispense with. This may mean increasing sales, or at least stable sales if competitors act in the same way. Fourth, it may improve the environmental image of the companies who choose to cut down on travel. Fifth, it may increase competitiveness in the labour market, since many competent people may see it as an advantage to be able to travel less and still have an interesting job.

It might still be difficult to persuade people that they can have meetings of the same quality over the video as they can have in person. There are, however, at least two strong reasons why these new opportunities should decrease travel:

1. Customers may no longer want to pay for their suppliers' travel. If suppliers insist that their managers and salespersons should travel at the same frequency as before to meet customers, suppliers may have to be able to prove that these costs actually add much more value to the relationship than would the alternative. The alternative may be a 50 per cent decrease in travel, and video meetings could be used as a complement making it possible to hold meetings much more frequently than in a situation where personal meetings would be the preferred alternative.
2. Shareholders may be interested to know why travel expenses cannot be brought down as new technology is acquired.

If no company at all learns to make use of the new technologies in order to decrease travel expenses, nothing will change, but if one company in each industry learns how to save millions each year by decreasing travel, competitors will surely follow suite.

> In a free trade an effectual combination cannot be established but by the unanimous consent of every single trader, and it cannot last longer than every single trader continues of the same mind. (Smith, 1997)

In the extreme scenario, we may assume that business travel could conceivably decrease by as much as 50 per cent within 5 years. If this were the case, it would have dramatic effects on all companies dependent on the transportation of people for their turnover and profit.

The first companies to suffer from such a decrease would be the ones most intimately associated with our infrastructure. Airlines and railway companies would be among the first in line to get hit. Next would be the producers of vehicles. Manufacturers of trains, planes and cars would be strongly affected, as would the construction companies that build roads and railroads.

Some readers will think that we will still need the same number of roads and railroads since we will still need to transport goods. This is undoubtedly true, but we would not have to expand the road or railway network further, since the capacity already in place would suffice for the next few years. Besides, there would not be the money to invest in these projects since the decrease in business travel would take away a large share of the money from these industries and the reasons to continue with this type of project would also be removed.

After the producers of vehicles and the construction companies had taken the blow, the next ones to experience a decline would be their suppliers, and the suppliers of these suppliers in turn. On the fringe of this development, hotels and restaurants catering to business travellers would see their volumes diminish. Companies in the leisure travel industries would be affected as well, since it would probably become much more expensive to travel on holiday if volumes in all parts of the business travel sector went down. Decreasing numbers of planes, trains and cars being produced would increase the price of each vehicle, and decreasing numbers of travellers on the established networks would increase ticket prices for tourists as well.

It should be noted that the increase in the number of jobs created in the electronics industries as a prerequisite for this development would be extremely small compared with the fall in jobs that would be the total effect of the development. Moreover, it is possible, but not necessary, that a large share of these new jobs would be created in countries other than those from which the jobs related to infrastructure had disappeared.

The paper industry

For many years, there have been predictions that the development of IT will result in the so-called 'paperless office', which means that it should be possible to work in an office without any printed papers. Contrary to this prediction, we have observed a steady increase in the consumption of paper, and the use of new technologies with the creation of new opportunities to print and reproduce written material easily has increased, rather than decreased, the use of paper in all organisations.

In this chapter, we will look at how the paper industry and paper production could be affected by the latest developments in IT. It may be true that we will never see the paperless office in reality, meaning that we will not see a technological development that sweeps away the total need for paper in society. We can, however, see that the development proposed in this book has the power to alter our use of paper and to decrease many aspects of it, not because we will give up the convenient uses, but because we will change our ways of getting information. When we discuss the future of paper, we must not forget that the main use of paper today is as a bearer of information.

The case of modest technological diffusion

We tend to think that paper-based systems for the collection and distribution of information are necessary. It is hard for us to conceive of a society in which we do not use paper in the same way as we do today. Everything on paper, from our morning newspaper to attractive product catalogues, are such basic pillars of our life, that we believe we will always have them in their present form.

Changes in paper use through transparency and real-time

Consumers will be able to access information about products over the Internet, where transparency will make it possible for us to compare different products and different service offerings to identify the alternative that suits us best. When we have found what we are looking for, we may want to print information about some of the offerings, but since most of us will have to pay for the paper ourselves, we are likely to try to print only the things in which we have a real interest.

If we compare this situation with how we do it today, we can consider a situation in which we are about to buy something that we do not buy every day, for example a trip abroad or new flooring for the kitchen. In these situations, we tend to collect a number of catalogues from the different suppliers of these products. A catalogue from a tour operator may be more than 100 pages thick, and we may collect half a dozen of them each time we think of going abroad. In the same way, producers of flooring will present their products in glossy catalogues printed on high-quality paper. In the future, we may use our computer screens to make a preliminary screening of the alternatives, use some of the opportunities to get additional information from secondary sources on the Internet, for example test results, and choose to print some pages of the catalogues to study further.

This means that the transparency of the Internet will make it possible for us to decrease our use of paper for purposes such as product catalogues and brochures, which will in its turn decrease costs for the companies that manage to make their customers choose this way of obtaining information. Savings through this decrease in paper usage could be used to decrease product prices, and customers could get information more rapidly over the Internet, which is an effect of the real-time society.

This development would also make it possible for companies to provide more updated information on all kinds of issue, than is possible to do today using a paper-based format.

Effects of concept transformation

Many large users of paper currently have a paper-based distribution concept as one of the cornerstones of their business ideas. In this case, we could think of newspapers and magazines. If customers start to use their computers in new ways, it could become necessary for these businesses to transform their concepts from the paper-based distribution of information to electronic distribution.

Printed newspapers and magazines have a couple of disadvantages that could prove fatal for the whole concept. The first of these is the fact that it is more difficult and costly to customise the product to the needs of each individual customer if these companies stick to the paper format. When we look in a paper, we see that only a small portion of the contents is really what we think of as 'news'. The rest consists of advertisements, columns and articles of general interest that readers may want to access when they need or if they have a particular interest in the subject in question. Advertisements could serve better as product information related to a specific need, which may arise at any point in time other than on the day the advertisement happened to be in the paper.

The obvious solution would be for new companies or our present newspaper and magazine publishers to offer customers written material in the form of articles, columns or advertisements in a large database on the Internet, where we could access articles of general interest on thousands of subjects at the same time and only print the ones we would like to read. In the same manner, we could look at advertisements for bikes when we actually needed to buy one, or could try to sell our old car through a small advertisement on the Internet in a location where presumptive buyers of used cars could look. Most news we could get directly on the screen as short articles, accessing more in-depth material by a double-click on a 'button' on the screen.

This way of transforming the newspaper and magazine concepts (the magazine concept could, of course, be transformed in the same way as the newspaper one) would add flexibility through increased access to information. It would also decrease the cost for customers since the printing and distribution process of a newspaper represents well over 50 per cent of the total cost. One other result would be to increase competition in the news and publishing industries, because it would become possible to access articles from on-line newspapers on an article-by-article basis, instead of subscribing to a paper for a couple of months or a year. The competition would increase even more since professional journalists would have to compete with all individuals who wanted to publish the same type of information on their own homepages free of charge or for a small fee (small fees could be handled electronically over the Internet in the future).

The result would be that the way of accessing news and other information that we tend to look for in newspapers today could substantially decrease the demand for newsprint and other printed papers. Some of these decreased volumes would show up as an increase in the use of plain white printing paper for computer print-outs.

Effects of network intelligence

We have argued that the average size of companies will be smaller in the future than it is today. We now suggest that a large share of the paper used in business is employed for the purpose of administering large organisations. In our work as consultants, we see how people in administrative functions in a company often tend to overflow the company with administrative reports and collections of figures on which other employees are asked to express their opinion. There are also weekly and monthly bulletins from managers at all levels, not to mention internal news magazines and information material.

> Telia in Sweden has come a long way in publishing information on their intranet. In 1995/96, they started to publish company information exclusively via this medium, and people have become so used to this that they react negatively if somebody sends them internal information that has been printed on paper.

We argue that one of the savings that can be made in networks of small organisations is that these networks do not have to be formally organised and managed. A structure of small independent companies would eliminate many of these administrative functions because they would not add value to customers in a networked structure. It would be natural to assume that the paperwork of these employees would disappear at the same time as the positions. Even if positions did not disappear, tasks that did not add value to the customer would be easy to identify in a market-based organisation, which would mean that administrative tasks with purely internal purposes would be taken away.

This could decrease the use of paper for administrative purposes. In the same vein, the development towards electronic trade, which includes for example the electronic handling of order forms, confirmations and invoices, could decrease the use of paper for such purposes.

Summary of examples from the paper industry

We could assume that most people will want to read many things on paper in the future as well as today. The majority of paper that we use in society, however, is not the paper from which we actually read. Instead, the greatest volumes of paper are used for printed matter that we throw away largely unread. This is true for newspapers, magazines, sales brochures, memoranda, collections of statistics, letters and many other types of printed matter. Even some of the things we do read we could admit to doing equally well without and would never print if we received them on our computer screens. Our use of paper could decrease substantially if we only printed the papers that we actually wanted to read. This would also decrease our costs for the production and distribution of printed matter, and whole industries related to the printing and physical distribution of paper would disappear as an effect of such a development.

Real estate

At present, there are no signs that people in the real estate business are seeing any major shifts in the future demand for real estate. Thus rents are still high in central locations in large cities, and there are numerous projects being initiated that are intended to add new buildings to these sites. This optimism is, of course, based on the assumption that everything will remain the same regardless of the technological development.

Urbanisation could have a number of spurs, two of the most prominent being the need to live close to a major labour market, and the need to live close to a major market for goods and services. Both these reasons will weaken in the future society as Internet trade gains momentum.

The case of modest technological diffusion

The whole development towards working where people want to work is based on the development towards transparency of information in society. In the physical world, people have to be in the same place to be able to communicate efficiently. Regardless of how strong we think that the trend of moving out of the cities will be, we can already see signs that many people are taking the opportunity to work from home. We also find that the headquarters and administrative parts of major corporations are getting smaller as more and more specialist functions are replaced by consultants or are outsourced in other ways. The development of employment figures in production point in the same direction because production is gradually becoming more efficient.

Even if some of us like to think that there will be a stable demand for office space and apartments in city centres, we can assume that the opportunity for people and companies to move to areas where rents are lower than in the heart of cities such as London and New York would make people consider this alternative. If future customers no longer needed the physical closeness of a supplier, there would be many companies that could move without the risk of losing business.

The point here is not that city centres will in the future be desolate in the same way that the London docklands became almost desolate as the London harbours moved from the Thames towards the coast. No, the argument here is based on the fact that real estate companies make investments for the long term and are therefore very sensitive to small changes in demand. If real estate prices are three times higher in the central locations of a large city than in a smaller city, these differences are based on the fact that demand is so high in the best locations that each tenant who moves out will immediately be replaced by somebody else eager to move in. Historically, prices have remained relatively high during economic troughs because everyone has been convinced that the low demand will last for only a relatively short period of time.

If, on the other hand, many companies and individuals start to consider alternate ways of organising their businesses or their lives, the queue of new tenants to the best locations may still be there but will become shorter. The demand for these spaces will decrease. This may, then, not be for the short term but for the long term. If we learn how to organise companies and society in new ways, there will not be a trend towards reurbanisation after a couple of years.

Instead, the change towards smaller agglomerations may be as irreversible as the trend of urbanisation has been during the move from agricultural society to industrial society. Even if these fluctuations in demand exemplified in this 'low scenario' did come true, it would strike our major financial institutions very hard. This is because many banks, insurance companies and other large investors have invested in real estate in the large cities. Thus rapid decreases in demand caused by factors such as those mentioned here, with rapid declines in prices on real estate in central locations, would cause major strains on these companies, which are really some of the cornerstones of our economies.

The case of extreme diffusion

History has shown us that it is possible for changes in production and distribution structures to very rapidly, from an economic point of view, alter the demand for office space and apartments. The above-mentioned move from the docklands in London in the 1960s is one such example.

Another example is the move of large parts of the American car industry from the centre in or around Michigan, to Mexico. The latter move struck some cities especially hard, for example Flint, Michigan, whose inhabitants had this industry as their main source of income.

Luckily, these historical examples have been limited to one industry or one city at a time. Now we are talking about a situation in which the same development could affect real estate prices over the whole developed world at the same time. If this trend became a reality, it would be very difficult for investors in the real estate market to persuade people to move back into the cities in order to fill the empty spaces.

We could think of an extreme scenario, which may not be as likely to happen as rapidly in this industry as in others, simply because we do not have enough empty flats in the countryside or in smaller towns to house the people who may want to move out of the cities. Over time, it may become attractive, however, to build new houses in these places, instead of paying very high rents in the locations that are currently most sought after.

Such a development, in the extreme case, could in time mean that our cities would turn into desolate places where only the unfortunate wanted to live. If many people, perhaps the most wealthy and powerful in society, left the cities, it would become difficult to raise the money needed in order to change the city environment into one more attractive.

It is very difficult to speculate about what the effects of such a development would be, but it should be enough to indicate the possibility of this happening. Our opinion is that we should start immediately to analyse alternative actions to avoid this situation.

14 Emerging Industries

Electronic marketplaces

Business in the new electronic marketplace requires sites where customers and companies can meet. The valuescape, as we outlined it in Part II, is a description of how the future structure of the Internet market could look. We have also described the development in various existing industries, how they will evolve and how the companies that populate these industries may change to adapt to the new and challenging environment and conditions.

Somewhere in between this future market and the existing one, new industries will be born that will prosper and grow. One example of such an industry is that of electronic marketplaces. A number of companies have already targeted this niche and tried to position themselves as the entrance to electronic commerce. There are a number of reasons why this is a growing niche:

■ Companies and customers need a place where they can meet. Before people can create their own valuescapes, they need to know where to find products and services.

■ Companies need help to handle money transactions. One possible support that an electronic business place could offer is the secure handling of payments.

■ Customers need to know that they are dealing with companies they can trust. An electronic business place managed by a well-known and trusted company can give the extra feeling of security that new customers need in this new environment.

■ Companies need to have a location where many customers pass by. Newcomers on the electronic business arena need to be exposed to many potential customers; otherwise, they will have problems selling their products or services. A well-known and popular business place can attract enough customers.

On the Internet today, there are a number of these marketplaces that have become popular enough to attract many companies.

A typical example is Torget (www.torget.se). This is a business place provided by the Swedish mail. It has existed for a long time ('long' meaning more than a year in this market) and has positioned itself as a natural place to be for many Swedish companies. A wide range of services is offered from a large number of companies. It is possible to find almost anything in these marketplaces. At Torget (meaning 'market' in Swedish), there are providers under headings such as finding a job, retailers, entertainment, computers, gambling, sports, news and weather. Users get a place for a quick overview of what is offered, and where they can feel 'at home'. Companies get fast access to a large number of customers who would be hard to find on their own.

Another well-known example of a marketplace on the Internet is The Internet Mall (www.InternetMall.com), which has been up and running since 1994. This currently has more than 27,000 companies linked to it, which shows how far this development has proceeded. The issue now is not how to get more companies involved but how to find the best products to buy.

Virtual offices on the network

The Internet is rapidly becoming the main place to work and do business for many companies and people. People will spend their working lives on the Internet, communicating with other people, buying and selling services and scanning the market for new options. This means that many people will need a natural place to work on the network. They could, of course, create this environment themselves by buying computers, databases and communication equipment. With the decreasing prices for this type of equipment, it has become possible even for small companies to afford a representative interface to their Internet customers, but the development and pace of change are high, and it is costly to be in the lead. It had been very convenient to create, with some help and support, an efficient office with all the necessary appliances. To invest in expert help from consultants in this area is, of course, possible but not cheap.

All this points in one direction: that there is a clear need to help small companies and individuals to create and maintain a professional office environment on the Internet. This is interesting enough to be a candidate for the next growing industry on the Internet: to provide virtual offices on the network. The main focus is to offer all the tools necessary for a new company or an individual to use the Internet as the base for work. All the usual office tools can easily be provided to people independently of location. By having the office on the network itself, it is as close as possible to the new market, and it is easy to start a working life where things happen.

What are the main characteristics of a virtual office? They are, of course, more or less the same as those of a 'physical' office, some basic examples being:

- office software (word processors, drawing tools and spread sheets);
- e-mail;
- a site on the Internet (to secure a place in the electronic market);
- organisers;
- publishing tools;
- storage space;
- payment and money transaction support;
- travel booking on-line.

This environment can be offered directly on-line with very low requirements on the local computer used to access the network. This makes it possible for people to work independently of location. Small companies and home-workers can use this as a base for their activities without needing to invest a large amount of money.

The provision of this environment is likely to emerge as a new market on the Internet, with completely new players. We have found no complete examples of virtual offices offered over the Internet today, but there are embryos. Web hotels is such an example. They play an important role as the only opportunity for small companies, organisations and individuals to enter the Internet without the full costs of a connection to the network. The offer of 'mobile' mailboxes is another embryo of a virtual office. Anybody who has tried to stay in touch with the e-mail box during a business trip knows what this means. Difficulties turn up when we try to establish a connection to download e-mails. It is possible to facilitate this through a web connection to the mailbox. This makes it possible to access mail from any PC with an Internet connection. A virtual office will have these facilities, and independent companies can offer this as a part of a more comprehensive service.

An example showing that there are embryos of this type of service on the Internet is the Hotmail site (www.hotmail.com), which was started in 1995 and already has 8 million users. Hotmail offers free e-mail services, funded by customised advertising. Each user has to provide a personal profile of age, interests and education level, among other things, which is used in addressing advertisements. Besides the e-mail function, Hotmail users can access news, receive reminders of events such as birthdays or weekly meetings and use the Internet search engine that is provided on the site.

Through this tool, it becomes possible to send and receive e-mail regardless of physical location. The Hotmail site could be reached from any computer with access to the Internet. If other office functions were added to this, or some other similar site, so that users could not only send their e-mails, but also access word processing software, drawing tools and calculation tools, and save their work so that they could access it over the Internet, an Internet office would be created. At the end of 1997, Hotmail was acquired by Microsoft, which might indicate that the services provided by Hotmail will be developed in the future. The stock value of Hotmail was estimated to be $400m at the time of Microsoft's take-over.

The facilities of the virtual office mentioned above are only the very beginning of what can be offered on-line. More advanced support will soon be available. One interesting example is that of personal assistants. The idea is to mimic the behaviour of secretaries who carry out various tasks. A personal assistant can help the user to make travel arrangements, handle invoicing, manage mail and telephone calls, and translate information between different formats, for example turning voice messages into text. These assistants know the profile of the user so that they can perform tasks in a way that is suitable for each particular user. The user's profile can be enhanced step by step as the assistant gets more and more information of what the user wants. The advantages of customisation are tremendous when users carry out tasks such as booking tickets or arranging meetings. The user will be able to concentrate on things other than making detailed descriptions of requirements. Personal assistants can easily be implemented in a network where the user can access the assistant from anywhere in the world.

Local distribution centres and distribution systems

If people increase their on-line shopping in the future, there will be a need for a new system of local storage and transportation of goods that have been ordered over the Internet. When customers stop going to physical shops, they will not be able to transport their goods themselves from the shop to their homes. Instead, a number of different parcels will arrive at all times during the day and week to their address, and it would create difficulties for somebody to be at home all the time in order to wait for goods to be delivered. Many parcels will be so large that they will not fit in a mailbox or might require pre-payment because of credit risks (if SET or other secure payment standards have not been used).

This creates an opportunity for companies who want to create local distribution centres where people can themselves come to pick up goods or where companies running local delivery systems would be able to pick goods up for delivery when people are at home. It could also create an opportunity for existing transport companies to set up delivery systems to the door that bypassed all such local distribution centres and delivered from existing terminals.

An increase in Internet shopping would in any case create an increasing amount of goods in transport networks for smaller packages, and a decrease in the amount of goods in transport networks for large transports between producers and retailers. Instead of sending large volumes of goods from producers to retailers, to be carried home by the customer himself, the future picture might be that customers will receive their packages directly from producers to a greater extent than today.

15 Conclusions

Throughout the book, we have argued that there will probably be substantial changes to society in the near future. In order to further clarify the argument, we would like to emphasise some main conclusions.

First, we are moving towards a major paradigm shift in the way in which we do business. Many companies that have been successful within the old paradigm are likely to disappear totally as a result of this shift. Any company that wants to survive this shake-up needs to put this issue at the top of the strategic agenda before it is too late.

The development described in this book could start almost immediately. If all people with access to the Internet started to make a large part of their purchases through this medium, or if a large share of all companies that already have access to the Internet did the same, it would not take more than a few months until many of the developments described in this book would become a reality.

New solutions designed to help states, organisations and people into the new marketplace must be developed with a broad scope in mind. The old concepts have to be transformed rather than just adapted. Old industry borders and positions in the value chain have to be forgotten quickly; otherwise, it is impossible to see the real opportunities and spot the real competitors in the market.

The development of a new electronic marketplace based on the Internet is not an isolated phenomenon that will live a life of its own. On the contrary, services, products and, last but not least, price levels also influence the traditional market.

One of the key features of the electronic market is the fact that it is possible to get an overview of the whole world market more quickly than it takes to go down to the local shop. Supply and demand are totally visible to all players in the market, which leads to major changes in the way in which business is carried out. It leads to price pressure, focus on customer value, far-reaching customisation of products and services, rapid changes in the offers to increase profit margins and less customer loyalty. We call this new marketplace the transparent marketplace to stress that this is one of the key issues.

The electronic marketplace is not equal to electronic commerce to consumers (even if this is often the scope discussed in many organisations). Electronic trade will influence every single part of a value chain. New solutions will lead to radically lower costs of administrating organisations and entire value chains. This means that even with a traditional shop at the end of a value chain, the rest of the chain may be totally electronic and automated, with substantially lower costs and prices as a consequence.

Traditional organisational principles that have made it possible to arrive at our present level of affluence, through planned value creation, will have to give way to the market mechanism, which has the power substantially to increase the efficiency of society. However, the market mechanism is not something that managers in an organisation can plan and control. It will come out of an increasing spontaneity within organisations where people and groups develop their own niches and offers.

Just as companies and organisations have to take this development seriously, so too do states and legislators. The old tax and labour rules make no sense in the new marketplace. Those states which wait too long to deal with this will see themselves left behind in future development. Companies will easily move to the country where the rules are most favourable. Distance is no problem in this global electronic market.

Every person has a major role to play in this development. First, it is ultimately the customer or consumer who decides how fast this paradigm shift will go by starting to shop electronically or sticking with the more expensive 'physical' shopping experience. Second, we all have to prepare for the new marketplace and start to think of how we want to work, spend our spare time and distribute the resources that are freed when we are able to produce the same amount of products and services with fewer resources.

During the period of transition from the present to the new paradigm, we have to prepare for extreme instability and unexpected twists and turns, but in the long run the transparent society will become much more stable than the industrial society has ever been. The long-term effects of the development are also likely to be advantageous to society as a whole.

One of the main conclusions, that we have not made explicit, but which is substantiated in many ways throughout the book, is that electronic trade, if it takes a substantial portion of the total volume of trade, is likely to force us to reshape our whole economic system. Our present system and our thinking about economics is built on the assumption that increased efficiency leads to an increase in GDP. GDP is measured as the value of the work that we use to produce the total volume of goods and services in a country.

In the economy that we describe there seems to be more opportunities to take away jobs than to create new ones. If this is true it means that an increase in the efficiency of production reduces the value of the input used and all the resources that have been freed will not be used in any other type of value creation. Even if we try to increase our consumption, because of our increasing amount of free time, many of the things that we will consume will require less resources to produce than they would require today. This means that GDP would decrease as the efficiency of the economy increases. It must be the utmost challenge to economists to come up with an economic system that could handle this.

References

Barker, J. A. (1993) *Paradigms*. HarperCollins: New York.

Blanchard, K., Waghorn, T. and Ballard, J. (1996) *Mission Impossible*. McGraw-Hill: Maidenhead.

Kuhn, T. (1996) *The Structure of Scientific Revolutions*. Ingram International: La Vergne, Tennessee.

Ricardo, D. (1996 [1817]) *Principles of Political Economy and Taxation*. Prometheus Books: Amherst, New York.

Smith, A. (1997 [1776]) *An Inquiry into the Nature and Causes of the Wealth of Nations*. Penguin: London.

Index